Six
Ingredients
or Less ®

Diabetic Cookbook

Also by Carlean Johnson

Six Ingredients or Less Cookbook

Six Ingredients or Less Chicken Cookbook

Six Ingredients or Less Cooking Light & Healthy

Six Ingredients or Less Pasta & Casseroles

Six Ingredients or Less Slow Cooker Cookbook

Six Ingredients or Less Low-Carb Cookbook

Six ingredients or Less Families on the Go

Six Ingredients or Less ®

Diabetic Cookbook

Carlean Johnson

CJ
Books
Washington

Six Ingredients or Less   Diabetic Cookbook

Cover Design by CarrotStick Marketing
Typography and production design by Linda Hazen

Library of Congress Control Number: 2005902158
ISBN: 0-942878-08-6

CJ Books
PO Box 922
Gig Harbor, WA 98335
1-800-423-7184
www.sixingredientsorless.com
email:carlean@sixingredientsorless.com

Dedication

This book is dedicated to my friend Dorothy Lovelace, who as a mother and nurse has dedicated her life to caring for others.

Acknowledgements

Until I wrote this cookbook I don't think I fully realized just how complicated diabetes is and how much it affects ones daily life-style. It has made me appreciate even more, those with diabetes who work so hard to keep it under control.

I would like to thank my daughter, Linda Hazen, for the many hours devoted to getting this book to press on time. I know with a family to take care of, it wasn't always easy. Linda is not only a wonderful daughter, but I am always happier and less stressed when we are working on a project together. Thank you again for your dedication, loyalty and support.

Another big thank you also, to Darlene Lindmark for her many hours spent proofreading the text. This is not an easy job and I appreciate all the long hours and weekends dedicated to getting the job done on time.

Carlean Johnson

Table of Contents

Ingredient List

Baking Mix - We used Bisquick all-purpose baking mix.

Barbecue Sauce - We used low-carb Westbrae, unsweetened un-ketchup at 1 carb per tablespoon.

Breads- Purchase breads with the lowest fat and/or carbs depending on your needs.

Cheese - Used reduced fat in most recipes.

Chocolate- I used *Low Effective Carb* sugarfree chocolate. It comes in dark, milk and white chocolate. It comes in 3.5 ounce packages and is reasonably priced. Call 516-706-6178 to locate stores in your area.

Cooking Spray - A vegetable cooking spray such as Pam.

Deli Meats - Compare deli meats. Some meats have higher fat, sodium and sugar contents.

Ice Cream - We used nonfat ice cream, but you could also use frozen yogurt. There are also ice creams which are low-fat and no sugar added. Use which best fits your needs.

Jams - We used Smucker's sugar free jams.

Low-Carb Products - We have used a few low-carb products because they also had the lowest fat and sugar content.

Maple Syrup - We used *Joseph's Maple Syrup*, a product that tastes just like real syrup and has 0 carbs and only 35 calories per 1/4 cup. but it is hard to find. Call 505-546-2839 to see who carries it in your area.

Margarine - Land 0' Lakes Fresh Buttery Taste Spread because it can be used for cooking and baking. If using your own recipes, you may have to do a little experimenting. If a recipe calls for stick margarine, I used Imperial Spread.

Ingredient List

Mayonnaise - Used light mayonnaise. You may want to experiment and use the one you like best.

Oils - Extra light olive oil and canola oil are the oils I like to use. I use extra light olive oil most often, merely because it is so convenient to have on hand. Unlike the other olive oils, it can withstand higher temperatures and can be used for all your cooking and baking needs as well as for salads and dressings.

Pasta - Dreamfield's pasta is lower in carbs and fat and tastes just like pasta should taste. At 5 net carbs and 1 fat gram per 2 ounces it is the lowest and best I have found on the market. Currently, they are working on the diabetic exchanges of their pasta, but this information was not available at our press time. You should be able to find their pastas in most supermarkets. At this time they make spaghetti, linguine, penne and elbow pasta. Go to www.Dreamfields.com or call 800-250-1917 for additional information.

Sour Cream - We used nonfat, but you may want to experiment and use the one you like best with the fat grams you are allowed.

Spaghetti Sauce - We used Carb Options, found in most supermarkets. You may want to compare to others.

Sugar - Used in a few recipes when a very small amount was needed.

Sugar Free Syrups - These are used most often in coffee and cold drinks. Can usually be found in coffee shops and supermarkets.

Tortillas - We used La Tortilla Factory low-carb and Mission's lowfat flour Tortilla.

Unsweetened Shredded Coconut - We used Bob's Red Mill found in most supermarkets. Again, you may want to compare and may find some lower in fat.

Introduction

This cookbook is not a specific diet plan, but a collection of recipes to be used as determined by your doctor or dietitian.

I think it is important to spend as much time as possible checking out books on diabetes and then choosing those recipes that best suit your specific needs. We have included the carbohydrates, net carbohydrates and diabetic exchanges in our recipes. With your diet plan chosen and a variety of Six Ingredients or Less quick and easy recipes, you should be well on your way to a happy and healthy lifestyle.

Healthy Cooking!

Carlean

About the Author

Carlean's love of cooking has inspired her to write a series of popular cookbooks called Six Ingredients or Less. The new Diabetic cookbook is the latest in her series. Carlean resides in Gig Harbor, Washington.

Appetizers and Beverages

- Appetizers
- Dips
- Cold Drinks
- Hot Drinks

Pineapple Cheese Spread

MAKES 3-1/4 CUPS

A most requested recipe for over 30 years now.

2 (8-oz) packages light cream cheese
1 (8-oz) can crushed pineapple, drained
1 cup finely chopped pecans
¼ cup finely chopped green pepper
2 tablespoons finely chopped onion
1 tablespoon seasoning salt

1. Beat cream cheese until smooth and light. Add remaining ingredients and mix thoroughly. Spoon into a serving bowl, cover and chill at least 2 hours before serving.

Per tablespoon: 38 Cal, 5 Fat, 1g Sat F, 5mg Chol, 86mg Sod, 1 Pro, <1g Sug, 1g Carb, <1g Fib

Exchanges   Net Carbs
Fat 1/2   <1

Vegetable Tray

Use as a vegetable tray for entertaining or keep in the refrigerator for snacks.

Suggestions:

Artichokes
Asparagus
Bell peppers
Broccoli
Cauliflower
Celery sticks
Cherry tomatoes
Cucumber spears
Green onions
Jicama
Mushrooms
Radishes
Snap peas
Zucchini

Quesadillas

MAKES 12 WEDGES

Good served with salsa or guacamole.

4   (7-inch) low-carb tortillas
1   cup (4-oz) reduced fat Cheddar
     cheese, shredded
¼   cup chopped black olives
¼   cup chopped green onion
¼   cup diced tomatoes

1. Preheat oven to 400°F. Place tortillas on a baking sheet and bake 2 minutes.
2. Remove from oven and sprinkle 2 tortillas with cheese, then remaining ingredients. Top with remaining tortillas. Bake until cheese is melted, 3 to 4 minutes. Cut each tortilla into 6 wedges.

Per wedge: 38 Cal, 2g Fat, <1g Sat F, 2mg Chol, 156mg Sod, 4g Pro, <1g Sug, 4g Carb, 3g Fib

Exchanges   Net Carbs
Very Lean Meat 1/2   1

Cheese Quesadilla

MAKES 1 SERVING

A lunch time favorite.

1   (7-inch) low-carb tortilla
½   cup (2-oz) reduced fat shredded
     cheese blend

1. Sprinkle cheese over half of tortilla. Fold over to enclose cheese.
2. Heat a lightly sprayed skillet over medium-high heat. Add tortilla and cook until lightly browned on both sides, turning once.

variations: A choice of these additions can be added:

    Cooked, crumbled bacon
    Diced chicken or turkey
    Salsa
    Diced tomatoes
    Chopped green onions
    Diced bell peppers
    Jalapeno peppers
    Cooked sausage

Per serving: 148 Cal, 6g Fat, 2g Sat F, 12mg Chol, 567mg Sod, 19g Pro, <1g Sug, 12g Carb, 8g Fib

Exchanges   Net Carbs
Fat 1/2   4
Very Lean Meat 2

Stuffed Pepper Shells

MAKES 8 SERVINGS

A wonderful addition to a vegetable tray.

4   small red peppers, halved, seeded
1   cup (4-oz) reduced fat Mozzarella
    cheese, shredded
2   tablespoons pesto

1. Preheat oven to 375°F. Fill peppers with cheese, mounding slightly. Place on a baking sheet and drizzle with pesto. Bake 10 to 12 minutes to melt the cheese. Serve hot.

Per serving: 45 Cal, 2g Fat, 1g Sat F, 5mg Chol, 101mg Sod, 4g Pro, 2g Sug, 3g Carb, 1g Fib

Exchanges   Net Carbs
Meat 1/2   2

Little Tomatoes with Cheese

PER TOMATO

These are those beautiful little tomatoes that are still attached to the vine.

1   small red tomato, about 1½-inches
1   tablespoon Pepper Jack cheese,
    shredded
¼   teaspoon sliced almonds, coarsely
    crumbled
    Chopped parsley

1. Preheat oven to 350°F. Remove a ¼- inch slice from top side of tomatoes. Remove pulp and place upside down on paper towels to drain.
2. Form cheese into a sort of ball and fill tomato. There should be a slight mound above the tomato. Sprinkle with almonds and parsley. Bake 5 minutes to melt cheese. Don't overcook or the tomatoes will be too soft.

Per tomato: 47 Cal, 3g Fat, 2g Sat F, 8mg Chol, 52mg Sod, 3g Pro, 2g Sug, 4g Carb, 1g Fib

Exchanges   Net Carbs
Veg 1/2   3

Antipasto

Deli ham, halved and rolled
Marinated artichoke hearts
Marinated mushrooms
Reduced fat cheese, cubed
Kalamata olives, pitted
Red and yellow cherry tomatoes
Pepperoncini peppers

Cheese Kabobs

MAKES 16 KABOBS

These are also nice served as a side-dish.

16 broccoli florets
2 cups (8-oz) reduced fat Monterey Jack cheese, cut into ¾-inch cubes (32 cubes)
16 pitted ripe olives
16 small cherry tomatoes

1. Thread 1 broccoli, 2 cheese cubes, 1 olive and one tomato on each small skewer.

Per kabob: 51 Cal, 4g Fat, 2g Sat F, 10mg Chol, 162mg Sod, 4g Pro, <1g Sug, 2g Carb, 1g Fib

Exchanges   Net Carbs
Fat 1/2   1
Meat 1/2

Chicken-Bacon Bites

MAKES 32 APPETIZERS

These can be made ahead and reheated.

2 chicken breast halves, skinned, boned and cut into 32 bite-size pieces
⅓ cup nonfat vinaigrette dressing
16 bacon slices, halved crosswise

1. Marinate chicken in dressing for 30 minutes.
2. Preheat oven to 425°F. Wrap chicken with bacon and secure with wooden toothpicks. Place on a foil-lined 15x10-inch pan and bake 15 to 20 minutes until cooked through.

Per 4 pieces: 114 Cal, 6g Fat, 2g Sat F, 32mg Chol, 391mg Sod, 11g Pro, 1g Sug, 2g Carb, 0g Fib

Exchanges   Net Carbs
Fat 1   2
Meat 1/2
Very Lean Meat 1

Celery Boats

MAKES ABOUT 60, 2-INCH PIECES

Always a favorite on a appetizer tray.

1 small bunch celery
1 (8-oz) package light cream cheese
1 (8-oz) can crushed pineapple, drained
   Paprika

1. Trim celery stalks; wash and dry thoroughly.
2. Combine cream cheese and pineapple. Spoon into celery and level with a knife. Sprinkle lightly with paprika. Cover and chill.
3. Cut celery into 2-inch pieces and serve.

Per piece: 12 Cal, 1g Fat, 4g Sat F,
2mg Chol, 20mg Sod, <1g Pro,
1g Sug, 1g Carb, <1g Fib

Exchanges	Net Carbs
Free	1

Cook's Tip Nuts make a nice between meal snack, but watch the carb count.

Teriyaki Kabobs

MAKES 20 KABOBS

These go really fast. Wooden skewers should be soaked in water for 20 minutes.

1 pound beef sirloin
⅓ cup brown Sugar Twin®
⅓ cup low sodium soy sauce
2 tablespoons white vinegar
1½ tablespoons Worcestershire sauce
2 thin slices fresh ginger

1. Cut sirloin crosswise into thin strips.
2. Combine remaining ingredients. Add meat; cover and marinate in refrigerator at least 2 hours.
3. Thread about 2 strips of meat on each 4-inch wooden skewer. Place on an oiled, heated grill and cook about 2 minutes. Brush with marinade, turn and cook 1 to 2 minutes or until cooked to desired doneness. For safety reasons do not brush with marinade a second time.

Per kabob: 33 Cal, 1g Fat, 1g Sat F,
10mg Chol, 35mg Sod, 5g Pro,
0g Sug, 0g Carb, 0g Fib

Exchanges	Net Carbs
Meat 1	0

Tortilla Appetizers

MAKES 40 APPETIZERS

A nice make-ahead appetizer.

2 (8-oz) packages light cream cheese
1 (1-oz) package Ranch dressing mix
¼ cup chopped green onions
½ cup finely chopped red peppers
½ cup chopped black olives
4 (10-inch) low-carb tortillas

1. Beat cream cheese until light. Add dressing mix and beat until blended. Add remaining ingredients and spread on the tortillas. Roll up tightly and wrap in wax paper, twisting ends. Chill at least 2 hours. Cut into 1-inch slices.

Per appetizer: 43 Cal, 3g Fat, 1g Sat F, 7mg Chol, 136mg Sod, 2g Pro, <1g Sug, 4g Carb, 2g Fib

Exchanges   Net Carbs
Fat 1/2   2

Bacon-Pineapple Appetizers

MAKES 1 SERVING

Pineapple adds a wonderful flavor to these appetizers..

Per Appetizer:

1 slice bacon, halved crosswise
1 whole water chestnut, halved
1 pineapple chunk, drained
1 teaspoon low sodium soy sauce

1. Preheat oven to 400°F. Wrap bacon slice around a pineapple chunk and water chestnut. Secure with a wooden toothpick. Bake on rack in a shallow pan for 15 minutes. Brush with soy sauce and bake 5 to 10 minutes or until bacon is crisp.

Per serving: 25 Cal, 1g Fat, <1g Sat F, 3mg Chol, 118mg Sod, 1g Pro, 1g Sug, 2g Carb, <1g Fib

Exchanges   Net Carbs
0   2

Ham Rolls

MAKES 30 APPETIZERS

Ham must be thinly sliced to allow for easy rolling. Asparagus should not be too soft.

1 (8-oz) container Herb Cheese Spread, softened
6 thin slices deli boiled ham
12 cooked asparagus spears

1. Spread cheese evenly over ham. Place 2 asparagus spears on long edge of ham and roll tightly. Wrap each roll in wax paper, twisting ends. Chill at least 2 hours.
2. Cut each roll into 5 slices and place on serving plate.

Per appetizer: 32 Cal, 3g Fat, 0g Sat F, 2mg Chol, 62mg Sod, 2g Pro, <1g Sug, <1g Carb, <1g Fib

Exchanges   Net Carbs
0   <1

> ### Hint
> Have an appetizer party and have everyone bring their favorite appetizer.

Sweet-Sour Wrap-Ups

MAKES 48 APPETIZERS

These go fast. To make ahead, prepare bacon and water chestnuts. Make sauce and refrigerate both until ready to bake.

1 pound lean bacon
2 (8-oz) cans water chestnuts
1½ cups low-carb ketchup
16 packets Splenda®
3 tablespoons lemon juice

1. Preheat oven to 350°F. Cut bacon crosswise into thirds. Cut water chestnuts in half. Wrap 1 piece bacon around each water chestnut. Secure with wooden toothpicks. Place in a sprayed 13x9-inch baking dish and bake for 30 minutes. Drain off fat.
2. Combine remaining ingredients and pour over top. Reduce heat to 325°F. Bake 20 to 30 minutes, basting occasionally, until bacon is crisp. Serve hot.

Per appetizer: 24 Cal, 1g Fat, <1 Sat F, 3mg Chol, 88mg Sod, 1g Pro, <1g Sug, 2g Carb, <1g Fib

Exchanges   Net Carbs
0   2

Linda's Guacamole

MAKES 2 CUPS

If not serving right away, cover with a thin layer of light mayonnaise, spreading to the edge; cover and refrigerate.

2 ripe avocados
1 garlic clove, minced
1 tablespoon lime juice
   Dash hot pepper sauce
1 small tomato, diced
   Salt and pepper to taste

1. Peel and slice avocados. Combine with garlic, lime juice and pepper sauce, mashing with a fork until blended. Add tomato, salt and pepper. When ready to serve, simply stir in the mayonnaise, if using.

Per ¼ cup: 84 Cal, 7g Fat, 1g Sat F, 0mg Chol, 24mg Sod, 1g Pro, 1g Sug, 5g Carb, 4g Fib

Exchanges
Fat 1-1/2
Fruit 1/2

Net Carbs
1

Baked Tortilla Chips

MAKES 24 CHIPS

Use with dips or with Taco Salads.

2 (7-inch) low-carb white tortillas
   Salt (optional)

1. Preheat oven to 425°F. Place tortillas on baking sheet and spray both sides with cooking spray. Sprinkle lightly with salt, if using.
2. Cut each tortilla into 12 even wedges. Separate slightly. Bake 5 to 7 minutes or until lightly browned.

Per chip: 4 Cal, <1g Fat, 0g Sat F, 0mg Chol, 73mg Sod, <1g Pro, 0g Sug, <1g Carb, <1g Fib

Exchanges
Fat 1/2

Net Carbs
<1

Apricot Almond Cheese

MAKES 8 SERVINGS

Serve with low-fat crackers.

1 (8-oz) package light cream cheese
5 tablespoons sugar free orange marmalade
1 teaspoon Grand Marnier
1 tablespoon sliced almonds

1. Place cheese on serving plate and let soften.
2. In small saucepan, heat marmalade and Grand Marnier until hot, but not boiling. Spoon over cheese and sprinkle with almonds.

Per serving: 87 Cal, 5g Fat, 3g Sat F, 16mg Chol, 84mg Sod, 3g Pro, 3g Sug, 6g Carb, 0g Fib

Exchanges   Net Carbs
Fat 1   6
Meat 1/2

Artichoke and Dill Dip

MAKES 4 SERVINGS

Kids love to dip these little leaves into the sauce.

2 artichokes
1/3 cup light mayonnaise
1/2 teaspoon dried dill weed

1. Wrap each artichoke in a paper towel and microwave until tender. Time varies according to wattage so watch carefully not to overcook. Serve warm or cold.
2. Combine mayonnaise and dill weed. Serve as a dip with the artichokes.

Per serving: 64 Cal, 3g Fat, 1g Sat F, 0mg Chol, 229mg Sod, 2g Pro, 2g Sug, 9g Carb, 3g Fib

Exchanges   Net Carbs
Fat 1/2   6
Veg 1

MENU

Ham Rolls
Tortilla Appetizers
Vegetable Tray
Celery Boats
Easy Salsa

Ranch Dip

Serve with your favorite low-carb vegetables.

½   cup Ranch dressing
½   cup light mayonnaise
½   cup nonfat sour cream
⅓   cup grated Parmesan cheese
½   cup crumbled cooked bacon

1. Combine first 4 ingredients. Cover and chill 1 to 2 hours. Add bacon just before serving.

Per ¼ cup: 150 Cal, 13g Fat, 3g Sat F, 11mg Chol, 433mg Sod, 3g Pro, 2g Sug, 6g Carb, 0g Fib

Exchanges   Net Carbs

Fat 2   6
Meat 1/2

Heavenly Fruit Dip

My favorite dip to serve with fresh fruit.

1   (1-oz) package sugar-free vanilla
     pudding mix
2   cups fat-free half and half
1   tablespoon sugar
½   teaspoon rum extract
½   teaspoon vanilla extract

1. Combine ingredients and beat with a whisk about 2 minutes. Cover and chill at least two hours to blend flavors.

Per ¼ cup: 30 Cal, <1g Fat, <1g Sat F, 2 mg Chol, 97mg Sod, 1g Pro, 2g Sug, 5g Carb, 0g Fib

Exchanges   Net Carbs

0   5

Jicama

JICAMA (HEE-kah-mah) is that wonderful, but funny looking vegetable with a thin brown skin. It should be peeled before serving. The crunchy white flesh is similar to a potato or water chestnut, only sweeter. It can be steamed, baked, boiled or fried and retains its crisp texture when cooked briefly. At only 2.5 net carbs per 1/2 cup, this is a vegetable that should become a staple in your kitchen.

Dill Dip

MAKES 1-1/3 CUPS

Serve with Jicama sticks and enjoy anytime, especially on those days when you are tempted to go off your diet.

⅔   **cup light mayonnaise**
⅔   **cup nonfat sour cream**
1   **teaspoon dry minced onion**
1   **teaspoon dill weed**
1   **teaspoon Beau Monde seasoning**

1. Combine ingredients; cover and chill several hours to blend flavors.

Per ¼ cup: 72 Cal, 4g Fat, 1g Sat F, 2mg Chol, 301mg Sod, 1g Pro, 2g Sug, 8g Carb, 0g Fib

Exchanges	Net Carbs
Fat 1	8

Artichoke Dip

MAKES 2-1/2 CUPS

Serve with vegetable sticks or toasted bread triangles.

1   **(14-oz) can artichoke hearts, drained, coarsely chopped**
1   **(4-oz) can chopped green chilies**
1   **cup light mayonnaise**
1   **cup grated Parmesan cheese**

1. Combine ingredients in a medium saucepan and heat through. Serve hot.
variation: add 1 cup cubed cooked chicken.

Per ¼ cup: 87 Cal, 5g Fat, 2g Sat F, 7mg Chol, 443mg Sod, 4g Pro, 2g Sug, 6g Carb, <1g Fib

Exchanges	Net Carbs
Fat 1	6
Meat 1/2	
Veg 1/2	

Clam Dip

MAKES 1 CUP

Can also be gently heated and served hot.

1 (8-oz) package light cream cheese
1 (6½-oz) can minced clams, save juice
1 small garlic clove, minced
1 teaspoon lemon juice
¼ teaspoon Worcestershire sauce
   Salt to taste

1. Combine cream cheese and clams. Add enough juice to make a nice consistency for dipping. Add remaining ingredients. Serve or cover and chill.

Per 2 tablespoons: 90 Cal, 5g Fat, 3 Sat F, 27mg Chol, 104mg Sod, 7g Pro, 0g Sug, 3g Carb, 0g Fib

Exchanges   Net Carbs

Fat 1   3
Meat 1/2
VL Meat 1/2

Hot Crab Dip

MAKES 8 SERVINGS

Serve with toasted bread triangles.

1 (8-oz) package light cream cheese, softened
1 cup light mayonnaise
½ cup grated Parmesan cheese, reserve 2 tablespoons for top
2 tablespoons finely chopped onion
½ cup chopped artichoke hearts
1 (6-oz) can crab, drained

1. Preheat oven to 350°F. Beat cream cheese until light. Add remaining ingredients, except crab, and beat until blended. Stir in crab.
2. Spoon into sprayed shallow dish. You want the mixture about 1-inch thick. Smooth top. Sprinkle with reserved Parmesan. Bake 15 to 20 minutes or until heated through.
variation: Top with 1 tablespoon sliced almonds.

Per serving: 163 Cal, 11g Fat, 5g Sat F, 39mg Chol, 522mg Sod, 10g Pro, 2g Sug, 7g Carb, 0g Fib

Exchanges   Net Carbs

Fat 2   7
Meat 1/2
Very Lean Meat 1/2

Vegetable Dip

MAKES 2 CUPS

Vegetable dippers could be snap peas, zucchini spears, red peppers and jicama.

2   (3-oz) packages light cream cheese
1   cup nonfat sour cream
1   tablespoon chopped green onion
⅓   cup finely chopped cucumber
1   small garlic clove, minced
    Dash Salt

1. Beat cream cheese until light; beat in sour cream. Add remaining ingredients. Cover and chill.

Per ¼ cup: 70 Cal, 4g Fat, 2g Sat F, 14mg Chol, 100mg Sod, 3g Pro, <1g Sug, 6g Carb, 0g Fib

Exchanges   Net Carbs
Fat 1   6
Meat 1/2

Easy Salsa

MAKES 3-1/2 CUPS

Serve as a dip or as a topping for meats, salads and hamburgers.

3   cups chopped Plum tomatoes
¼   cup chopped onion
1   (4-oz) can chopped green chilies
1   tablespoon oil
1   tablespoon apple cider vinegar
¾   teaspoon salt

1. Combine ingredients; cover and chill several hours to blend flavors.

Per ¼ cup: 18 Cal, 1g Fat, 0g Sat F, 0g Chol, 115mg Sod, <1g Pro, 1g Sug, 2g Carb, 1g Fib

Exchanges   Net Carbs
Fat 1/2   1

Pineapple Salsa

MAKES 1-1/2 CUPS

Serve on salmon fillets or grilled chicken.

1   cup coarsely chopped fresh pineapple
½   cup chopped Plum tomatoes
¼   cup chopped cilantro
1   teaspoon minced fresh jalapeños
¼   teaspoon salt

1. Combine ingredients and mix well.

Per ¼ cup: 41 Cal, 0g Fat, 0g Sat F,
0mg Chol, 101mg Sod, 0g Pro,
2g Sug, 4g Carb, <1 Fib

Exchanges   Net Carbs
0   4

Tomato Salsa

MAKES 2 CUPS

Serve over grilled chicken or fish.

1   cup chopped red tomato
1   cup chopped yellow tomato
1   tablespoon red wine vinegar
½   teaspoon dried basil

1. Combine ingredients; cover and chill several hours to blend flavors.

Per ¼ cup: 7 Cal, 0g Fat, 0g Sat F,
0mg Chol, 5mg Sod, <1g Pro,
<1g Sug, 1g Carb, 0g Fib

Exchanges   Net Carbs
0   1

Cook's Tip
Pork Rinds are good when you want something crispy to use with dips and salsa.

Almond Iced Tea

MAKES 11 CUPS

*Lemon and almond is a
refreshing combination.*

6   tea bags
1   tub Crystal Light® lemonade mix
24 packets Splenda®
½ teaspoon almond extract

1. Heat 2 cups water to boiling. Add tea
bags and let steep 5 minutes.
2. Remove tea bags and add remaining
ingredients. In large container, combine
mixture with 9 cups water. You may wish to
adjust sweetener to taste. Serve over ice.

Per cup: 13 Cal, 0g Fat, 0g Sat F,
0mg Chol, 7mg Sod, 0g Pro,
0g Sug, 2g Carb, 0g Fib,

Exchanges	Net Carbs
Free	2

Sun Tea

MAKES 1 GALLON

*This is very easy to make,
especially for a crowd.*

1   gallon cold water
7   tea bags

1. Fill a gallon glass jar with water. Add
tea bags; put lid on. Place outside in sun and
leave several hours or until desired strength
is achieved.

Per cup: 0 Cal, 0g Fat, 0g Sat F,
0mg Chol, 7mg Sod, 0g Pro,
0g Sug, 0g Carb, 0g Fib,

Exchanges	Net Carbs
Free	0

Strawberry Lemonade

A little bit rich, but oh so good.

6   cups sliced strawberries
1½ cups Splenda®
1   tub Crystal Light® lemonade mix
9   cups diet lemon-lime soda, chilled

1. Purée strawberries in blender or food processor. Combine purée with Splenda, lemonade mix and 6 cups water. Cover and chill.

2. When ready to serve, mix equal parts strawberry mixture with soda, or to taste.

Per cup: 30 Cal, <1g Fat, 0g Sat F, 0mg Chol, 19mg Sod, <1g Pro, 3g Sug, 6g Carb, 1g Fib

*E*xchanges   *N*et Carbs
0   5

Paulina's Italian Cream Soda

MAKES 1 SERVING

If desired, garnish with a dollop of whipped topping and a strawberry slice.

2   tablespoons sugar-free strawberry syrup, or to taste
1   cup chilled club soda
1   tablespoon fat-free half & half

1. Pour syrup into a glass filled with ice cubes. Add club soda. Stir in the half & half.

Per serving: 9 Cal, <1g Fat, <1 Sat F, 1mg Chol, 86mg Sod, <1g Pro, <1g Sug, 1g Carb, 0g Fib,

*E*xchanges   *N*et Carbs
Free   1

Peach Fizz

Just the thing to make when you get a craving for something sweet.

1 (12-oz) can diet golden peach soda
1 tablespoon fat free half & half

1. Pour soda into a tall glass. Add half & half and stir.

Per serving: 9 Cal, <1g Fat, <1g Sat F, <1mg Chol, 22mg Sod, <1g Pro, 1g Sug, 1g Carb, 0g Fib

Exchanges   Net Carbs
Free   1

Cook's Tip
If you are strictly counting carbs and if a recipe calls for milk, combine 2 tablespoons heavy cream with water to measure 1 cup. This combination is 0.8g carbs compared to 11 carbs for 1 cup whole milk, however if you are watching your fat as well, you may wish to experiment with fat free half & half.

Vanilla-Raspberry Treat

This makes that little-bitty ½ cup serving of ice cream go a little farther.

½ cup nonfat vanilla ice cream
½ cup diet raspberry soda, chilled

1. Place ice cream in a 12-ounce glass and pour raspberry soda over top.

Per cup: 90 Cal, 0g Fat, 0g Sat F, 0mg Chol, 15mg Sod, 3g Pro, 16g Sug, 19g Carb, <1g Fib

Exchanges   Net Carbs
Other Carbs 1   19

Raspberry Drink

MAKES 2 CUPS

You may also use any choice of flavors.

1 cup nonfat vanilla ice cream
2 tablespoons sugar-free raspberry syrup
1 cup diet lemon-lime soda

1. Place ingredients in blender and blend until smooth.

Per cup: 140 Cal, 0g Fat, 0g Sat F, 0mg Chol, 85mg Sod, 3g Pro, 16g Sug, 19g Carb, <1g Fib

Exchanges   Net Carbs

Other Carbs 1   19

Root Beer Float

MAKES 1 SERVING

Let the kids make these.

½ cup nonfat vanilla ice cream
1 (12-oz) can diet root beer, chilled

1. Place ice cream in a tall glass and slowly add root beer.
variation: Vanilla ice cream and diet orange soda.

Per cup: 140 Cal, 0g Fat, 0g Sat F, 0mg Chol, 125mg Sod, 3g Pro, 16g Sug, 19g Carb, <1g Fib

Exchanges   Net Carbs

Other Carbs 1   19

Cappuccino

At home, Cappuccino can be made by pouring hot milk and hot espresso into a blender and processing until frothy. Sprinkle with nutmeg or cinnamon. Or, top with whipped topping and chocolate sprinkles.

Lime Spritzer

*Good wine choices are: Chardonnay,
Chablis, Reisling, etc.*

½ **cup dry white wine**
1 **lime (1 tablespoon juice and 1 slice)**
½ **cup diet lemon-lime soda, or to taste**

1. Combine wine, lime juice and soda.
Pour over ice. Garnish with a lime slice.

Per serving: 84 Cal, 0g Fat, 0g Sat F,
0mg Chol, 21mg Sod, <1g Pro,
<1g Sug, 2g Carb, 0g Fib

Exchanges   Net Carbs

Other Carbs 1   2

7-Up Punch

MAKES 36 PUNCH CUP SERVINGS

This makes a nice holiday punch.

2 **quarts nonfat vanilla ice cream**
3 **quarts diet 7-Up, chilled**

1. Spoon ice cream into a large punch
bowl. Stir in 7-Up, leaving small bits of ice
cream.

Per serving: 40 Cal, 0g Fat, 0g Sat F,
 0mg Chol, 38mg Sod, 1g Pro,
 7g Sug, 9g Carb, <1g Fib

Exchanges   Net Carbs

Other Carbs 1/2   9

Mochalicious

MAKES 1 SERVING

Delicious! The taste testers loved this one.

1	cup hot coffee
¼	cup low-fat spray whipped cream
1	tablespoon low-carb dark chocolate, grated

1. Pour coffee into mugs. Top with about ¼ cup spray whipped cream and sprinkle with grated chocolate.

Per serving: 113 Cal, 11g Fat, 7g Sat F, 33mg Chol, 17mg Sod, 1g Pro, 0g Sug, 2g Carb, 1g Fib

Exchanges	*Net Carbs*
Fat 2	1

Frappacino

MAKES 4 SERVINGS

For a more flavorful drink, you need to use strong brewed coffee.

4	cups strong decaf coffee
1	cup fat-free half & half
6	packets Splenda®, or to taste

1. Combine ingredients and chill. Serve over ice.

Per serving: 41 Cal, 1g Fat, 1g Sat F, 3mg Chol, 91mg Sod, 2g Pro, 3g Sug, 7g Carb, 0g Fib

Exchanges	*Net Carbs*
0	7

Easy Entertaining ideas

- Serve dessert coffees such as the ones on these pages.

- Serve a nice dessert and coffee or tea.

- Serve sliced fruit with Heavenly Fruit Dip.

Spiced Coffee

MAKES 4 CUPS

Can you believe our passion for flavored coffees.

- 4 cups water
- 1 cinnamon stick
- 1 teaspoon whole allspice
  Dash nutmeg
- 2 packets Splenda
- 1 tablespoon instant coffee

1. In large saucepan, combine first 4 ingredients. Bring mixture to a boil; remove from heat. Stir in Splenda and coffee. Serve hot.

Per cup: 5 Cal, 0g Fat, 0g Sat F, 0mg Chol, 33mg Sod, 0g Pro, 0g Sug, 1g Carb, 0g Fib

Exchanges	Net Carbs
Free	1

Dessert Coffee

MAKES 1 SERVING

Sugar-free syrup makes this a wonderful low-carb drink.

- 1 cup hot decaf coffee
- 2 tablespoons fat-free half & half
- 2 teaspoons sugar free white chocolate syrup
- 1 packet Splenda®

1. Combine all ingredients in a mug and enjoy.

Per serving: 22 Cal, 1g Fat, 1g Sat F, 3mg Chol, 91mg Sod, 2g Pro, 3g Sug, 7g Carb, 0g Fib

Exchanges	Net Carbs
0	7

Caramel Coffee Delight

Variations can be easily made by using Irish cream, hazelnut or other assorted sugar-free syrups.

1 **tablespoon sugar-free caramel syrup (or to taste)**
1 **cup hot decaf coffee**
2 **tablespoons frozen Lite whipped topping, thawed**

1. Pour syrup into a 10-ounce mug. Add coffee and top with whipped topping. If desired, garnish with cocoa powder or grated chocolate.

Per serving: 21 Cal, 1g Fat, 1g Sat F, 0mg Chol, 11mg Sod, 1g Pro, 2g Sug, 2g Carb, 0g Fib

Exchanges   Net Carbs
Free   2

Maple Coffee Drink

MAKES 2 SERVINGS

Can't always make it to Starbucks. You can make this delicious coffee drink at home.

½ **cup fat-free half & half**
1 **to 2 tablespoons no-carb maple syrup**
1 **cup hot decaf coffee**

1. Combine ingredients until mixed. Heat in microwave and serve.

Per serving: 42 Cal, 1g Fat, 1g Sat F, 3mg Chol, 94mg Sod, 2g Pro, 3g Sug, 5g Carb, 0g Fib

Exchanges   Net Carbs
0   5

Breads

- 🧑‍🍳 Breakfast
- 🧑‍🍳 Breads
- 🧑‍🍳 Muffins

Oven Pancake

This is delicious and fun to make. Pancake will puff up like a large bowl. Then it will fall after removing from oven.

2   **tablespoons reduced calorie margarine**
2   **large eggs, lightly beaten**
½   **cup nonfat milk**
½   **cup flour**

1. Preheat oven to 425°F. Place margarine in 9-inch pie dish and melt in oven.

2. Meanwhile, combine remaining ingredients. Pour into pie dish and bake 12 to 15 minutes or until golden. Serve immediately.

Per serving: 199 Cal, 10g Fat, 2g Sat F, 142mg Chol, 112mg Sod, 9g Pro, 2g Sug, 20g Carb, 1g Fib

Exchanges   Net Carbs
Fat 1-1/2   19
Meat 1/2
Starch 1

Maple Butter

MAKES 2/3 CUP

Use as a topping for French toast, pancakes or waffles.

½   **cup reduced calorie margarine, softened**
¼   **cup no-carb maple syrup**

1. In a mixer bowl, beat margarine until fluffy.

2. Gradually add maple syrup, beating until well-mixed and light.

NET CARBS: 0

The Basic Muffin

MAKES 12 MUFFINS

Nothing fancy, but good with almost any meal.

2 cups flour
½ cup Splenda
1 tablespoon baking powder
5 tablespoons vegetable oil
2 egg whites
¾ cup nonfat milk

1. Preheat oven to 400°F. Combine first 3 ingredients in medium bowl, stirring to blend. Thoroughly combine remaining ingredients in a small bowl; pour into flour mixture. Stir gently just until flour is moistened.

2. Spoon into paper-lined muffin tins, filling about 2/3 full. Bake 15 to 20 minutes or until center tests done.

Per muffin: 143 Cal, 6g Fat, 1g Sat F, 0mg Chol, 139mg Sod, 4g Pro, 1g Sug, 19g Carb, 1g Fib

Exchanges   Net Carbs
Fat 1   18
Starch 1

VARIATION: Add one or two of the following:
1 cup blueberries
½ cup chopped nuts
1 tablespoon freshly grated lemon peel
1 tablespoon freshly grated orange peel

Whole Wheat Muffins

MAKES 12 MUFFINS

Use regular sugar in this recipe.

2 cups whole wheat flour
½ cup sugar
3½ teaspoons baking powder
2 egg whites
3 tablespoons reduced calorie margarine, small pieces
1½ cups non-fat milk

1. Preheat oven to 375°F. In mixing bowl, combine flour, sugar and baking powder. Combine remaining ingredients. Add to dry mixture; stir just enough to moisten (do not overmix.)

2. Pour into sprayed muffin tins, filling ¾ full. Bake 25 to 30 minutes or until center tests done.

Per muffin: 127 Cal, 3g Fat, 1g Sat F, 0mg Chol, 33mg Sod, 3g Pro, 8g Sug, 23g Carb, 2g Fib

Exchanges   Net Carbs
Fat 1/2   21
Other Carbs 1/2
Starch 1

Bran Muffins

A delicious bran muffin "without" sugar.

2   cups nonfat milk
2   cups All-Bran cereal
¼   cup reduced calorie stick margarine
2   eggs
5   teaspoons baking powder
2   cups flour

1. Preheat oven to 375°F. In small mixing bowl, pour milk over cereal. Let stand until soft (about 5 minutes).

2. Cream margarine in mixer bowl. Add eggs and beat until smooth. Add bran mixture. Combine baking powder and flour. Add to bran mixture, stirring just enough to moisten the flour. Spoon into sprayed muffin tins, filling almost full. Bake 25 to 30 minutes or until center tests done. Serve hot.

Per muffin: 161 Cal, 5g Fat, 1g Sat F, 36mg Chol, 284mg Sod, 7g Pro, 4g Sug, 27g Carb, 3g Fib

Exchanges   Net Carbs

Fat 1   24
Starch 1-1/2

Biscuits

Buttermilk biscuits are always a favorite.

2   cups flour
½   teaspoon salt
3   teaspoons baking powder
1   tablespoon, plus 2 teaspoons reduced calorie margarine, melted
¾   cup nonfat milk

1. Preheat oven to 450°F. In medium mixing bowl, combine flour, salt and baking powder. Stir to mix. Add the 1 tablespoon margarine to the milk. Add to flour mixture; stir quickly and gently to blend.

2. Place on lightly floured surface. Knead lightly until smooth (this doesn't take long.) Gently pat into a circle about ¾-inch thick. Cut with a 2½-inch biscuit cutter into 12 biscuits. Scraps can be gently re-rolled.

3. Place on a sprayed baking sheet. Brush lightly with remaining margarine. Bake for 10 to 12 minutes or until light golden.
tip: For crisper biscuits, do not allow biscuits to touch. For softer, place biscuits close together.

Per biscuit: 99 Cal, 2g Fat, <1g Sat F, <1mg Chol, 126mg Sod, 4g Pro, 1g Sug, 18g Carb, 1g Fib

Exchanges   Net Carbs

Fat 1/2   17
Starch 1

Bread

Bread is a delicious part of our diet, but we do need to control the fat. For that reason, the fat in these recipes has been kept as low as possible.

I have also included some easy to make yeast breads. Depending on the size of your bread machine, most of the recipes can be made on the dough cycle. This eliminates having to knead the dough. Just mix, put in the pan and let rise.

Buttermilk Biscuits

MAKES 20 BISCUITS

Buttermilk adds a rich flavor.

2   **cups flour**
2   **teaspoons baking powder**
¾   **teaspoon baking soda**
1   **tablespoon sugar**
5   **tablespoons reduced calorie margarine, chilled**
1   **cup low-fat buttermilk**

1. Preheat oven to 400°F. In medium bowl, combine flour, baking powder, baking soda and sugar. Add margarine; cut in with a fork or pastry blender until very small balls form. Add buttermilk; stir just until moistened. Mixture will be quite moist.

2. Turn out on floured surface. Gently knead, about 10 to 15 turns, until smooth. Dough will be quite soft and feel light to the touch. Pat out to ½-inch thick. Cut with floured 2-inch round cutter.

3. Place on a sprayed baking sheet. Bake 10 to 12 minutes or until cooked through. TIP: Scraps can be used, but treat gently or biscuits will be tough.

Per biscuit: 80 Cal, 3g Fat, 1g Sat F, 1mg Chol, 85mg Sod, 2g Pro, 1g Sug, 12g Carb, <1g Fib

Exchanges   Net Carbs

Fat 1/2   12
Starch 1/2

Blueberry Drop Biscuits

This is such an easy way to make biscuits.

1   **cup flour**
½   **teaspoon salt**
1½ **teaspoons baking powder**
2   **tablespoons reduced calorie margarine**
½   **cup nonfat milk**
½   **cup fresh blueberries**

1. Preheat oven to 375°F. Combine flour, salt and baking powder in a mixing bowl. Cut in margarine with two knives or a pastry blender. Add milk, stirring just enough to moisten. Carefully fold in blueberries. Drop by tablespoon onto a sprayed baking sheet. Bake 12 to 14 minutes or until lightly browned.

Per biscuit: 64 Cal, 2g Fat, <1g Sat F, <1mg Chol, 179mg Sod, 2g Pro, 1g Sug, 10g Carb, <1g Fib

Exchanges   Net Carbs

Fat 1/2   10
Starch 1/2

Orange Sweet Rolls

You will love these.

1   **(1-lb) loaf frozen bread dough, thawed**
1/3 **cup sugar free apricot preserves**
2   **tablespoons dried cranberries**
1/2 **cup sifted powdered sugar**
1/2 **teaspoon freshly grated orange peel**
1   **tablespoon orange juice**

1. Roll the bread dough into a 12x8-inch rectangle and spread with apricot preserves. Sprinkle with cranberries. Roll up, starting with the long side. Pinch dough to seal.

2. Cut into 12 one inch slices. Place in a sprayed muffin tin. Lightly cover and let rise until doubled, about 50 to 60 minutes.

3. Meanwhile, preheat oven to 350°F. Bake 15 to 20 minutes or until golden. Remove and place on rack.

4. Combine powdered sugar and orange peel with just enough of the orange juice to make a glaze. Drizzle over warm rolls.

Per roll: 134 Cal, 2g Fat, 0g Sat F, 0mg Chol, 212mg Sod, 4g Pro, 7g Sug, 27g Carb, 2g Fib

Exchanges   Net Carbs

Other Carbs 1/2   25
Starch 1

Quick Cinnamon Rolls

These can be ready to bake in less than 5 minutes.

4   (10-oz) can refrigerated pizza crust
1   tablespoon reduced calorie margarine
2   tablespoons cinnamon sugar (made with Splenda)
½   cup sifted powdered sugar

1. Preheat oven to 375°F. Spray an 8-inch cake pan with cooking spray. Unroll pizza dough; press slightly to straighten edges. You should have about a 10x13-inch rectangle.
2. Spread margarine evenly over dough. Sprinkle with cinnamon sugar. Roll up tightly, starting with the 10-inch side. Press edges to seal.
3. Cut into 8 slices. Place, cut-side up, in pan. Bake 18 to 20 minutes or until golden. Remove from pan; place right side up on serving dish. Combine powdered sugar with just enough water to make a glaze. Drizzle over hot rolls, serve hot.

Per roll: 137 Cal, 3g Fat, <1g Sat F, 0mg Chol, 248mg Sod, 3g Pro, 9g Sug, 25g Carb, 1g Fib

Exchanges   Net Carbs
Fat 1/2   24
Other Carbs 1/2
Starch 1

Tomato-Garlic Pizza Bread

A nice light pizza.

1   (10-oz) package refrigerated pizza crust
2   small garlic cloves, minced
½   teaspoon dried oregano
1   cup (4-oz) reduced fat Mozzarella cheese, shredded
2   plum tomatoes, chopped

1. Preheat oven to 425°F. On a sprayed baking sheet, pat dough into about a 12x8-inch rectangle. Sprinkle with garlic, oregano, and cheese. Top with chopped tomato. Bake 10 to 12 minutes or until crust is golden and cheese has melted.

Per serving: 132 Cal, 3g Fat, 1g Sat F, 5mg Chol, 337mg Sod, 7g Pro, 2g Sug, 18g Carb, 1g Fib

Exchanges   Net Carbs
Meat 1/2   17
Starch 1

Supper Cheese Bread

MAKES 6 SERVINGS

A cheese bread that goes with almost everything.

1½ cups baking mix
1 large egg
¼ cup nonfat milk
1 cup (4-oz) reduced fat Cheddar
cheese, shredded, divided
1 teaspoon poppy seeds
2 tablespoons reduced calorie
margarine, melted

1. Preheat oven to 400°F. Combine baking mix, egg, milk and ½ cup of the cheese; stir just until moistened. The dough will be quite sticky. Pat dough evenly onto bottom of a sprayed 9-inch pie pan. Sprinkle with cheese and poppy seeds; pour margarine over top. Bake 20 to 25 minutes or until lightly browned. Cut into wedges and serve hot.

Per serving: 207 Cal, 11g Fat, 3g Sat F, 40mg Chol, 540mg Sod, 8g Pro, 1g Sug, 20g Carb, 1g Fib

Exchanges   Net Carbs

Fat 1   19
Starch 1
Very Lean Meat 1

Easy Graham Bread

MAKES 1 LOAF OF 16 SLICES

*I like to make this bread when
I have leftover buttermilk.*

2 cups graham flour (or whole wheat)
1 cup flour
½ cup sugar
1 teaspoon salt
1 teaspoon baking soda
2 cups low-fat buttermilk

1. Preheat oven to 375°F. Combine both flours, sugar and salt. Combine baking soda and buttermilk. Stir into flour mixture just until blended.

2. Pour into a sprayed 9x5-inch loaf pan. Bake 60 to 70 minutes or until center tests done. Remove from pan and cool on rack.

Per slice: 122 Cal, 1g Fat, <1g Sat F, 1mg Chol, 178mg Sod, 4g Pro, 8g Sug, 26g Carb, 2g Fib

Exchanges   Net Carbs

Other Carbs 1/2   24
Starch 1

Corn Bread Sticks

*I call this recipe amazing because it really is
amazing what you can do with a few ingredients.*

1   can (8.75-oz) cream corn
2   cups all-purpose baking mix
2   tablespoons reduced calorie
    margarine, melted
    Parmesan cheese

1. Preheat oven to 450°F. Combine corn
and baking mix. Turn out onto a floured
surface and knead no more than 8 to 10 times
using more flour as needed. Pat into a 10x6-
inch rectangle Cut lengthwise in half, then
crosswise into 10 strips.

2. Carefully place bread on a sprayed
baking pan, about 1-inch apart. Brush with
margarine and sprinkle with cheese. Bake 10
to 12 minutes or until lightly browned and
cooked through.

Per bread stick: 70 Cal, 3g Fat, 1g Sat F,
<1mg Chol, 205mg Sod, 1g Pro,
1g Sug, 10g Carb, <1g Fib

Exchanges   Net Carbs

Fat 1/2   10
Starch 1/2

Tomato Herb Toast

*These are excellent for an
appetizer tray or with salads.*

4   slices low-fat white bread
1   tablespoon oil
2   small Plum tomatoes, chopped
½   teaspoon dried basil
    Salt and pepper to taste
½   cup (2-oz) reduced fat Cheddar
    cheese, shredded

1. Preheat oven to 375°F. Brush top side
of bread with oil. Place on baking sheet and
bake 6 to 8 minutes or until toasted.

2. Combine tomato and basil. Add salt and
pepper to taste. Spoon onto bread slices.
Sprinkle with cheese. Bake 3 to 4 minutes to
melt cheese. Cut into triangles.

Per serving: 117 Cal, 2g Fat, 1g Sat F,
3mg Chol, 280mg Sod, 7g Pro,
1g Sug, 18g Carb, 1g Fib

Exchanges   Net Carbs

Starch 1   17
Very Lean Meat 1/2
Vegetable 1/2

Easy Cheese Rolls

MAKES 15 ROLLS

A nice bread machine recipe.

1½ cups nonfat milk
1 cup (4-oz) reduced fat Cheddar cheese, shredded
1 tablespoon sugar
1 teaspoon salt
4 cups flour
1 package dry yeast

1. Combine ingredients in pan in order given or as directed for your bread machine. Start dough cycle and mix thoroughly, adding a small amount of water or flour if needed to make a nice dough that isn't sticky or dry.
2. When kneading cycle is completed, remove from pan and punch down. Divide into 15 pieces. Form each into a smooth ball and place in sprayed muffin cups. Cover with towel or waxed paper and let rise until doubled in size, about 45 to 60 minutes.
3. Preheat oven to 400°F. Bake 12 to 14 minutes or until golden. Remove and serve or let cool.

Per roll: 154 Cal, 1g Fat, <1g Sat F, 2mg Chol, 214mg Sod, 8g Pro, 2g Sug, 30g Carb, 1g Fib

Exchanges   Net Carbs
Starch 1-1/2   29
Very Lean Meat 1/2

Croutons

MAKES 2 CUPS

4 slices low-fat white bread
1½ tablespoons oil
3 tablespoons grated Parmesan cheese

1. Preheat oven to 400°F. Cut bread into small cubes and place in bowl.
2. Toss with oil and Parmesan. Spread in a single layer in shallow baking pan and bake 5 to 8 minutes or until golden.

Per ¼ cup: 74 Cal, 4g Fat, 1g Sat F, 2mg Chol, 125mg Sod, 2g Pro, 0g Sug, 8g Carb, <1g Fib

Exchanges   Net Carbs
Fat 1/2   8
Starch 1/2

Pizza Dough

*Pizza dough is very easy to make
using a bread machine.*

1½   cups water
3¼   to 4 cups flour
½   teaspoon salt
1   package dry yeast

1. Combine ingredients in pan in order given or as directed for your bread machine. Start dough cycle and mix thoroughly, adding a small amount of flour or water if needed to make a smooth dough.

2. When kneading kneading cycle is completed, remove from pan and punch down. Press dough into desired pans.

3. Preheat oven to 425°F. Add toppings to dough and bake until cooked through and cheese is melted.

Makes:
   two 16-inch thin crust pizzas
   two 12-inch thick crust pizzas
   five 9-inch individual pizzas

Nutritional analysis will vary.

Batter Bread

MAKES 1 LOAF OF 16 SLICES

Quick and easy.

1   package dry yeast
1¼   cups water (105 to 115 F)
2   tablespoons honey
2   tablespoons reduced calorie stick margarine
1   teaspoon salt
3   cups flour

1. Combine yeast, water and honey in small bowl; stir slightly. Let stand until doubled in size, about 10 minutes.

2. In large bowl, combine yeast mixture, margarine, salt and 2 cups of the flour. If using mixer, beat on low speed until blended. Beat at medium speed for about 1 minutes. Stir in remaining flour with wooden spoon. Cover and let rise in warm place, about 1 hour or until doubled.

3. Stir batter down; spoon into a sprayed 9x5-inch loaf pan. Cover and let rise in warm place, about 45 minutes or until doubled.

4. Preheat oven to 375°F. Bake 35 to 45 minutes or until browned and loaf sounds

hollow when tapped. Remove from pan and cool on rack. Makes 1 loaf.

Per slice: 112 Cal, 2g Fat, <1g Sat F, 0mg Chol, 162mg Sod, 4g Pro, 2g Sug, 22g Carb, 1g Fib

Exchanges

Fat 1/2
Starch 1

Net Carbs

21

Focaccia

MAKES 10 SERVINGS

This recipe can also be mixed in your bread machine using the dough cycle.

1   **package dry yeast**
2   **to 2½ cups flour**
1   **teaspoon sugar**
½   **teaspoon salt**
1   **tablespoon, plus 1 teaspoon olive oil**
     Garlic salt or grated Pamesan cheese

1. In large mixer bowl, combine yeast, 1½ cups of the flour, sugar and salt. Add ¾ cup hot tap water and the 1 tablespoon oil. Beat until smooth. By hand, stir in enough of the remaining flour to make a soft, but not sticky dough. Place on a floured surface and knead about 5 minutes. Place in a lightly greased bowl. Cover and set in warm place until doubled, about 60 minutes.

2. Lightly spray a 12-inch pizza pan. Flatten dough into an 11-inch circle. Prick surface of dough with fork. Brush with remaining olive oil. Sprinkle lightly with garlic salt or Parmesan. Let rise in warm place 30 minutes. Preheat oven to 425°F. Bake 18 to 20 minutes or until golden. Best served warm.

Per serving: 128 Cal, 2g Fat, <1g Sat F, 0mg Chol, 221mg Sod, 5g Pro, <1g Sug, 24g Carb, 1g Fib

Exchanges

Fat 1/2
Starch 1-1/2

Net Carbs

23

Cook's Tip

Focaccia can be used as a bread serving or split and fill with your favorite sandwich ingredients.

Swedish Rye Bread

MAKES 1 LOAF OF 16 SLICES

You may decide to make bread more often after you try this recipe.

1   **package dry yeast**
2   **tablespoons honey**
2   **tablespoons oil**
1   **cup dark rye flour**
1   **teaspoon salt**
2¾   **cups flour**

1. In a mixer bowl, dissolve the yeast and honey in 1¼ cups water (105-110°F). Add oil and rye flour, and with the paddle attachment, beat until smooth. Add salt and flour and beat until well mixed. Switch to the hook attachment and beat 4 to 5 minutes or until smooth and elastic.

2. Place dough in a large sprayed bowl; turn to coat the top. Cover and let rise in a warm place until doubled, about 45 to 60 minutes.

3. Punch down the dough, shape into a loaf and place in a sprayed 9x5-inch loaf pan. Loosely cover and let rise until doubled, about 45-60 minutes. Preheat oven to 375°F. Bake 35 to 45 minutes or until browned and bottom of bread sounds hollow when tapped. It's okay to return the bread to the pan and continue baking, if necessary.

variation: Add 2 teaspoons caraway seeds when adding rye flour.

Per slice: 133 Cal, 2g Fat, <1g Sat F, 0mg Chol, 146mg Sod, 5g Pro, 2g Sug, 26g Carb, 2g Fib

Exchanges
Fat 1/2
Starch 1-1/2

Net Carbs
24

Bread Crumbs How-To

Soft Bread Crumbs

Soft bread crumbs are made from fresh low-fat white bread. Process in a blender or food processor until soft crumbs form.

TWO SLICES WILL MAKE 1 CUP

Dry Bread Crumbs

Place low-fat white bread on a baking sheet and bake at 350°F 10 to 12 minutes or until bread is quite dry. Break into smaller pieces and process in blender or food processor to make dry crumbs.

FOUR SLICES WILL MAKE 1 CUP

Rosemary Batter Bread

MAKES 1 LOAF OF 16 SLICES

Great with Italian food.

3 cups flour, divided
1 teaspoon salt
2 1 package dry yeast
1 tablespoon sugar
2 tablespoons shortening
1 teaspoon crushed dried rosemary leaves

1. In mixer bowl, combine 2 cups of the flour, salt, sugar and yeast. Add 1¼ cups very warm water (120-130° F), shortening and rosemary. Beat on medium speed about 2 minutes, scraping bowl frequently. By hand, stir in remaining 1 cup flour until batter is smooth.

2. Spoon into a sprayed 9x5-inch loaf pan. Cover and let rise until double, about 45 to 60 minutes.

3. Preheat oven to 375°F. Bake 35 to 45 minutes or until bread sounds hollow when tapped. Remove and cool on rack.

Per slice: 106 Cal, 2g Fat, <1g Sat F, 0mg Chol, 146mg Sod, 4g Pro, 0g Sug, 20g Carb, 1g Fib

Exchanges   Net Carbs
Fat 1/2   19
Starch 1

Whole Wheat Bread

MAKES 1 LARGE LOAF OF 16 SLICES

---

1   package dry yeast
2   tablespoons reduced calorie stick
    margarine
4   cups all-purpose flour
1⅓ cups whole wheat flour
2   teaspoons salt

1. Dissolve yeast in ½ cup warm water (105-110°F). Place in mixer bowl along with the margarine.

2. Combine flour, whole wheat flour and salt. Place 3½ cups flour mixture in mixer bowl along with 2 cups water. Beat with paddle attachment until smooth. Add enough of the remaining flour to make a soft, but not sticky dough; you may not need all the flour. Switch to hook attachment and beat until dough is smooth and clears the side of the bowl, about 4 to 5 minutes.

3. Remove and place on a lightly floured surface, kneading just until smooth. Place in a sprayed bowl, turning to coat top. Cover and let rise about 60 minutes or until doubled in size.

4. Punch down dough. Shape into one large round and place on a large lightly sprayed baking sheet. Cover with a tea towel and let rise until double, about 30 to 45 minutes. Preheat oven to 375°F. Bake 20 to 25 minutes or until lightly browned and bottom sounds hollow when tapped.

Per slice: 168 Cal, 2g Fat, <1g Sat F, 0mg Chol, 308mg Sod, 7g Pro, 0g Sug, 33g Carb, 2g Fib

Exchanges   Net Carbs
Fat 1/2   31
Starch 2

Barnes & Noble Booksellers #2230
11380 Legacy Ave
Palm Beach Gardens, FL 33410
561-625-3932

STR:2230 REG:007 TRN:3556 CSHR:Joanne G

Girl Who Played with Fir
9780739384176   T1
(1 @ 39.95) PROMO 20% (7.99)
(1 @ 31.96)   31.96
Diabetic Cookbook: Delic
9780942878080   T1
(1 @ 19.95)   19.95
Six Ingredients or Less
9780942878073   T1
(1 @ 19.95)   19.95

Subtotal   71.86
Sales Tax T1 (6.000%)   4.31
TOTAL   76.17
AMEX   76.17
  Card#: XXXXXXXXXXX5000
  Expdate: XX/XX
  Auth: 586110
  Entry Method: Swiped

A MEMBER WOULD HAVE SAVED   7.20

Thanks for shopping at
Barnes & Noble

101.25B   04/04/2011 01:35PM

CUSTOMER COPY

Barnes & Noble Booksellers #2230
11380 Legacy Ave
Palm Beach, FL 33410

Return Policy

<u>With a sales receipt</u>, a full refund in the original form of payment
will be issued from any Barnes & Noble store for returns of new
and unread books (except textbooks) and unopened
music/DVDs/audio made within (i) 14 days of purchase from a
Barnes & Noble retail store (except for purchases made by check
less than 7 days prior to the date of return) or (ii) 14 days of
delivery date for Barnes & Noble.com purchases (except for
purchases made via PayPal). A store credit for the purchase price
will be issued for (i) purchases made by check less than 7 days
prior to the date of return, (ii) when a gift receipt is presented
within 60 days of purchase, (iii) textbooks returned with a receipt
within 14 days of purchase, or (iv) original purchase was made
through Barnes & Noble.com via PayPal. Opened music/DVDs/
audio may not be returned, but can be exchanged only for the
same title if defective.

<u>After 14 days or without a sales receipt</u>, returns or exchanges will
not be permitted.

Magazines, newspapers, and used books are not returnable.
Product not carried by Barnes & Noble or Barnes & Noble.com will
not be accepted for return.

Policy on receipt may appear in two sections.

Subtotal
Sa
TOTAL
AMEX

Auth: 985110
Edit Method

A MEMBER WOULD HAVE SAVED   7.20

Thanks for shopping at

Return Policy

<u>With a sales receipt</u>, a full refund in the original form of payment
will be issued from any Barnes & Noble store for returns of new
and unread books (except textbooks) and unopened
music/DVDs/audio made within (i) 14 days of purchase from a
Barnes & Noble retail store (except for purchases made by check
less than 7 days prior to the date of return) or (ii) 14 days of
delivery date for Barnes & Noble.com purchases (except for
purchases made via PayPal). A store credit for the purchase price
will be issued for (i) purchases made by check less than 7 days
prior to the date of return, (ii) when a gift receipt is presented
within 60 days of purchase, (iii) textbooks returned with a receipt
within 14 days of purchase, or (iv) original purchase was made

Eggs & Cheese

✿ Omelets
✿ Casseroles
✿ Quiches

Basic Omelet

MAKES 2 SERVINGS

Once you learn the basics you can make a variety of your favorite omelets.

¾ **egg substitute**
   Salt and pepper

1. Place a sprayed 9-inch nonstick skillet over medium heat.
2. Combine egg substitute, salt, pepper and 1 tablespoon water, mixing until lightly blended. Add to skillet. As mixture begins to set, lift edges to allow uncooked portions to flow underneath. When eggs are lightly set, fold, then cut in half to serve.

Per serving: 80 Cal, 3g Fat, 1g Sat F, 1mg Chol, 167mg Sod, 11g Pro, 1g Sug, 1g Carb, 0g Fib

Exchanges   Net Carbs
     Fat 1/2   1
Very Lean Meat 1-1/2

MENU

Ham & Cheese Omelet
Orange Sweet Rolls
Fresh Fruit

Ham & Cheese Omelet

MAKES 1 SERVING

I added a little apple here, not much, just 1 tablespoon, but a treat!

1   **tablespoon diced apple**
¼ **egg substitute**
1   **large egg**
¼ **cup diced Canadian Bacon**
¼ **cup (1-oz) reduced fat Swiss cheese, shredded**

1. In a sprayed 9-inch nonstick skillet cook apple until just tender. Remove apple and set aside.
2. Combine egg substitute with 1 tablespoon water. Add to skillet and cook until eggs begin to set. Then gently lift edges to allow egg to flow underneath. When eggs are lightly set, spoon apple, ham, and cheese over one side. Let cook about 1 minute. Fold in half and serve.

Per serving: 214 Cal, 10g Fat, 3 g Sat F, 232mg Chol, 490mg Sod, 26g Pro, 2g Sug, 3g Carb, <1g Fib

Exchanges   Net Carbs
     Fat 1/2   3
     Meat 1
Very Lean Meat 3

Omelet For Two

*Quick and easy. Just what
you need in the morning.*

¼ **cup finely chopped onion.**
¾ **cup egg substitute**
1 **egg**
   Salt and pepper

1. In a sprayed 9-inch nonstick skillet add onion and cook until soft.

2. Combine egg substitute with salt, pepper and 2 tablespoons water. Add to skillet and cook over medium heat, lifting gently to allow uncooked portion to flow underneath. When eggs are lightly set, fold, then cut in half to serve.

Per serving: 124 Cal, 1g Fat, 1g Sat F, 106mg Chol, 198mg Sod, 15g Pro, 2g Sug, 3g Carb, <1g Fib

Exchanges   Net Carbs

Fat 1/2   3
Very Lean Meat 1-1/2
Veg 1/2

Omelet Crepes

There's a restaurant in Missouri that makes their omelets this way, filling them with all sorts of delicious fillings and toppings. If you have trouble making omelets, try this easy method.

2 **large eggs**

1. Thoroughly combine eggs with 2 tablespoons water, whisking until smooth.

2. Heat a sprayed 9-inch nonstick skillet over medium heat. Add eggs and cook until top is only slightly moist. Turn and cook 2 to 3 seconds. Remove. Fill omelets, non-browned side out, with desired filling and/or toppings. Roll up and serve.

Per serving: 147 Cal, 10g Fat, 3g Sat F, 422mg Chol, 124mg Sod, 13g Pro, 1g Sug, 1g Carb, 0g Fib

Exchanges   Net Carbs

Fat 1   1
Meat 2

Cook's Tip
Omelets are easier to make if cooked in a slope-sided nonstick skillet.

Chicken Frittata

Just a small amount of chicken is all you need for this recipe.

2 tablespoons reduced calorie margarine
1 cup cubed cooked chicken
1 tablespoon fat-free half & half
1½ cups egg substitute
¼ teaspoon salt
½ cup salsa

1. Heat margarine in an oven-proof 10-inch skillet. Spoon chicken over bottom. Combine half & half, egg substitute, salt and 3 tablespoons water and pour over chicken. Spoon salsa over top.

2. Cook over low heat 6 to 8 minutes or until almost set.

3. Broil about 6 inches from heat, 2 to 3 minutes, or until set.

Per serving: 171 Cal, 10g Fat, 2g Sat F, 19mg Chol, 381mg Sod, 18g Pro, 1g Sug, 2g Carb, <1g Fib

Exchanges   Net Carbs
Fat 1-1/2   2
Very Lean Meat 2-1/2

Sausage Egg Scramble

Mixture can be served in a low-carb tortilla. Just add 3 carbs per serving.

4 ounces low-fat turkey sausage
¼ cup chopped onion
2 tablespoons chopped green pepper
3 large eggs
¾ cup egg substitute
½ cup (2-oz) reduced fat Monterey Jack cheese, shredded

1. Cook sausage, onion and green pepper in a medium skillet; drain.

2. Combine eggs and egg substitute with ¼-cup water. Add to sausage and cook over medium heat, stirring occasionally. Sprinkle with cheese and serve.

Per serving: 190 Cal, 13g Fat, 5g Sat F, 344mg Chol, 470mg Sod, 17g Pro, 1g Sug, 2g Carb, <1g Fib

Exchanges   Net Carbs
Fat 1   2
Meat 1-1/2
Very Lean Meat 1

Ham and Egg Scramble

An easy way to use up that last little bit of ham.

1 tablespoon reduced calorie margarine
2 tablespoons chopped onion
¼ cup chopped mushrooms
¼ cup diced ham
2 large eggs, lightly beaten
½ cup egg substitute

1. Melt margarine in a medium skillet. Add onion and cook until almost soft. Add mushrooms and cook through. Stir in the ham.

2. Add eggs, salt and pepper. Cook, stirring frequently, until almost set.

Per serving: 198 Cal, 12g Fat, 3g Sat F, 221mg Chol, 443mg Sod, 19g Pro, 1g Sug, 2g Carb, < 1g Fib

Exchanges   Net Carbs
Fat 2   2
Meat 1
Very Lean Meat 1-1/2

Egg Nests

MAKES 1 SERVING

Not just for kids.

1 slice nonfat French bread
1 large egg
   Salt and pepper

1. Make a hole in center of bread and place both pieces in a heated sprayed skillet. Drop egg into hole and sprinkle with salt and pepper. Cook over medium heat until toasted on bottom. Turn both pieces and cook as desired.

Per serving: 161 Cal, 5g Fat, 2g Sat F, 211mg Chol, 257mg Sod, 9g Pro, <1g Sug, 17g Carb, 1g Fib

Exchanges   Net Carbs
Fat 1/2   16
Meat 1
Starch 1

Sausage & Egg Casserole

MAKES 8 SERVINGS

For mushroom lovers. Spicy with a chewy cheese topping.

6   large eggs
¼   cup nonfat sour cream
12 ounces low-fat turkey sausage
4   ounces fresh mushrooms, sliced
1   (4-oz) can diced green chilies
2   cups (8-oz) reduced fat Mozzarella cheese, shredded

1. Preheat oven to 400°F. Combine eggs and sour cream. Pour into a sprayed 13x9-inch baking dish. Bake 10 to 12 minutes or until set, but not firm.
2. Meanwhile, cook sausage; drain. Add mushrooms and chilies and cook 2 to 3 minutes. Spoon over eggs. Sprinkle with cheese. Bake 10 to 15 minutes or until golden.

Per serving: 197 Cal, 12g Fat, 5g Sat F, 200mg Chol, 498mg Sod, 19g Pro, 1g Sug, 4g Carb, <1g Fib

Exchanges   Net Carbs
Fat 1   4
Meat 2-1/2

Asparagus-Egg Dish

MAKES 1 SERVING

Vegetable, meat and dairy, all in one recipe.

4   cooked asparagus spears
1   poached or fried egg
2   tablespoons diced ham

1. Place asparagus on a serving dish. Top with egg and ham.

Per serving: 101 Cal, 5g Fat, 2g Sat F, 217mg Chol, 173mg Sod, 10g Pro, 1g Sug, 3g Carb, 1g Fib

Exchanges   Net Carbs
Fat 1/2   2
Very Lean Meat 1/2
Vegetable 1/2

MENU
Sausage Egg Casserole
Blueberry Muffins
Orange Juice

Tortilla Egg Casserole

MAKES 6 SERVINGS

This is a little on the hot side.

3   large eggs
1¼ cup egg substitute
½   medium green pepper, chopped
1½ cups (6-oz) reduced fat Monterey
    Jack cheese, shredded
6   (7-inch) low-carb white flour tortillas

1. Preheat oven to 350°F. Lightly beat eggs with ¼ cup water. Cook along with green peppers in a medium skillet until scrambled, but still moist.

2. Spoon ¹/₆ of the mixture down center of each tortilla. Sprinkle with half the cheese. Roll tightly and place, seam-side down, in a sprayed 8x8-inch baking dish. Sprinkle with remaining cheese. Bake 15 to 20 minutes or until heated through.

Per serving: 242 Cal, 15g Fat, 7g Sat F, 168mg Chol, 493mg Sod, 24g Pro, 1g Sug, 13g Carb, 8g Fib

Exchanges   Net Carbs

Fat 1   5
Meat 2
Vegetable 1

Deviled Eggs

MAKES 16 HALVES

This may seem like a lot, but they make great snacks.

8   hard-boiled eggs
3   tablespoons light mayonnaise
2   teaspoons dill pickle relish
¼   cup finely chopped ham
    Salt and pepper to taste

1. Slice eggs in half lengthwise.
2. Remove yolks and combine with remaining ingredients. Fill whites. Cover and chill until ready to serve.

note: Fill deviled eggs by spooning egg mixture in a small resealable plastic bag. Cut off one corner of the bag and squeeze to fill.

Per half: 42 Cal, 3g Fat, 1g Sat F, 94mg Chol, 81mg Sod, 3g Pro, <1g Sug, <1g Carb, 0g Fib

Exchanges   Net Carbs

Fat 1/2   <1
Meat 1/2

Sunny-Side Up Eggs

MAKES 1 SERVING

If you have problems getting your eggs just right, try this method.

1 **large egg**
  Salt and pepper

1. Cook egg in a heavily small sprayed skillet until white is set.
2. Add 1 tablespoon water. Cover and let cook briefly until yolk is cooked to desired firmness.

Per serving: 73 Cal, 5g Fat, 2g Sat F, 212mg Chol, 62mg Sod, 6g Pro, <1g Sug, <1g Carb, 0g Fib

Exchanges   Net Carbs
Fat 1/2   <1
Meat 1

Hard-Boiled Eggs

This is the way I like to hard-boil eggs. I place the eggs in a single layer in a saucepan. Add water to cover eggs by 1 inch. Bring water to a boil then immediately remove from the heat. Let stand 20 minutes. Drain and rinse with cold water until eggs are cool.

note:
Overcooking the eggs will cause those unattractive green rings around the yolks.

Eggs Creole

MAKES 4 SERVINGS

Tomatoes add a nice touch to egg dishes.

⅓ **cup sliced mushrooms**
2 **tablespoons chopped onion**
1 **tablespoon reduced calorie margarine**
¾ **cup chopped Plum tomatoes**
2 **large eggs, lightly beaten**
1 **cup egg substitute**

1. Sauté mushrooms and onion in margarine until tender. Add tomatoes and heat through.
2. Add eggs and cook until scrambled, but not firm, stirring gently. Serve immediately.

Per serving: 120 Cal, 7g Fat, 2g Sat F, 106mg Chol, 163mg Sod, 11g Pro, 2g Sug, 3g Carb, 1g Fib

Exchanges   Net Carbs
Fat 1   2
Meat 1/2
Very Lean Meat 1
Vegetable 1/2

Hamburger Quiche

When you don't know what to cook for breakfast, lunch or dinner--make a quiche.

½   **pound extra lean ground beef**
1½   **cups (6-oz) reduced fat Swiss cheese, shredded**
⅔   **cup nonfat milk**
1   **tablespoon cornstarch**
¾   **cup egg substitute**

1. Preheat oven to 350°F. Brown ground beef; drain thoroughly.

2. Meanwhile, sprinkle cheese in a sprayed 9-inch pie dish. Top with ground beef.

3. Combine milk and cornstarch. Add egg substitute and mix well. Pour over ground beef. Bake 30 to 40 minutes or until custard is set.

note: Not as good reheated.

Per serving: 148 Cal, 5g Fat, 2g Sat F, 34mg Chol, 162mg Sod, 22g Pro, 2g Sug, 4g Carb, 0g Fib

Exchanges   Net Carbs

Fat 1/2   4
Very Lean Meat 3

Chicken-Broccoli Quiche

MAKES 6 SERVINGS

A nice creamy quiche

2   **cups small broccoli florets**
1   **cup (4-oz) reduced fat Swiss cheese, shredded**
1   **cup cubed cooked chicken**
½   **egg substitute**
1   **cup fat-free half & half**

1. Preheat oven to 350°F. Place broccoli in a sprayed 9-inch pie dish; add cheese and chicken.

2. Combine egg substitute and half & half until well mixed. Pour over chicken mixture, pressing down to cover ingredients as much as possible. Bake 30 to 40 minutes or until custard is set. Let stand 5 to 10 minutes before serving.

Per serving: 105 Cal, 3g Fat, 1g Sat F, 21mg Chol, 161mg Sod, 14g Pro, 2g Sug, 6g Carb, 1g Fib

Exchanges   Net Carbs

Fat 1/2   5
Very Lean Meat 2

Meats & Seafoods

- Ground Beef
- Beef
- Pork
- Lamb
- Salmon
- White Fish
- Shellfish

Selecting the Best Roasts

When selecting meat, freshness is of the utmost importance. There should be no offensive odors, yellow or brown discoloration on fat or sticky surfaces. The color should be bright and without dark spots.

Beef

Unlike some cuts of meat, a beef roast should have some marbling of fat. Restaurants usually get the Prime cuts of meat, so most of our choices will be Choice or Select, with Choice being the better of the two. Many supermarkets carry only Select cuts. These are okay, but if cooked beyond medium-rare stage, they may tend to be dry and less tender.

Pork

Pork tends to be lean with very little marbling. The meat should be firm and slightly moist. The color should be a pale reddish-pink. To prevent dryness, most pork should be cooked to no more that 140°. The temperature will rise as it stands. Pork is a great choice for brining, see page 206, but make sure the pork doesn't have additives. This may be labeled on the package as tender or flavor enhanced.

Lamb

I sometimes have a hard time finding good lamb, but look for meat that is light red in color. The fat should be smooth and white. As with pork, lamb should not be overcooked.

When cooking meats, I highly recommend you invest in an accurate thermometer. The one I like best has an external display that you can place on your counter with a cord attached to a probe that you insert into the meat. You simply set the desired temperature and the thermometer will beep to alert you when it has reached that degree. Do not rely on thermometers that have preset temperatures for Rare, Medium Rare, etc., we usually find these settings to be too high. Probably the most important thing to remember when cooking roasts, turkey or a whole chicken is to allow time for the meat to stand after roasting. Your meat will be juicier and easier to carve.

Beef Roasting Chart

Beef Cut	Oven Temp	Lbs	Approx. Total Cooking Hours	Remove when Temp Reaches
Eye Round Roast	325°F	2-3	Med. Rare: 1½ to 1¾	135° F
Rib Eye Roast (small end)	350° F	4-6 6-8	Med. Rare: 1¾ -2 / Med: 2-2½ Med. Rare: 2¼ / Med: 2½-2¾	135° F / 140° F 135° F / 140° F
Rib Eye Roast (large end)	350° F	4-6 6-8	Med. Rare: 2-2½ / Med: 2½-3 Med. Rare: 2¼-2½ / Med: 2½-3	135° F / 140° F 135° F / 140° F
Rib Roast (prime rib)	350° F	6-8 8-10	Med. Rare: 2¼-2½ / Med: ¾-3 Med. Rare: 2½-3 / Med: 3-3½	135° F / 140° F 135° F / 140° F
Round Tip Roast	325° F	4-6 6-8	Med. Rare: 2-2½ / Med: 2½-3 Med. Rare: 2½-3 / Med: 3-3½	140° F / 150° F 140° F / 150° F
Tenderloin Roast	425° F	2-3 4-5	Med. Rare: 35-40 min. / Med. 45-50 min Med. Rare: 50-60 min. / Med. 60-70 min	135° F / 140° F 135° F / 140° F
Tri-Tip Roast	425° F	1½-2	Med. Rare: 30-40 min. / Med. 40-45 min	135° F / 140° F
Ground Beef				160°F

Olive Oils

Extra Virgin Olive Oil	Fragrant and strong flavor. Drizzle on pasta, meats and vegetables. Not for high temperature cooking.
Virgin Olive Oil	Lighter and less fruity. Can use the same as extra virgin oil but doesn't have the same flavor.
Refined Olive Oil	Made from lower-quality oils. Use in frying, cooking and salad dressings.
Pure Olive Oil	Has a mild flavor. Cheaper than above oils. Use as an all-purpose oil, and in dressings, salads and marinades.
Extra Light Olive Oil	Composed of refined olive oils and virgin olive oils. A mild taste and light color. Can withstand higher temperatures. ***This is the one I used for this book.***
Pomace	Made from previous pressings. Bland flavor, but good for dressings, cooking and deep-frying.

Menu Ideas

Organization is the key to stress-free cooking. In the long run, it will save you time as well as money.

Make it simple and plan a 4-week cycle of menus. Once this is done, the hardest part is over and you are on your way to preparing more nutritious meals for your family.

As long as you know what the main course is, filling in the rest is fairly easy. At least once a week, prepare a ham, roast, chicken or turkey and plan for the use of leftovers.

A sample weekly menu might be:

> Sun - Ham
> Mon - Pizza
> Tue - Noodles & Ham Casserole
> Wed - Roasted Chicken
> Thur - Fish
> Fri - Ham Fettuccine
> Sat - A Chicken Casserole

Tortilla Hamburgers

MAKES 4 SERVINGS

A different twist on how to serve a hamburger.

1   pound extra lean ground beef
⅓   cup finely chopped onion
1   teaspoon salt
4   (7-inch) low-carb tortillas
2   cups shredded lettuce
¼   cup salsa

1. Combine first 3 ingredients and shape into 4 patties. Broil or grill patties until cooked (160°).

2. Warm tortillas if desired, and place on serving plates. Top with lettuce, burger patty and salsa.

Per serving: 289 Cal, 8g Fat, 3g Sat F, 70mg Chol, 922mg Sod, 23g Pro, 1g Sug, 24g Carb, 2g Fib

Exchanges   Net Carbs

Fat 1   22
Very Lean Meat 4
Vegetable 1/2

Ground Beef

Safety reasons show that all ground beef must be cooked to 160°F. The correct temperature is extremely important and well worth the investment in an accurate thermometer with the sensor in the tip, thus reducing any margin for error.

Burger Towers

MAKES 6 SERVINGS

Nice for even your carb friends.

1½   pounds extra lean ground beef
1   teaspoon seasoning salt
4   ounces mushrooms, sliced
2   tablespoons reduced calorie margarine
2   medium tomatoes

1. Lightly mix ground beef with salt. Shape into 6 patties about 1-inch thick. Pan-fry, grill or broil until cooked (160°), turning once.

2. Meanwhile, cook mushrooms in margarine until tender; drain.

3. Place meat patties on serving plates. Slice tomatoes and place on patties. Top with mushrooms.

Per serving: 211 Cal, 9g Fat, 3g Sat F, 70mg Chol, 257mg Sod, 27g Pro, 2g Sug, 3g Carb, 1g Fib

Exchanges   Net Carbs

Fat 1-1/2   2
Very Lean Meat 3-1/2
Vegetable 1/2

Taco Burgers

Like a taco, just minus the shell.

1   pound extra lean ground beef
½   cup salsa
4   slices reduced fat Cheddar cheese
1   cup shredded lettuce
2   Plum tomatoes, chopped

1. Combine ground beef and salsa. Form ground beef into 2 oval patties, about 3/4 inch thick. Broil or grill until cooked to 160°.
2. Top each with cheese, lettuce and tomato.

Per serving: 230 Cal, 8g Fat, 4g Sat F, 76mg Chol, 235mg Sod, 34g Pro, 3g Sug, 6g Carb, 2g Fib

Exchanges   Net Carbs

Fat 1   4
Very Lean Meat 5
Vegetable 1/2

Southwestern Cheeseburgers

Any cheese can be substituted for the Monterey Jack.

1   pound extra lean ground beef
¼   cup finely chopped onion
4   slices reduced fat Monterey Jack cheese
4   tomato slices

1. Combine ground beef and onion. Divide and shape into 8 thin slices. Top 4 patties with cheese, cutting cheese to fit. Cover with remaining patties and seal. Broil or grill until cooked to 160°. Top with tomato slice and serve.

Per serving: 253 Cal, 12g Fat, 7g Sat F, 90mg Chol, 297mg Sod, 34g Pro, 1g Sug, 2g Carb, 0g Fib

Exchanges   Net Carbs

Fat 1-1/2   2
Meat 1
Very Lean Meat 4

Swiss with Dill Burgers

MAKES 4 SERVINGS

Serve hamburgers with your choice of condiments and fresh vegetables.

1 **pound extra lean ground beef**
2 **tablespoons nonfat sour cream**
¼ **teaspoon dried dill weed**
4 **(1-oz) slices reduced fat Swiss cheese**

1. Combine first 3 ingredients, mixing lightly. Shape into 4 patties and grill over direct heat until cooked through (160°). Top with cheese and cook until melted.

Per serving: 224 Cal, 8g Fat, 4g Sat F, 81mg Chol, 140mg Sod, 35g Pro, 0g Sug, 2g Carb, 0g Fib

Exchanges   Net Carbs
Fat 1   2
Very Lean Meat 5

Swiss Burgers

MAKES 4SERVINGS

If desired, meat can be divided into smaller burgers.

1 **pound extra lean ground beef**
   Salt and pepper
4 **(1-oz) slices reduced fat Swiss cheese**
4 **dill pickle spears**

1. Form ground beef into 4 patties. Broil or grill until cooked through (160°). Sprinkle with salt and pepper and top with cheese last couple minutes of cooking time.
2. Serve with pickles.

Per serving: 224 Cal, 8g Fat, 4g Sat F, 80mg Chol, 514mg Sod, 35g Pro, 1g Sug, 2g Carb, 0g Fib

Exchanges   Net Carbs
Fat 1   2
Very Lean Meat 5

Reuben Burgers

MAKES 4 SERVINGS

A delicious way to serve a beef patty.

1 **pound extra lean ground beef**
1 **cup sauerkraut, drained**
4 **(1-oz) slices reduced fat Swiss cheese**

1. Shape ground beef into 4 oval patties and grill or cook as desired, to 160°.

2. Top each patty with sauerkraut, then cheese. Place under broiler to melt the cheese.

Per serving: 225 Cal, 8g Fat, 4g Sat F, 80mg Chol, 364mg Sod, 35g Pro, 1g Sug, 2g Carb, 1g Fib

Exchanges	Net Carbs
Fat 1	1
Very Lean Meat 5	
Vegetable 1/2	

MENU

Reuben Burgers
Spinach-Orange Salad
Quick Angel Cake

Soft Tacos

MAKES 8 SERVINGS

Low-carb taco shells are just as good as the full carb ones.

1 **pound extra lean ground beef**
1 **(1.25-oz) package taco seasoning mix**
8 **low carb tortillas**
½ **cup (2-oz) reduced fat Cheddar cheese, shredded**
1 **cup shredded lettuce**
½ **cup chopped tomatoes**

1. Brown ground beef and drain. Add seasoning mix and ¾-cup water. Bring to a boil, reduce heat, and simmer 10 to 15 minutes or until liquid is absorbed.

2. Spoon onto tortillas. Sprinkle with cheese, lettuce and tomato and roll up.
note: Recipe can be cut in half.

Per serving: 162 Cal, 6g Fat, 2g Sat F, 37mg Chol, 560mg Sod, 20g Pro, <1g Sug, 14g Carb, 8g Fib

Exchanges	Net Carbs
Fat 1/2	6
Very Lean Meat 2	

Ground Beef Fajitas

A slight twist to the popular beef fajitas.

1   pound extra lean ground beef
1   medium green pepper, cut into narrow strips
1   small onion, thinly sliced
8   (7-inch) low-carb tortillas
¾   cup well-drained salsa
½   cup nonfat sour cream

1. Brown ground beef, green pepper and onion in a large skillet. Cook until beef is lightly browned and cooked through. Drain off fat.

2. Divide mixture evenly and spoon onto tortillas. Top each with 2 tablespoons salsa and 1 tablespoon sour cream. Roll up and serve.

Per serving: 155 Cal, 5g Fat, 1g Sat F, 36mg Chol, 270mg Sod, 19g Pro, 1g Sug, 16g Carb, 9g Fib

Exchanges   Net Carbs

Fat 1/2   7
Very Lean Meat 2

Spaghetti Sauce with Red Peppers

Everyone enjoys Linda's spaghetti. The mild flavor of the red pepper blends well with the spaghetti sauce giving it a slightly sweet taste. Serve over spaghetti squash or low carb pasta.

1   pound extra lean ground beef
4   ounces fresh mushrooms, sliced
1   small red pepper, coarsely chopped
3   cups low-fat spaghetti sauce
    Salt and pepper to taste

1. Brown the ground beef. Add mushrooms toward end of cooking time; drain.

2. Add remaining ingredients and bring to a boil. Reduce heat and simmer 15 to 20 minutes or to desired thickness.

Per serving: 205 Cal, 10g Fat, 2g Sat F, 55mg Chol, 573mg Sod, 17g Pro, 1g Sug, 12g Carb, 3g Fib

Exchanges   Net Carbs

Fat 1/2   9
Meat 2
Other Carbs 1/2

Swedish Meatballs

MAKES 40 MEATBALLS

If desired, meatballs can be served in a gravy. Make gravy, add meatballs and heat through.

2   **pounds, extra lean ground beef**
1½ **cups low-fat white soft bread crumbs, crust removed**
⅓   **cup very finely chopped onion**
1   **teaspoon salt**
½   **teaspoon nutmeg**
1   **(14.5-oz) can low sodium beef broth**

1. Preheat oven to 425°F. Combine first 5 ingredients. Form into walnut-size meatballs. Place in a shallow baking pan and bake 10 minutes.
2. Add broth to pan. Cover tightly with foil and bake 8 minutes or until cooked to 160°.

Per 4 meatballs: 161 Cal, 5g Fat, 2g Sat F, 56mg Chol, 336mg Sod, 22g Pro, <1g Sug, 4g Carb, <1g Fib

Exchanges   Net Carbs

Fat 1/2   4
Very Lean Meat 3

Italian Meatballs

MAKES 16 MEATBALLS

If you can afford the carbs, serve meatballs with low-carb spaghetti sauce and low-carb pasta. Otherwise, enjoy just the meatballs.

1   **pound extra lean ground beef**
½   **cup low-fat soft white bread crumbs**
1   **teaspoon Italian seasoning**
¼   **cup egg substitute**
¼   **cup lowfat spaghetti sauce**
½   **cup (2-oz) reduced fat Mozzarella cheese**

1. Preheat oven to 400°F. Combine first 5 ingredients. Mix lightly.
2. Cut cheese into 16 cubes. Divide meat mixture into 16 parts and shape around cheese cubes. Place in a shallow baking pan and bake 18 to 20 minutes or until cooked to 160°.
variation: Make larger meatballs by dividing meat mixture and cheese into 8 portions.

Per 4 meatballs: 247 Cal, 10g Fat, 4g Sat F, 76mg Chol, 303mg Sod, 33g Pro, <1g Sug, 5g Carb, <1g Fib

Exchanges   Net Carbs

Fat 1-1/2   5
Very Lean Meat 4-1/2

Stuffed Green Peppers

MAKES 8 SERVINGS

Serve these when peppers are on sale.

1 **pound extra lean ground beef**
¾ **cup chopped onion**
4 **Plum tomatoes, chopped**
  Salt and pepper to taste
4 **medium green peppers**
1 **(8-oz) can tomato sauce**

1. In a large skillet, brown ground beef and onion; drain. Add tomatoes, salt and pepper.
2. Preheat oven to 325°F. Meanwhile, cut peppers in half lengthwise; remove seeds. Place, cut-side up, in a sprayed 13x9-inch baking dish. Fill with meat mixture. Spoon remaining mixture around peppers. Pour tomato sauce over top. Add ¼ cup water to dish. Bake 50 to 60 minutes or until peppers are tender.

Per serving: 113 Cal, 3g Fat, 1g Sat F, 35mg Chol, 265mg Sod, 14g Pro, 4g Sug, 7g Carb, 1g Fib

Exchanges   Net Carbs
   Fat 1/2   6
Very Lean Meat 2

MENU

Stuffed Green Peppers

Spinach-Orange Salad

Muffins

Grilled Steaks

Use steaks such as New York strip, porterhouse, T-bone or sirloin.

1 (4-oz) sirloin steak
Minced garlic
Freshly ground black pepper
Salt

1. Trim steak of excess fat. Firmly rub steak with garlic (both sides). Sprinkle with pepper. Set aside while preparing coals. Sprinkle 1 side of steak with salt. Place salt-side down, on grill. Sprinkle with salt. Cook 4 to 6 minutes. Turn and cook to desired doneness.

Per serving: 175 Cal, 8g Fat, 3g Sat F, 60mg Chol, 51mg Sod, 24g Pro, 0g Sug, 0g Carb, 0g Fib

Exchanges   Net Carbs

Very Lean Meat 3-1/2   0

Teriyaki Tri-Tip Steaks

Allow time for meat to marinate 6 to 8 hours.

1 (1½) pound tri-tip beef steak
½ cup low sodium soy sauce
2 tablespoons brown Sugar Twin®
½ teaspoon ground ginger

1. Place meat in a large resealable bag. Combine remaining ingredients with ¼ cup water. Pour over meat. Seal. Marinate in refrigerator for 6 to 8 hours.
2. Grill over hot coals until cooked to desired doneness, turning once.
note: Tri-tip steaks are sometimes cut into 4 to 6-ounce boneless steaks and sometimes cut into long narrow strips that can also be used for beef kabobs.

Per 4 oz serving: 139 Cal, 6g Fat, 2g Sat F, 54mg Chol, 113mg Sod, 20g Pro, 0g Sug, 0g Carb, 0g Fib

Exchanges   Net Carbs

Meat 3   0

MENU

Teriyaki Tri-Tip Steaks
Family Favorite Asparagus
Crisp Green Salad

Teriyaki Strips

MAKES 4 SERVINGS

Remember to pre-soak wooden skewers.

1 (1-lb) flank steak
¼ cup low sodium soy sauce
¼ cup dry sherry
1½ teaspoons freshly grated ginger
1 small garlic clove, minced

1. Cut beef crosswise into thin strips.
2. Combine remaining ingredients in a shallow dish. Add beef and marinate 1 hour.
3. Place beef, accordian style, on 4 skewers. Grill or broil until cooked through, turning at least once.

Per 4 oz serving: 173 Cal, 8g Fat, 3g Sat F, 43mg Chol, 98mg Sod, 24g Pro, 0g Sug, 0g Carb, 0g Fib

Exchanges   Net Carbs

Fat 1   0
Very Lean Meat 3-1/2

Beef Kabobs

MAKES 4 SERVINGS

If using wooden skewers, don't forget to soak in water for about 20 minutes.

1 (1¼-lb) top sirloin
1 cup dry white wine
⅔ cup oil
⅓ cup low sodium soy sauce
2 large garlic cloves, minced
1 medium onion (8 wedges)

1. Cut meat into 16 (1½ inch) cubes. Combine next 4 ingredients. Reserve ¼-cup for basting. Add meat; cover and marinate in refrigerator at least 2 hours.
2. Thread the meat with onion on 4 skewers. Place on grill or under broiler and cook to desired doneness or about 3 minutes per side, basting frequently with the ¼ cup sauce.

Per kabob: 236 Cal, 10g Fat, 4g Sat F, 75mg Chol, 135mg Sod, 31g Pro, 1g Sug, 3g Carb, <1g Fib

Exchanges   Net Carbs

Meat 4-1/2   3
Vegetable 1/2

Stuffed Flank Steak

MAKES 6 SERVINGS

For a 2 ingredient recipe, this one has a lot of flavor. And leftover steak makes delicious sandwiches.

1   (1 to 1½-lb) flank steak
12 ounces low-fat turkey sausage

1. Preheat oven to 350°F. Pound steak, rounded side down, to flatten and make even.

2. Crumble sausage over meat to within one inch of edge. Starting at the short end, roll tightly. Tie with kitchen string in 5 or 6 places, making sure ends are tied to enclose filling. String should be tight, making a compact loaf.

3. Place, seam-side down, on a rack in a roasting pan. Bake 75 to 85 minutes or until both meats are cooked through. Slice into ¼-inch slices.

Per 4-oz serving: 210 Cal, 11g Fat, 4g Sat F, 67mg Chol, 284mg Sod, 28g Pro, 0g Sug, 0g Carb, 0g Fib

Exchanges   Net Carbs

Fat 1   0
Meat 1
Very Lean Meat 3

Kid's Favorite Flank Steak

MAKES 4 SERVINGS

Simple and delicious

1   (1¼-lb) flank steak
¼ cup low sodium soy sauce

1. Place steak in a large resealable bag. Add soy sauce and seal bag. Marinate in refrigerator 60 minutes, turning bag frequently.

2. Grill or broil steak to 140°, turning once. Do not overcook. Slice crosswise to serve.

Per serving: 214 Cal, 10g Fat, 4g Sat F, 54mg Chol, 109mg Sod, 29g Pro, 0g Sug, 0g Carb, 0g Fib

Exchanges   Net Carbs

Fat 1-1/2   0
Very Lean Meat 4

Tri-Tip Roast

A tri-tip roast is a delicious and economical roast that has become quite popular in recent years. Meat should be cooked at a high temperature.

1 (1½ to 2½-lb) beef tri-tip roast
  Salt and pepper

1. Generously sprinkle meat all over with salt and pepper. Rub into meat and let stand at room termperature for 1 hour.
2. Preheat oven to 450°F. Place meat, fat-side up, on a rack in a shallow roasting pan. Place in oven and begin checking temperature after 20 minutes. For rare, remove at 120°. For medium-rare, remove at 140°. Temperature will rise as meat stands. Let stand 10 minutes. Carve into thin slices across the grain.

Per 4 oz serving: 206 Cal, 9g Fat, 4g Sat F, 81mg Chol, 62mg Sod, 30g Pro, 0g Sug, 0g Carb, 0g Fib

Exchanges   Net Carbs
Meat 4-1/2   0

Swiss Steak

Let bake in the oven while you are busy doing other things.

1 (2-lb) round steak, 1 inch thick
  Salt and pepper
1 tablespoon oil
½ cup chopped onion
1 (16-oz) can diced tomatoes, with juice

1. Preheat oven to 350°F. Sprinkle meat with salt and pepper.
2. Heat oil in a Dutch oven or large skillet; add meat and brown both sides. Top with onion and tomatoes. Cover and bake 1½ to 2 hours or until tender, adding water if necessary.

Per 4-oz serving: 180 Cal, 6g Fat, 2g Sat F, 65mg Chol, 197mg Sod, 26g Pro, 2g Sug, 3g Carb, 1g Fib

Exchanges   Net Carbs
Fat 1   2
Very Lean Meat 3-1/2

Mushroom Round Steak

An easy economical meal.

1   **(1-lb) top round steak**
4   **ounces fresh mushrooms, sliced**
1   **medium onion, sliced**
1   **(14.5-oz) can low sodium beef broth**
    Salt and pepper to taste
2   **tablespoons cornstarch**

1. Preheat oven to 325°F. Cut meat into 4 serving size pieces. Place in a Dutch oven. Add mushrooms, onion, broth, and salt and pepper. Cover. Bake 2½ to 3 hours or until tender.

2. Remove meat and keep warm. Combine cornstarch with about ½ cup water. Stir into broth mixture. Place on a burner and cook over medium heat until thickened. Taste for seasoning.

Per serving: 200 Cal, 5g Fat, 2g Sat F, 65mg Chol, 66mg Sod, 28g Pro, 2g Sug, 7g Carb, 1g Fib

Exchanges   Net Carbs

Exchanges	Net Carbs
Fat 1/2	6
Meat 1/2	
Very Lean Meat 3-1/2	
Vegetable 1/2	

Pepper Steak

MAKES 4 SERVINGS

A quick top of the stove meal.

1   **(1-lb) top round steak**
1   **teaspoon cornstarch**
2   **tablespoons low sodium soy sauce**
1   **tablespoon Splenda®**
2   **medium green peppers, cut into narrow strips**
2   **medium tomatoes**

1. Cut steak crosswise into ⅛-inch strips
2. Combine cornstarch, soy sauce and Splenda. Pour over steak; marinate in refrigerator 2 to 3 hours or overnight.
3. When ready to serve, quickly brown steak in a sprayed nonstick skillet. (Do not overcook or meat will be tough).
4. Remove meat from pan. Add green peppers, cook until just crisp-tender. If peppers stick to pan, add a little oil. Add tomatoes and beef and cook until heated through.

Per serving: 190 Cal, 5g Fat, 2g Sat F, 65mg Chol, 303mg Sod, 28g Pro, 4g Sug, 8g Carb, 2g Fib

Exchanges   Net Carbs

Exchanges	Net Carbs
Fat 1/2	6
Very Lean Meat 3-1/2.	

Marinated Beef Fajitas

MAKES 6 MEAT SERVINGS OF 2 FAJITAS EACH

Low-carb and low-fat tortillas allow us to have Fajitas again.

1   (1-lb) flank steak
1   tablespoon oil
2   tablespoons fresh lime juice
½   teaspoon ground cumin
1   teaspoon chili powder
¼   teaspoon garlic powder

1. Trim any fat from meat and place in a shallow dish. Combine remaining ingredients; pour over meat, turning to coat. Cover and refrigerate 2 to 3 hours.

2. When ready to cook, remove meat from marinade. Slice, across the grain, into ⅛-inch slices.

3. Cook about ¼ of the meat at a time in a nonstick skillet, adding more oil if needed. Heat should be fairly hot to cook meat quickly.

note: Serve with warm low-carb tortillas, sautéed peppers and onions, salsa and nonfat sour cream.

Per serving: 137 Cal, 8g Fat, 2g Sat F, 29mg Chol, 35mg Sod, 16g Pro, < 1g Sug, <1g Carb, <1g Fib

Exchanges	*Net Carbs*
Fat 1	<1
Very Lean Meat 2	

Pork Roasts

In case you were wondering, picnic shoulder roasts and pork leg (fresh ham) roasts are not cooked the same way as pork loin roasts. They are cooked at a lower oven temperature of 325° and to a higher internal temperature of 185°. Because of their size and cooking variables, the exact cooking time is hard to pin down. The nice thing is that while the meat is standing before carving, you can put the final touches to the rest of your meal.

Pork Gravy

Skim off the fat from drippings in pan. Add 1 cup chicken broth (can use part dry white wine). Bring to a boil, stirring to loosen brown pieces in bottom of pan. Cook over medium-high heat 2 to 3 minutes. Pour over meat slices on platter and serve. Less than one carb per serving (per 8 servings).

Roasted Fresh Ham

MAKES 15 TO 20 SERVINGS

The whole pork leg is known as a fresh un-cured ham. When cooked. it doesn't look like ham, but is very tender and moist and ideal for large holiday dinners. For more accurate cooking time and doneness, use a reliable meat thermometer.

1   (15-20-lb) bone-in pork leg (fresh ham)
    Salt and pepper
2   teaspoons dried oregano or rosemary
2   cups dry white wine

1. Preheat oven to 425°F. Remove skin from pork; score fat. Combine seasonings and rub into roast. Place in a large roasting pan.
2. Bake 30 minutes, then reduce tempera-ture to 325°. Bake 60 minutes; pour wine over meat. Cook 2½ to 3½ hours or until meat reaches 185°. Cover loosely with foil and let stand 30 to 60 minutes before slicing.

Per 4 oz serving: 240 Cal, 11g Fat, 4g Sat F, 98mg Chol, 67mg Sod, 33g Pro, 0g Sug, 0g Carb, 0g Fib

Exchanges   Net Carbs
Meat 4   0

Maple Ham

MAKES ABOUT 10 SERVINGS

For the holidays, you may want to purchase a 12 pound ham, otherwise, a 7 or 8 pound ham is an ideal size.

1   (7-lb) fully cooked bone-in ham
1   teaspoon dry mustard
2   teaspoons cider vinegar
½   cup no-carb maple syrup

1. Preheat oven to 350°F. Trim ham of excess fat. Score top of ham. Place, fat-side up, on a rack in a shallow roasting pan.
2. Bake 15 to20 minutes per pound or until temperature reaches 140°, about 1½ hours.
3. Meanwhile, combine remaining ingredi-ents and spoon over ham last 30 minutes of cooking time. I usually add this after ham has baked about an hour. Then I baste a couple of times. Let stand 10 minutes before slicing.

Per 4 oz serving: 178 Cal, 6g Fat, 2g Sat F, 62mg Chol, 1500mg Sod, 28g Pro, 0g Sug, 0g Carb, 0g Fib

Exchanges   Net Carbs
Fat 1   0
Very Lean Meat 4

Grilled Pork Loin Roast

MAKES 8 SERVINGS

Grilling is one of my favorite ways to cook pork. I like to use a charcoal grill which imparts a wonderful smoky flavor, but other grills will work. If desired, you can choose to use a dry rub, page 85.

1 (2½-lb) boneless pork loin
Salt and pepper

1. Sprinkle pork with salt and pepper. The heat in the grill should be low, around 200°F to 250°F. Place pork, fat-side up, over indirect heat. Cover grill and cook about 1½ to 2 hours or until meat registers 140°.
2. Wrap in foil and let stand 10 to 15 minutes before slicing.

Per 4 oz serving: 264 Cal, 16g Fat, 6g Sat F, 87mg Chol, 63mg Sod, 29g Pro, 0g Sug, 0g Carb, 0g Fib

Exchanges   Net Carbs

    Fat 1   0
    Meat 4

Pork Roast Dijon

MAKES 6 SERVINGS

An easy family or company roast.

1 (2½-lb) boneless pork loin
2 teaspoons Dijon mustard
½ teaspoon dried rosemary
**   Salt and pepper**

1. Preheat oven to 350°F. Place roast on a rack in a roasting pan; spread with mustard and sprinkle with rosemary, salt and pepper.
2. Bake 40 to 50 minutes or until meat reaches 140°. Cover with foil and let stand 15 minutes before slicing.

Per 4 oz serving: 264 Cal, 16g Fat, 6g Sat F, 87mg Chol, 63mg Sod, 29g Pro, 0g Sug, 0g Carb, 0g Fib

Exchanges   Net Carbs

    Fat 1   0
    Meat 4

Cook's Tip **Cooking spray should be sprayed on grill before heating.**

Pan-Fried Pork Chops

MAKES 4 SERVINGS

Today's pork is very lean, but can be tough and dry if overcooked. Brining will help increase the pork's moisture content and tenderness.

¼ cup kosher salt
4 (½-inch) center loin pork chops
   Salt and pepper
1 tablespoon oil

1. Combine kosher salt with 4½ cups water, stirring until melted. Put in a large resealable bag. Add pork chops and seal bag. Let stand in refrigerator at least 8 hours.

2. Remove pork chops and pat dry. Sprinkle with salt and pepper.

3. Heat oil in large skillet and cook over medium-high heat, to 140°F, turning once.

Per serving: 189 Cal, 10g Fat, 3g Sat F, 67mg Chol, 745mg Sod, 24g Pro, 0g Sug, 0g Carb, 0g Fib

Exchanges   Net Carbs
   Fat 1-1/2   0
Very Lean Meat 3-1/2

Dry Rub Recipe

MAKES 1/2 CUP

2 tablespoons salt
2 tablespoons Splenda®
2 teaspoons pepper
2 teaspoons paprika
2 teaspoons fresh lemon peel

Combine ingredients and mix well. Amounts can be increased as needed. I use about 1 recipe per rack of baby back ribs. Can also be used on chicken.

Lemon Pepper Pork Chops

MAKES 4 SERVINGS

Watch carefully and do not overcook.

4   (½-inch) center loin pork chops
1   tablespoon oil
    Lemon pepper
1   cup low sodium chicken broth

1. Brown pork chops quickly in heated oil over medium-high heat, about 2 minutes per side. Sprinkle with lemon pepper. Add broth and cook over low heat until cooked through and temperature reaches 140°, about 5 to 6 minutes.

Per serving: 189 Cal, 10g Fat, 3g Sat F, 65mg Chol, 60mg Sod, 24g Pro, 0g Sug, 0g Carb, 0g Fib

Exchanges   Net Carbs
   Fat 1-1/2   0
Very Lean Meat 3-1/2

Sweet & Sour Pork Chops

MAKES 4 SERVINGS

You must try this recipe. It's a winner.

4   (½-inch) center loin pork chops
2   tablespoons oil
2   teaspoons low sodium soy sauce
¼   cup cider vinegar
4   packets Splenda®
1   medium onion, sliced

1. Brown pork chops, in heated oil in a large skillet over medium-high heat, turning once.
2. Combine soy sauce, vinegar and Splenda and pour over meat.
3. Separate onion into rings and add to skillet.
4. Cover skillet and cook on low heat about 40 to 45 minutes or until meat is tender. Check occasionally making sure heat isn't too high. You want some of those tasty juices to remain in the pan.
variation: Substitute 4 ounces sliced fresh mushrooms for the onions.

Per serving: 209 Cal, 10g Fat, 3g Sat F, 65mg Chol, 137mg Sod, 24g Pro, 2g Sug, 5g Carb, <1g Fib

Exchanges   Net Carbs
   Fat 1-1/2   5
Very Lean Meat 3-1/2

Grilled Pork Chops Dijon

Due to their lower fat content, pork chops should not be overcooked.

4 (½-inch) center loin pork chops
3 tablespoons Dijon mustard
¼ teaspoon dried tarragon
¼ teaspoon garlic powder
  Cracked pepper

1. Trim pork chops of all fat. Place on a heated grill that was sprayed with cooking spray. Cook 4 minutes; turn.
2. Combine mustard, tarragon and garlic powder. Brush on top of each pork chop. Cook 2 to 3 minutes or until cooked through or 140°. Temperature will rise after cooking. Sprinkle lightly with pepper.

Per serving: 175 Cal, 7g Fat, 2g Sat F, 65mg Chol, 332mg Sod, 25g Pro, 0g Sug, 2g Carb, <1g Fib

Exchanges   Net Carbs

Fat 1   2
Very Lean Meat 3-1/2

Pork-Mushroom Kabobs

To prevent ingredients from falling off the skewers, top off with a large garlic clove.

1 (1-lb) pork tenderloin
8 ounces fresh mushrooms
1 medium onion, cut into 8 wedges
⅓ cup nonfat vinaigrette dressing

1. Trim fat and silver skin from pork. Cut into 1½-inch cubes.
2. Thread meat and vegetables on five 12-inch skewers, leaving some space between each.
3. Grill kabobs on a sprayed rack over direct heat. Cook 12 to 14 minutes, turning occasionally, and brushing with dressing until cooked through. Do not overcook or pork will be dry.

Per kabob: 140 Cal, 3g Fat, 1g Sat F, 50mg Chol, 170mg Sod, 20g Pro, 3g Sug, 7g Carb, 1g Fib

Exchanges   Net Carbs

Fat 1/2   6
Very Lean Meat 2-1/2
Vegetable 1/2

Roast Pork Tenderloin

MAKES 6 SERVINGS

Pork tenderloin is the most tender cut of pork.

2   (¾-lb) pork tenderloins
1   tablespoon coarse grain mustard
½   teaspoon salt
½   teaspoon pepper
1   tablespoon oil
¼   cup dry white wine

1. Trim pork and remove silver skin. Place in a resealable bag.

2. Combine remaining ingredients and pour over pork. Release air from bag and seal. Marinate 2 hours in refrigerator. Drain.

3. Preheat oven to 400°F. Place tenderloins in a sprayed 11x7-inch baking dish. Bake 25 to 30 minutes or until temperature reaches 140°. Remove and let stand 10 minutes before slicing.

Per serving: 134 Cal, 4g Fat, 1g Sat F, 63mg Chol, 68mg Sod, 23g Pro, 0g Sug, 0g Carb, 0g Fib

Exchanges   Net Carbs
Fat 1/2   0
Very Lean Meat 3

Sausage-Cheese Meatballs

MAKES 8 LARGE MEATBALLS

These are so easy to make I like to keep some in the refrigerator or freezer at all times. Serve with eggs, omelets, spaghetti, etc.

1   pound lowfat turkey sausage
3   ounces reduced fat Mozzarella cheese

1. Preheat oven to 425°F. Divide sausage into 8 sections. Cut cheese into 8 cubes.

2. Form sausage evenly around a cheese cube, sealing completely. Place in a shallow baking pan. Bake 20 to 25 minutes or until browned and cooked through.

Per meatball: 95Cal, 6g Fat, 2g Sat F, 37mg Chol, 316mg Sod, 10g Pro, <1g Sug, <1g Carb, 0g Fib

Exchanges   Net Carbs
Fat 1/2   <1
Meat 1-1/2

Company Maple Sausages

MAKES 4 SERVINGS

A nice change. Serve with Orange Sweet Rolls, page 43, and scrambled eggs.

16 **turkey sausage links**
¼ **cup brown Sugar Twin®**
½ **cup no-carb maple syrup**

1. Place sausages in a 12-inch nonstick skillet and cook, turning occasionally, until browned and cooked through, but not overcooked.

2. Combine sugar and syrup and pour over sausages. Bring to a boil, reduce heat and simmer until nicely glazed, 10 to 15 minutes.

Per serving: 207 Cal, 11g Fat, 3g Sat F, 86mg Chol, 966mg Sod, 21g Pro, 1g Sug, 1g Carb, 0g Fib

Exchanges	Net Carbs
Fat 1/2	1
Meat 3	

∽ Baked Bacon ∾

A very easy way to cook bacon.

1 **pound bacon (more or less)**

1. Preheat oven to 350°F. Arrange bacon slices on a roasting pan rack. Bake 20 to 25 minutes or until cooked through. Drain on paper towels.

Per serving: 105 Cal, 11g Fat, 3g Sat F, 27mg Chol, 576mg Sod, 9g Pro, 0g Sug, 0g Carb, 0g Fib

1-1/2 Fat exchange
1-1/2 Meat exchange

Cooking Time for Fish

Measure fish at its thickest point.
Estimate 10 minutes total cooking time per inch.

Total cooking time applies to whatever cooking method is being used—baking, broiling, frying, etc. If baking a salmon or other fish and the fish measures 3 inches at its thickest point, bake 30 minutes at 450°. If broiling a steak 1½ inches thick, divide the total time and broil 7½ minutes on each side. Cooking times may vary somewhat according to the thickness and size of the fish, the temperature of the fish at cooking time and how hot your oven bakes. Watch carefully though, and remember that the fish will continue to cook somewhat after removing from heat. The internal temperature of fish should be 137 degrees. Salmon cooked in foil or stuffed may take a little longer.

Baked Whole Salmon

SERVING SIZE IS 4 OUNCES

A great Pacific Northwest treat.

Whole salmon, cleaned, wiped dry
Salt & pepper
1 large lemon, sliced
1 medium onion, sliced
6 slices bacon

1. Preheat oven to 450°F. Sprinkle salmon with salt and pepper, inside and out. Place on a large sheet of heavy duty foil in a large shallow baking pan.

2. Place 3 bacon slices lengthwise inside salmon. Stuff with lemon and onion slices. Place remaining bacon on top. Wrap foil to seal.

3. Bake 10 minutes per inch measuring salmon at its thickest part (a large salmon may take a little longer). Test for doneness with a toothpick or knife tip. When opaque all the way through, it should be done. Discard bacon, lemon and onion.

tip: Salmon cooked in foil or stuffed may take a little longer to cook.

Per 4 oz serving: 158 Cal, 5g Fat, 1g Sat F, 62mg Chol, 66mg Sod, 27g Pro, 0g Sug, 0g Carb, 0g Fib

Exchanges   Net Carbs
Fat 1/2   0
Very Lean Meat 3-1/2

Baked Salmon Fillets

MAKES 4 SERVINGS

Salmon is a "good" high fat fish.

4 (4-oz) salmon fillets
2 tablespoons reduced calorie margarine, melted
½ teaspoon Worcestershire sauce
1 teaspoon fresh lemon juice

1. Preheat oven to 450°F. Place salmon in a sprayed shallow baking pan.

2. Combine remaining ingredients and brush salmon with some of the sauce. Bake for 10 minutes, basting occasionally with the sauce. Test for doneness after 8 minutes.

Per serving: 172 Cal, 8g Fat, 2g Sat F, 53mg Chol, 97mg Sod, 23g Pro, <1g Sug, <1g Carb, 0g Fib

Exchanges   Net Carbs
Fat 1   <1

Tarragon Salmon Fillet

MAKES 4 SERVINGS

Tarragon teams well with salmon.

4   (4-oz) salmon fillets
½   teaspoon oil
¼   teaspoon dried tarragon
1   tablespoon Dijon mustard
¼   cup white wine
1   tablespoon reduced calorie margarine

1. Preheat oven to 450°F. Place fillets, skin-side down, on a sprayed shallow baking pan.
2. Combine remaining ingredients in a small saucepan. Bring to a boil; reduce heat and simmer about 2 minutes. Pour over salmon. Bake 10 to 12 minutes or until fish tests done. Cut crosswise into 4 pieces.

Per serving: 179 Cal, 8g Fat, 2g Sat F, 53mg Chol, 175mg Sod, 23g Pro, 0g Sug, 1g Carb, 0g Fib

Exchanges   Net Carbs

Fat 1   1
Very Lean Meat 3

Salmon Steaks

MAKES 4 SERVINGS

A quick, easy dinner.

4   (4-oz) salmon fillets
1   tablespoons oil
2   tablespoons lemon juice
1   garlic clove, minced
2   tablespoons minced fresh basil

1. Pat salmon dry and place on a broiler pan.
2. Combine remaining ingredients; brush some of the mixture over salmon. Broil 8 to 10 minutes, or until cooked through, basting once or twice with the sauce. You do not need to turn the salmon.

Per serving: 160 Cal, 7g Fat, 1g Sat F, 53mg Chol, 56mg Sod, 23g Pro, <1g Sug, 1g Carb, <1g Fib

Exchanges   Net Carbs

Fat 1   1
Very Lean Meat 3

Baked Salmon with Sour Cream

The sour cream keeps the salmon moist.

6 (4-oz) salmon fillets
   Salt and pepper
2 tablespoons fresh lemon juice
1 cup nonfat sour cream
2 teaspoons finely chopped onion

1. Preheat oven to 450°F. Place salmon in a sprayed 13x9-inch baking dish. Season with salt and pepper; sprinkle with lemon juice.

2. Spread sour cream over top, then the onion. Bake 10 minutes per inch, measuring at its thickest point.

Per serving: 152 Cal, 4 Fat, 1g Sat F, 55mg Chol, 87mg Sod, 23g Pro, <1g Sug, 4g Carb, 0g Fib

Exchanges   Net Carbs
   Fat 1/2   4
Very Lean Meat 3

Teriyaki Salmon Steaks

MAKES 4 SERVINGS

Serve with vegetable kabobs.

4 (4-oz) salmon fillets
¼ cup oil
2 tablespoons fresh lemon juice
2 tablespoons low sodium soy sauce
½ teaspoon dry mustard
½ teaspoon ground ginger

1. Place salmon in a sprayed 11x7-inch baking dish. Combine remaining ingredients; pour over top. Marinate 1 hour in refrigerator.

2. Drain off marinade. Place salmon on rack in broiling pan. Broil 5 minutes, turn and broil 5 minutes more or until cooked through. Brush lightly with additional oil if salmon appears dry.

Per serving: 135 Cal, 4g Fat, 1g Sat F, 53mg Chol, 83mg Sod, 23g Pro, 0g Sug, <1g Carb, <1g Fib

Exchanges   Net Carbs
   Fat 1/2   <1
Very Lean Meat 3

Red Snapper & Peppers

Lots of color in this recipe

1   (1-lb) red snapper fillet
4   teaspoons low sodium soy sauce
¼   teaspoon ground ginger
1   tablespoon olive oil
2   small peppers (1 red, 1 green), julienned
4   ounces fresh mushrooms, sliced

1. Preheat broiler. Place fillet in a sprayed shallow baking pan.
2. Combine soy sauce and ginger; brush over fish. Place under broiler and broil about 8 to 10 minutes or until fish tests done.
3. Meanwhile, heat oil in a large nonstick skillet. Cook peppers and mushrooms until just crisp-tender. Serve with or over the snapper.

Per serving: 157 Cal, 5g Fat, 1g Sat F, 40mg Chol, 386mg Sod, 24g Pro, 2g Sug, 3g Carb, 1g Fib

Exchanges   Net Carbs

Fat 1/2   2
Very Lean Meat 3
Vegetable 1/2

Red Snapper Fillets

Easy and good.

4   (4-oz) red snapper fillets
1   teaspoons oil
   Salt and pepper
2   tablespoons lime juice
1   tablespoon reduced calorie margarine, melted

1. Preheat grill to medium-hot. Brush fillets with oil and sprinkle generously with salt and pepper. Grill until cooked through, turning once. Approximately 8 to 10 minutes total cooking time.
2. Brush with lime juice and spoon margarine over top.

Per serving: 141 Cal, 5g Fat, 1g Sat F, 40mg Chol, 67mg Sod, 22g Pro, <1g Sug, 1g Carb, 0g Fib

Exchanges   Net Carbs

Fat 1/2   1
Very Lean Meat 3

Cook's Tip

It's always a good idea to check your oven temperature before each use. You will be surprised at the fluctuation in temperature in various ovens.

Halibut & Tomato

Halibut is low in carbs, fat and calories.

1   (1-lb) halibut, 1 inch thick
¼   cup fresh lemon juice
2   Plum tomatoes, chopped
2   green onions, sliced diagonally
¼   teaspoon dried basil
¼   teaspoon salt

1. Preheat oven to 450°F. Place halibut in a sprayed shallow baking dish. Pour lemon juice over fish. Sprinkle remaining ingredients over top.
2. Bake 10 minutes or until fish tests done.

Per serving: 142 Cal, 3g Fat, <1g Sat F, 38mg Chol, 212mg Sod, 24g Pro, 1g Sug, 3g Carb, 1g Fib

Exchanges   Net Carbs
Fat 1/2   2
Very Lean Meat 3

MENU
Baked Halibut
Family Favorite Asparagus
Caesar Salad

Baked Halibut

MAKES 4 SERVINGS

The lemon juice and onion adds a lot of flavor.

4   (4-oz) halibut steaks
3   tablespoons fresh lemon juice
1   teaspoon salt
½   teaspoon paprika
½   cup chopped onion
2   tablespoons reduced calorie margarine

1. Combine lemon juice, salt and paprika in a shallow dish. Add halibut, turning to coat. Chill 1 hour to marinate, turning once or twice.
2. Preheat oven to 450°F. Sauté onion in heated margarine until soft. Place halibut in a sprayed 11x7-inch baking dish; top with onions. Bake 10 minutes or until cooked through.

Per serving: 161 Cal, 6g Fat, 1g Sat F, 38mg Chol, 146mg Sod, 25g Pro, 1g Sug, 2g Carb, <1g Fib

Exchanges   Net Carbs
Fat 1   2
Very Lean Meat 3

Linda's Favorite Halibut

MAKES 4 SERVINGS

This recipe is good with most white fish.

1   **(1-lb) halibut, 1-inch thick**
½   **teaspoon garlic salt**
3   **tablespoons nonfat sour cream**
1   **green onion, chopped**
2   **tablespoons grated Parmesan cheese**

1. Preheat oven to 450°F. Place halibut in a sprayed shallow baking dish. Sprinkle with garlic salt.

2. Combine sour cream and onion; spread over fish. Sprinkle with Parmesan. Bake 10 minutes or until cooked through.

Per serving: 156 Cal, 3g Fat, 1g Sat F, 42mg Chol, 250mg Sod, 26g Pro, <1g Sug, 3g Carb, 0g Fib

Exchanges   Net Carbs

Fat 1/2   3
Very Lean Meat 3

Easy Grilled Halibut

MAKES 4 SERVINGS

Simple is often the best.

4   **(4-oz) halibut fillets, skin on**
    Salt and pepper

1. Sprinkle halibut with salt and pepper. Spray with cooking spray and place, flesh side down, on a sprayed heated grill. Grill about 5 minutes.

2. Spray skin with cooking spray and turn. Cook 4 to 5 minutes or until the center turns white.

Per serving: 130 Cal, 3g Fat, <1 Sat F, 38mg Chol, 64mg Sod, 25g Pro, 0g Sug, 0g Carb, 0g Fib

Exchanges   Net Carbs

Fat 1/2   0
Very Lean Meat 3

Ling Cod Fillets

MAKES 4 SERVINGS

Can be made in about 15 minutes.

1 **(1-lb) ling cod fillet**
1 **tablespoon reduced calorie
   margarine, melted**
1 **teaspoons dry mustard**
¼ **teaspoon lemon pepper**

1. Preheat broiler. Cut fish into 4 serving pieces. Place in a shallow sprayed baking pan.
2. Combine remaining ingredients; brush on the fillets. Place under broiler and cook 5 to 10 minutes, or until fish tests done.

Per serving: 128 Cal, 4g Fat, 1g Sat F, 62mg Chol, 116mg Sod, 21g Pro, 0g Sug, <1g Carb, <1g Fib

Exchanges   Net Carbs
   Fat 1/2   1
Very Lean Meat 3

Baked Ling Cod

MAKES 4 SERVINGS

Another low carb, low-fat and low calorie fish.

4 **(4-oz) ling cod fillets
   Salt and pepper**
1 **(14.5-oz) can diced Italian-style
   tomatoes, drained**
¼ **cup chopped ripe olives**

1. Preheat oven to 450°F. Place fillets in a sprayed 13x9-inch baking dish. Sprinkle with salt and pepper. Spoon tomatoes and olives over top. Bake 10 to 12 minutes or until cooked through.

Per serving: 139 Cal, 2g Fat, <1 Sat F, 65mg Chol, 461mg Sod, 23g Pro, 4 Sug, 6g Carb, 1g Fib

Exchanges   Net Carbs
Very Lean Meat 3   5

Baked Catfish Parmesan

MAKES 4 SERVINGS

The Parmesan coating isn't exactly a Southern or Mid-western way to cook catfish, but do give it a try. It is delicious. (I still haven't convinced my Mother that there are other ways to cook catfish, other than just cornmeal and/or flour).

1   (1-lb) catfish fillet
3   tablespoons nonfat sour cream
⅓   cup grated Parmesan cheese
2   tablespoons flour
⅛   teaspoon pepper
¼   teaspoon paprika

1. Preheat oven to 450°F. Cut fish into 4 equal portions. Brush lightly with sour cream.
2. Combine remaining ingredients. Dip fish in mixture, turning to coat both sides. Place on a sprayed shallow baking pan. Bake 8 to 12 minutes, or until fish tests done.

Per serving: 200 Cal, 9g Fat, 3g Sat F, 67 Chol, 202mg Sod, 21g Pro, 0g Sug, 7g Carb, <1g Fib

Exchanges	Net Carbs
Fat 1/2	7
Meat 3	

Jamaican Jerk Mahi-Mahi

MAKES 4 SERVINGS

Jerk seasoning isn't for everyone, but it takes beautifully to grilled fish, pork, and chicken. Team with a fruity salsa. In case you are wondering, jerk seasoning is not the same as Cajun seasoning.

4   (4-oz) mahi-mahi fillets or steaks
1   tablespoon oil
2   tablespoons Jamaican jerk seasoning

1. Lightly spray the grill rack. Place over medium-hot heat.
2. Brush mahi-mahi with oil. Sprinkle with seasoning and rub over fish. Grill, turning once until opaque in the center, about 3 to 4 minutes per side.

note: Any firm white fish may be substituted for the mahi-mahi.

Per serving: 154 Cal, 5g Fat, 1g Sat F, 107mg Chol, 548mg Sod, 27g Pro, 0g Sug, 0g Carb, 0g Fib

Exchanges	Net Carbs
Fat 1/2	0
Very Lean Meat 3-1/2	

Easy Skillet Fish Dish

MAKES 4 SERVINGS

This makes a colorful dish, but only if you remember to remove from heat when the peppers are still a bright color.

1 **pound orange roughy**
1 **tablespoon oil**
2 **small peppers (1 red, 1 green), julienned**
½ **cup coarsely chopped onion**
½ **teaspoon dried basil**
   Salt and pepper to taste

1. Cut fish into 4 serving pieces.
2. Heat oil in a large nonstick skillet. Add peppers and onion. Arrange fish on top. Sprinkle with seasonings. Cover; cook over low heat 8 to 10 minutes. Uncover; continue cooking until fish tests done and vegetables are crisp tender.

Per serving: 128 Cal, 4g Fat, 1g Sat F, 24mg Chol, 77mg Sod, 18g Pro, 2g Sug, 4g Carb, 1g Fib

Exchanges   Net Carbs
Fat 1/2   3
Very Lean Meat 2-1/2

Fillet of Sole with Dill

MAKES 4 SERVINGS

Use fresh dill if you just happen to have some.

4 **(4-oz) sole fillets**
2 **tablespoons fresh lime juice**
1 **small garlic clove, minced**
¼ **teaspoon dried dill weed**
   Salt and pepper

1. Preheat broiler. Place fillets in a sprayed shallow baking pan.
2. Combine lime juice, garlic and dill weed. Brush some of the sauce on fillets. Sprinkle lightly with salt and pepper. Place under broiler; cook 5 to 10 minutes, depending on thickness, brushing occasionally with remaining sauce.

Per serving: 95 Cal, 1g Fat, 0g Sat F, 53mg Chol, 83mg Sod, 19g Pro, <1g Sug, 1g Carb, 0g Fib

Exchanges   Net Carbs
Very Lean Meat 3   1

Lemon Pepper Spice

MAKES ABOUT 1/2 CUP

Especially good on meats, seafood and poultry.

5   tablespoons lemon pepper
1   tablespoon seasoning salt
2½ teaspoons garlic powder

Combine ingredients and store tightly covered.

Easy Bake Parmesan Sole

MAKES 4 SERVINGS

You could also use halibut or orange roughy in this recipe.

4   (4-oz) sole fillets
2   tablespoons reduced calorie margarine, melted
⅓   cup low-fat dry white bread crumbs
2   tablespoons grated Parmesan cheese
1   teaspoon paprika

1. Preheat oven to 450°F. Brush fillets with margarine. Combine bread crumbs, Parmesan and paprika. Dip sole in bread crumbs and place in a shallow sprayed baking pan.
2. Bake 8 to 10 minutes or until cooked through. If coating appears dry, brush with a little melted butter.

Per serving: 222 Cal, 8g Fat, 2g Sat F, 80mg Chol, 261mg Sod, 30g Pro, 1g Sug, 7g Carb, 1g Fib

Exchanges	Net Carbs
Fat 1	6
Starch 1/2	
Very Lean Meat 4	

Sautéed Scallops

Remember, scallops take very little time to cook.

1½ **pounds scallops**
  3 **tablespoons reduced calorie**
     margarine
  3 **slices fresh ginger**
     Salt and pepper
  1 **tablespoon chopped parsley**

1. Rinse scallops and pat dry. Melt margarine in a large skillet. Add ginger, then scallops, and cook until just heated through and lightly browned. Remove ginger. Sprinkle with salt, pepper and parsley.

Per serving: 148 Cal, 7g Fat, 1g Sat F, 36mg Chol, 234mg Sod, 19g Pro, 0g Sug, 3g Carb, 0g Fib

Exchanges   Net Carbs
      Fat 1   3
Very Lean Meat 2-1/2

"Fresh" Canned Shrimp

SERVING SIZE IS 3 OUNCES

This simple method really does improve the taste.

   Canned shrimp
  1 **teaspoon salt**

1. Drain shrimp and rinse several times. Place in a quart-size jar; add salt and cover with ice water. Refrigerate overnight.
2. Drain shrimp and pat dry.

Per serving: 102 Cal, 2g Fat, <1g Sat F, 147mg Chol, 144mg Sod, 20g Pro, 0g Sug, 1g Carb, 0g Fib

Exchanges   Net Carbs
Very Lean Meat 3   1

Grilled Shrimp Kabobs

MAKES 4 SERVINGS

Remember to soak wooden skewers in water for 20 minutes before using.

16 large shrimp
16 Chinese pea pods, cooked crisp-
    tender
 2 tablespoons reduced calorie
    margarine, melted
 2 teaspoons fresh lemon juice
 ¼ teaspoon dried dill weed
    Dash pepper

1. Spray grill with cooking spray and preheat. Wrap a pea pod around each shrimp and secure with a wooden toothpick. Place 4 on each skewer.

2. Combine remaining ingredients and brush shrimp with some of the sauce. Place on hot grill. Cooking time can vary according to the size of the shrimp and temperature of the grill. Cook on one side, turn and baste with sauce. Cook until cooked through.

Per serving: 52 Cal, 3g Fat, 1g Sat F, 43mg Chol, 73mg Sod, 5g Pro, <1g Sug, 1g Carb, <1g Fib

Exchanges   Net Carbs
Fat 1/2   1
Very Lean Meat 1/2

Spicy Garlic Shrimp

MAKES 4 SERVINGS

The red pepper is just what this recipe needs.

 1 tablespoon olive oil
1½ pounds large shrimp
    Salt and pepper
 3 small garlic cloves, chopped
 ¼ teaspoon crushed red pepper
 1 tablespoon lemon juice

1. Heat oil in a large skillet over medium-high heat. Add shrimp. Sprinkle with salt and pepper. Cook about 2 minutes, stirring frequently.

2. Stir in garlic and red pepper and cook over medium heat until shrimp is opaque and pink throughout - do not overcook. Remove from heat and add lemon juice.

Per serving: 162 Cal, 5g Fat, 1g Sat F, 252mg Chol, 290mg Sod, 27g Pro, <1g Sug, 1g Carb, 0g Fib

Exchanges   Net Carbs
Fat 1/2   1
Very Lean Meat 3-1/2

Poultry

♦ Chicken
♦ Turkey

Teriyaki Chicken

MAKES 4 SERVINGS

Serve with a low-fat rice dish.

4 chicken breast halves, skinned, boned
¼ cup chopped onions
1 medium garlic clove, minced
2 tablespoons Splenda®
½ teaspoon dried ginger
½ cup low sodium soy sauce

1. Place chicken in an 8x8-inch baking dish or re-sealable bag. Combine remaining ingredients with ¼-cup water. Pour over chicken. Marinate, in refrigerator, for one hour.

2. Preheat oven to 350°F. Place chicken in a shallow sprayed roasting pan. Pour marinade over top. Bake 20 minutes; turn chicken and bake 10 to 15 minutes or until cooked through, basting frequently with the sauce.

Per serving: 155 Cal, 3g Fat, 1g Sat F, 72mg Chol, 597mg Sod, 24g Pro, <1g Sug, 2g Carb, <1g Fib

Exchanges   Net Carbs
Very Lean Meat 3-1/2   2

Mock Chicken Cordon Bleu

MAKES 4 SERVINGS

Most of us enjoy Cordon Bleu, but lack the time or patience to prepare it. This version is easier.

4 chicken breast halves, skinned, boned
½ cup low-fat white bread crumbs
1 teaspoon seasoning salt
¼ cup nonfat sour cream
4 thin slices boiled ham
1 thin slice reduced fat Swiss cheese, about 5x8 inches, cut into 4 rectangles

1. Preheat oven to 350°F. Combine bread crumbs and seasoning salt. Brush chicken with sour cream. Sprinkle each side of breast with 1 tablespoon breadcrumbs. Place on a sprayed shallow baking pan and bake 30 to 40 minutes or until cooked through.

2. Top each chicken breast with a ham slice folded to fit. Top with a cheese slice. Bake long enough to melt cheese.

Per serving: 236 Cal, 4g Fat, 1g Sat F, 86mg Chol, 894mg Sod, 35g Pro, 1g Sug, 12g Carb, 1g Fib

Exchanges   Net Carbs
Fat 1/2   11
Starch 1
Very Lean Meat 4-1/2

Onion-Pepper Chicken

MAKES 4 SERVINGS

A nice blend of vegetables with the chicken.

4   chicken breast halves, skinned, boned
1   tablespoon oil
1   medium onion, sliced
½   medium red and green pepper, julienned
½   cup sliced fresh mushrooms
     Salt and pepper to taste

1. Heat oil in a medium skillet. Add chicken and cook until lightly browned, cooking each side 2 to 3 minutes or until cooked through. Remove and keep warm.
2. Add onion, peppers and mushrooms to skillet. Sprinkle with salt and pepper; cook until just crisp-tender. Serve over chicken.

Per serving: 190 Cal, 7g Fat, 1g Sat F, 72mg Chol, 65mg Sod, 27g Pro, 2g Sug, 5g Carb, 1g Fib

Exchanges   Net Carbs

Fat 1   4
Very Lean Meat 3-1/2
Vegetable 1

Diner's Chicken Plate

MAKES 4 SERVINGS

Can also garnish with fresh fruit.

4   chicken breast halves, skinned, boned
2   tablespoons nonfat vinaigrette
4   (1-oz) slices reduced fat Monterey Jack cheese
8   large lettuce leaves
8   tomato slices
8   thin onion slices

1. In a medium skillet, cook chicken in vinaigrette over medium heat until cooked through, turning once. Top with cheese and cook to melt.
2. Place chicken on lettuce on individual serving plates. Garnish with tomato and onion slices.

Per serving: 243 Cal, 9g Fat, 5g Sat F, 92mg Chol, 369mg Sod, 34g Pro, 3g Sug, 6g Carb, 1g Fib

Exchanges   Net Carbs

Fat 1   5
Meat 1
Very Lean Meat 3-1/2

Baked Fried Chicken

The easiest way there is to "fry" chicken.

8   chicken legs
    Salt and pepper
    Paprika
2   tablespoons reduced calorie
    margarine

1. Preheat oven to 400°F. Sprinkle chicken with salt, pepper and paprika. Place, skin-side down, in a shallow baking pan. Dot with margarine. Cover with foil and bake for 30 minutes.
2. Remove foil. Increase temperature to 425°, bake 30 minutes or until cooked through.

Per serving: 118 Cal, 6g Fat, 2g Sat F, 53mg Chol, 62mg Sod, 15g Pro, 0g Sug, 0g Carb, 0g Fib

Exchanges   Net Carbs

Fat 1   0
Very Lean Meat 2

MENU

Baked Fried Chicken
Onion Broccoli Stir-fry
Berry-Berry Fruit Salad
Raspberry Delight

Candied Chicken

The high heat is to help prevent sauce from getting too thin.

4   chicken breast halves, skinned, boned
    Salt and pepper
1   cup no-carb maple syrup
½   cup low-carb ketchup
¼   cup white vinegar

1. Preheat oven to 425°F. Sprinkle chicken with salt and pepper. Place in a sprayed 13x9-inch baking dish.
2. Combine remaining ingredients and pour over chicken. Bake 30 to 45 minutes, or until cooked through, basting every 15 minutes. Serve sauce with chicken.

Per serving: 178 Cal, 3g Fat, 1g Sat F, 72mg Chol, 175mg Sod, 26g Pro, 0g Sug, 2g Carb, 0g Fib

Exchanges   Net Carbs

Very Lean Meat 3-1/2   2

Chicken Italian

Dinner in about 30 minutes.

4   chicken breast halves, skinned, boned
1   tablespoon oil
1   medium garlic clove, minced
1   small onion, sliced, separated into
    rings
1   (14.5-oz) can Italian stewed whole
    tomatoes, with juice
¼   teaspoon salt

1. Lightly brown chicken in heated oil in a medium skillet. Remove chicken and set aside.

2. Add garlic and onion; cook over medium heat until onion is crisp-tender. Add tomatoes, chicken and salt. Cover and cook on low heat 15 to 20 minutes or until chicken is cooked through.

Per serving: 196 Cal, 7g Fat, 1g Sat F, 72mg Chol, 341mg Sod, 27g Pro, 3g Sug, 6g Carb, 1g Fib

Exchanges   Net Carbs

Fat 1   5
Very Lean Meat 3-1/2
Vegetable 1

Lemon Pepper Chicken

MAKES 4 SERVINGS

An easy way to prepare chicken on those days when you have very little time to cook.

4   chicken breast halves, skinned, boned
1   tablespoon olive oil
    Lemon pepper

1. Preheat oven to 375°F. Place chicken, skin-side up, on a shallow baking pan. Brush with oil. Sprinkle lightly with lemon pepper. Bake 30 to 40 minutes or until cooked through.

Per serving: 170 Cal, 6g Fat, 1g Sat F, 72mg Chol, 83mg Sod, 26g Pro, 0g Sug, 0g Carb, 0g Fib

Exchanges   Net Carbs

Fat 1   0
Very Lean Meat 3-1/2

Lemon Chicken Packet

MAKES 1 SERVING

Be careful when you open the packet, the steam is very hot.

1 chicken breast half, skinned, boned
1 tablespoon fresh lemon juice
  Dried tarragon or rosemary
  Salt and pepper
1 green onion, sliced

1. Preheat oven to 375°F. Place chicken on a large square of foil. Place in a shallow pan. Pour lemon juice over chicken. Sprinkle lightly with tarragon, salt, pepper, and then the onion. Cover chicken with the foil and seal tightly. Bake 30 to 40 minutes or until cooked through.

tip: Tarragon and rosemary are very strong herbs and should be used with a light hand.

Per serving: 147 Cal, 3g Fat, 1g Sat F, 72mg Chol, 66mg Sod, 27g Pro, <1g Sug, 2g Carb, <1g Fib

Exchanges   Net Carbs
Very Lean Meat 3-1/2   2

Swiss Onion Chicken

MAKES 4 SERVINGS

A great fix-it and put it in the oven recipe.

4 chicken breast halves, skinned, boned
  Salt
2 tablespoons Dijon mustard
3 green onions, sliced
½ cup (2-oz) reduced fat Swiss cheese, shredded
  Paprika

1. Preheat oven to 350°F. Place chicken in a sprayed shallow baking pan. Sprinkle lightly with salt. Brush with mustard. Sprinkle onions, cheese, and then paprika over chicken. Bake 20 to 25 minutes or until cooked through.

Per serving: 179 Cal, 4g Fat, 1g Sat F, 77mg Chol, 291mg Sod, 31g Pro, <1g Sug, 2g Carb, <1g Fib

Exchanges   Net Carbs
       Fat 1/2   2
Very Lean Meat 4-1/2

Chicken Broccoli Supreme

MAKES 1 SERVING

A colorful dish for a special person.

1   chicken breast half, skinned, boned
    Salt and pepper
1   broccoli spear, cooked crisp-tender
½   slice reduced fat Swiss cheese
    Paprika

1. Gently pound chicken to ¼-inch thickness. Cook chicken in sprayed medium nonstick skillet, turning once. Sprinkle with salt and pepper.

2. Top with broccoli spear. Place cheese on top. Sprinkle with paprika. Cover and heat just long enough to melt the cheese.

note: Broccoli spears can be cooked quickly by steaming on top of the stove or in the microwave with a small amount of water.

Per serving: 179 Cal, 4g Fat, 1g Sat F, 77mg Chol, 192mg Sod, 31g Pro, 1g Sug, 3g Carb, 1g Fib

Exchanges   Net Carbs

Fat 1/2	2
Very Lean Meat 4-1/2	
Vegetable 1/2	

Roast Chicken in Foil

MAKES 6-8 SERVINGS

Chicken should be very tender and moist. Also great for recipes requiring cubed or sliced chicken.

1   (3 to 3½-lb) chicken
½   teaspoon salt
¼   teaspoon pepper
¼   teaspoon garlic powder
¼   teaspoon dried rosemary

1. Preheat oven to 400°F. Place a large piece of heavy duty foil in a shallow baking pan. Place chicken on top.

2. Combine seasonings and sprinkle over chicken. Wrap foil tightly to seal. Bake 60 minutes; reduce heat and cook 20 to 30 minutes or until thigh registers 170°. Discard skin before serving.

tip: If browned chicken is desired, open foil last 20 minutes of cooking time.

Per 3 oz serving (average of white & dark meat: 162 Cal, 6g Fat, 2g Sat F, 76mg Chol, 73mg Sod, 25g Pro, 0g Sug, 0g Carb, 0g Fib

Exchanges   Net Carbs

Fat 1	0
Very Lean Meat 3-1/2	

Chicken Strips Stir-Fry

This marinade gives the chicken a subtle ginger flavor. Additional oil isn't needed for stir-frying.

- **4** **chicken breast halves, skinned, boned**
- **1** **tablespoon oil**
- **¼** **teaspoon salt**
- **5** **thin slices fresh ginger**

1. Cut chicken into narrow strips. Combine chicken with remaining ingredients. Cover and chill at least 1 hour.

2. Remove ginger slices and cook chicken in a medium skillet over medium-high heat. Cook quickly, stirring often, until cooked through. This doesn't take long. Remember that over-cooked chicken is dry and tough.

Per serving: 170 Cal, 6g Fat, 1g Sat F, 72mg Chol, 208mg Sod, 26g Pro, 0g Sug, 0g Carb, 0g Fib

Exchanges   Net Carbs
Fat 1   0
Very Lean Meat 3-1/2

Chicken-Vegetable Dish

MAKES 4 SERVINGS

A nice colorful main dish.

- **4** **chicken breast halves, skinned, boned**
  Salt and pepper
- **1** **tablespoon oil**
- **1¼** **cups chicken broth**
- **2** **cups broccoli florets**
- **1** **medium yellow squash, sliced**

1. Sprinkle chicken with salt and pepper. Heat oil in a large skillet and brown chicken on both sides. Add chicken broth; cover and cook 15 to 20 minutes or until chicken is cooked through.

2. Add vegetables and sprinkle lightly with salt and pepper. Cover and cook 5 to 6 minutes or until vegetables are just crisp-tender.

Per serving: 191 Cal, 6g Fat, 1g Sat F, 72mg Chol, 236mg Sod, 8g Pro, <1g Sug, 3g Carb, 2g Fib

Exchanges   Net Carbs
Fat 1   1
Very Lean Meat 3-1/2
Vegetable 1/2

Baked Chicken Italian

I hope your supermarket carries Bernstein dressings. They can be used in many chicken recipes, as well as your favorite salad combinations.

6 chicken breast halves, skinned, boned
¼ cup nonfat vinaigrette

1. Preheat oven to 400°F. Brush chicken with dressing. Place, skin-side up, on a baking pan. Bake 45 to 60 minutes, basting once or twice with dressing, until chicken is golden and cooked through.

Per serving: 150 Cal, 3g Fat, 1g Sat F, 72mg Chol, 146mg Sod, 26g Pro, 1g Sug, 2g Carb, 0g Fib

Exchanges   Net Carbs
Very Lean Meat 3-1/2   2

Garlic Butter Chicken

Another quick and easy recipe.

6 chicken breast halves, skinned, boned
¼ cup reduced calorie margarine, melted
1 tablespoon garlic salt
¼ teaspoon pepper

1. Preheat oven to 350°F. Place chicken, skin-side down, in a sprayed 13x9-inch baking dish.
2. Combine remaining ingredients. Brush chicken with some of the mixture and bake 30 minutes, basting twice. Turn chicken and bake 20 to 30 minutes or until cooked through, basting frequently.

Per serving: 206 Cal, 10g Fat, 2g Sat F, 72mg Chol, 471mg Sod, 26g Pro, 0g Sug, 0g Carb, 0g Fib

Exchanges   Net Carbs
Fat 1-1/2   0
Very Lean Meat 3-1/2

Broccoli-Tomato Chicken

MAKES 4 SERVINGS

A colorful dish.

2   chicken breast halves, skinned, boned
2   tablespoons oil, divided
2   small onions, sliced
2   cups broccoli florets
1   medium tomato (wedges)
    Salt and pepper

1. Cut chicken into bite-size pieces and toss with 1 tablespoon of the oil. Add to a large skillet and cook over high heat, stirring frequently, until just tender.
2. Add remaining oil and onion. Cook over medium heat, about 2 minutes. Add broccoli and tomato. Sprinkle with salt and pepper. Cover and cook 4 minutes or until vegetables are just crisp-tender.

Per serving: 132 Cal, 5g Fat, 1g Sat F, 36mg Chol, 198mg Sod, 15g Pro, 2g Sug, 7g Carb, 2g Fib,

Exchanges   Net Carbs

      Fat 1   5
Very Lean Meat 3-1/2
  Vegetable 1 1/2

Lemon Roasted Chicken

MAKES 6 SERVINGS

Nutritional analysis is based on skin removed before serving.

1   (4 -lb) roasting chicken
½   cup reduced calorie margarine, softened
1   tablespoon fresh lemon zest
    Salt and pepper

1. Preheat oven to 375°F. Place chicken on a rack in roasting pan.
2. Combine margarine with lemon zest. Add a little salt and pepper. Loosen the skin from the breast area and spread half the mixture under the skin. Rub remaining mixture over the chicken. Bake 1 to 1½ hours or until leg-thigh registers 170°, brushing occasionally with pan juices. Remove skin before serving.

Per 3 oz serving (average of white & dark meat): 195 Cal, 10g Fat, 2g Sat F, 76mg Chol, 104mg Sod, 25g Pro, 0g Sug, 0g Carb, 0g Fib

Exchanges   Net Carbs

      Fat 1-1/2   2
Very Lean Meat 3-1/2

Curried Chicken Bake

Delight your palate with just a touch of curry.

4   chicken breast halves, skinned, boned
⅓   cup light mayonnaise
1   teaspoons curry powder
½   teaspoon prepared horseradish
½   teaspoon low sodium soy sauce
½   teaspoon Dijon mustard

1. Preheat oven to 350°F. Place chicken, skin-side down, in a sprayed 13x9-inch baking dish. Combine remaining ingredients and brush chicken; turn and brush with remaining sauce. Bake 50 to 60 minutes or until browned and cooked through.

Per serving: 176 Cal, 6g Fat, 2g Sat F, 72mg Chol, 274mg Sod, 27g Pro, 1g Sug, 3g Carb, <1g Fib

Exchanges   Net Carbs
Fat 1/2   3
Very Lean Meat 3-1/2

Chicken-Bacon Rolls

MAKES 4 SERVINGS

The bacon keeps the chicken moist as well as adding lots of flavor.

4   chicken breast halves, skinned, boned
¼   cup drained oil-packed sun-dried tomatoes, chopped
    Salt and pepper
4   thin slices bacon

1. Preheat oven to 350°F. Pound chicken to ¼-inch thickness.
2. Top each with 1 tablespoon sun-dried tomatoes. Roll up to enclose filling. Sprinkle with salt and pepper.
3. Stretch bacon by running a knife down the slice and pulling at the same time. Wrap around chicken; secure with a wooden toothpick. Bake 20 to 30 minutes or until cooked through.

Per serving: 189 Cal, 7g Fat, 2g Sat F, 79mg Chol, 228mg Sod, 30g Pro, 0g Sug, 2g Carb, <1g Fib

Exchanges   Net Carbs
Fat 1   2
Meat 1/2
Very Lean Meat 3-1/2
Vegetable 1/2

Company Chicken

When you reach maintenance level, you can place a sliced pineapple ring between the ham and cheese slices.

4 chicken breast halves, skinned, boned
¼ cup flour
1 tablespoon oil
2 slices deli ham, halved
2 slices reduced fat Monterey Jack cheese, halved

1. Dip chicken in flour; shake off excess. Cook in heated oil over medium-high heat, turning once.
2. Top with a slice of ham and then the cheese. Cook until cheese is melted.

Per serving: 243 Cal, 10g Fat, 3g Sat F, 87mg Chol, 336mg Sod, 33g Pro, <1g Sug, 6g Carb, <1g Fib

Exchanges   Net Carbs

Fat 1   6
Meat 1/2
Starch 1/2
Very Lean Meat 4

Chicken Vegie Kabobs

Kabobs are made for grilling.

4 chicken breast halves, skinned, boned
   Salt and pepper
12 green pepper squares
12 small mushrooms
¼ cup reduced calorie margarine, melted

1. Cut chicken into 1½-inch pieces. Sprinkle with salt and pepper.
3. Thread chicken, peppers and mushrooms on skewers. Grill 4 to 5 minutes on each side, or until cooked through, basting frequently with margarine.

Per serving: 200 Cal, 8g Fat, 2g Sat F, 72mg Chol, 104mg Sod, 28g Pro, 2g Sug, 4g Carb, 1g Fib

Exchanges   Net Carbs

Fat 1   3
Very Lean Meat 3-1/2
Vegetable 1/2

Chicken Kabobs

The kabobs can be grilled or broiled. This is an easy recipe for family meals or entertaining.

4   chicken breast halves, skinned, boned
½   cup low sodium soy sauce
1   teaspoon grated fresh ginger

1. Cut chicken breasts into bite-size pieces. Combine soy sauce and ginger with 1 cup water and pour over chicken. Marinate at least 2 hours in refrigerator.

2. Place chicken on skewers and broil or grill, basting occasionally with marinade. Turn, do not baste, and cook until cooked through.

Per serving: 142Cal, 3g Fat, 1g Sat F, 72mg Chol, 152mg Sod, 26g Pro, 0g Sug, 0g Carb, 0g Fib

Exchanges   Net Carbs
Very Lean Meat 3-1/2   0

Quick Grill

Brush chicken pieces with Italian dressing and bake at 350°F for 30 to 45 minutes. If cooking for a crowd, I like to do this step ahead. Then place chicken on grill over medium coals. Brush with low-carb barbecue sauce and cook, basting frequently, until heated through.

Chicken Seafood Kabobs

A very low-carb recipe.

2   chicken breast halves, skinned, boned
8   small mushrooms
½   red pepper, cut into squares
8   jumbo shrimp, peeled, deveined
4   green onions, 4-inch lengths
2   tablespoons oil

1. Cut chicken into 1½ inch pieces. Alternate food on skewers beginning and ending with chicken. Brush with oil.

2. Grill, turning several times and basting with oil until cooked through.

Per skewer: 228 Cal, 6g Fat, 1g Sat F, 257mg Chol, 290mg Sod, 38g Pro, 2g Sug, 3g Carb, 1g Fib

Exchanges   Net Carbs
Fat 1   2
Very Lean Meat 5

Orange Chicken Kabobs

The kabobs can be grilled or broiled. This is an easy recipe for family meals or entertaining.

4   chicken breast halves, skinned, boned
⅓   cup reduced sugar orange marmalade
1   tablespoon Grand Marnier

1. Cut chicken breasts into bite-size pieces. Thread on 4 skewers, leaving a small space between each piece of chicken. Place on a heated grill and cook, turning once, until chicken is almost cooked through.

2. Combine remaining ingredients and brush some of the sauce over the chicken. Cook one side, turn and baste with sauce. Continue to cook until cooked through.

Per serving: 186 Cal, 3g Fat, 1g Sat F, 72mg Chol, 63mg Sod, 26g Pro, 8g Sug, 9g Carb, 0g Fib

Exchanges   Net Carbs
Other Carbs 1/2   9
Very Lean Meat 3-1/2

Broccoli-Cheese Chicken

MAKES 4 SERVINGS

Can also be baked in the oven.

4   chicken breast halves, skinned, boned
1   tablespoon oil
4   thin tomato slices
4   small broccoli spears, cooked
4   slices reduced fat Mozzarella cheese

1. Heat oil in a large skillet. Cook chicken 6 to 8 minutes or until cooked through, turning once.

2. Top chicken with remaining ingredients, cutting to fit if necessary. Cover skillet and cook to heat through and melt cheese.

Per serving: 256 Cal, 10g Fat, 3g Sat F, 82mg Chol, 280mg Sod, 35g Pro, 1g Sug, 4g Carb, 1g Fib

Exchanges   Net Carbs
Fat 1   3
Very Lean Meat 3-1/2
Vegetable 1/2

Easy Baked Chicken

This is about as easy as it gets.

1   **chicken, cut up**
⅓   **cup reduced calorie margarine**
    Paprika
    Salt and pepper

1. Preheat oven to 400°F. Place chicken, skin-side up, in a 13x9-inch baking dish. Dot with margarine and sprinkle with paprika and salt and pepper. Bake 50 to 60 minutes or until cooked through, basting occasionally with the butter. Discard chicken before serving.

Per 3-oz serving (average of white & dark meat): 203 Cal, 12g Fat, 3g Sat F, 75mg Chol, 70mg Sod, 23g Pro, 0g Sug, 0g Carb, 0g Fib

Exchanges   Net Carbs

Fat 1-1/2   0
Meat 3-1/2

Baked Garlic Chicken

A mild-flavored garlic chicken that is so tender it just falls off the bone.

6   **chicken breast halves, skinned, boned**
    Salt and pepper
¼   **cup flour**
2   **tablespoons oil**
30 **large garlic cloves, for flavor only**
½   **teaspoon Italian seasoning**

1. Preheat oven to 350°F. Sprinkle chicken with salt and pepper. Lightly coat with flour and brown in heated oil in a large pot or Dutch oven.
2. Remove paper-like covering from garlic, but do not peel. Add to pot and sprinkle with seasoning. Add ½ cup water. Cover and bake 1½ hours or until chicken is cooked through.
note: Count 1g of carbs per garlic clove. Keep this in mind if you would like to try one.

Per serving: 180 Cal, 5g Fat, 1g Sat F, 72mg Chol, 70mg Sod, 24g Pro, 0g Sug, 4g Carb, <1g Fib

Exchanges   Net Carbs

Fat 1/2   4
Very Lean Meat 3-1/2

Dilly Chicken

*If you like the flavor of dill, you
will enjoy this recipe.*

4   chicken breast halves, skinned, boned
¾   cup nonfat sour cream
1   cup chicken broth
2   tablespoons flour
1   teaspoon Splenda®
1   teaspoon dried dill weed

1. Preheat oven to 350°F. Place chicken in
a sprayed 13x9-inch baking dish.
2. Combine remaining ingredients in a
small saucepan. Bring to a boil and cook,
stirring frequently, until thickened. Pour over
chicken and bake 30 minutes. Increase
temperature to 375° and cook 15 minutes or
until cooked through.

Per serving (with 2 T sauce): 171 Cal,
3g Fat, 1g Sat F, 74mg Chol, 153mg Sod,
28g Pro, 0g Sug, 7g Carb, <1g Fib

Exchanges   Net Carbs
Very Lean Meat 3-1/2   7

Italiano Chicken

MAKES 4 SERVINGS

Your kitchen will smell "sooo" good!

4   chicken breast halves, skinned, boned
½   cup grated Parmesan cheese
½   teaspoon oregano
1   teaspoon garlic salt
¼   teaspoon pepper
2   tablespoons reduced calorie
    margarine, melted

1. Preheat oven to 375°F. Rinse chicken
and pat dry.
2. Combine next 4 ingredients. Dip chicken
in melted butter; coat with cheese mixture
and place in a shallow baking dish. Pour any
remaining butter over top. Bake 30 to 40
minutes or until chicken is cooked through.

Per serving: 234 Cal, 11g Fat, 4g Sat F,
81mg Chol, 502mg Sod, 30g Pro,
0g Sug, 1g Carb, <1g Fib

Exchanges   Net Carbs
Fat 1-1/2   1
Meat 1/2
Very Lean Meat 3-1/2

Sherry Glazed Chicken

This chicken is richly glazed, tender and delicious. A family favorite. If desired, garnish with sesame seeds.

4 **chicken breast halves, skinned, boned**
¼ **cup flour**
1 **tablespoon oil**
¼ **cup low sodium soy sauce**
2 **tablespoons dry sherry**
2 **tablespoons Splenda®**

1. Preheat oven to 350°F. Coat chicken with flour; shake off excess.

2. Heat oil in a large skillet and quickly brown chicken over high heat, turning once.

3. Place in a sprayed 11x7-inch baking dish. Bake 15 minutes. Combine remaining ingredients and baste chicken. Bake 15 minutes or until cooked through, basting every 5 minutes.

Per serving: 212 Cal, 7g Fat, 1g Sat F, 72mg Chol, 597mg Sod, 29g Pro, <1g Sug, 7g Carb, 0g Fib

Exchanges   Net Carbs

Fat 1   7
Other Carbs 1/2
Very Lean Meat 3-1/2

Stir-Fry Chicken

Another way to get your vegetables for the day.

4 **chicken breast halves, skinned boned**
1 **tablespoon oil**
1 **medium onion, sliced**
1 **red or green pepper, sliced**
2 **cups bean sprouts**
2 **tablespoons low sodium soy sauce**

1. Cut chicken into bite-size pieces. Heat oil in a large skillet; add chicken and cook, stirring frequently, until just tender. Remove chicken.

2. Add onions and pepper; cook until crisp-tender, adding more oil if needed. Add sprouts, soy sauce and chicken. Heat through, but do not overcook.

Per serving: 232 Cal, 9g Fat, 1g Sat F, 36mg Chol, 335mg Sod, 32g Pro, 4g Sug, 8g Carb, 1g Fib

Exchanges   Net Carbs

Fat 1   7
Very Lean Meat 4
Vegetable 1

Chicken Hawaiian

Another company favorite.

4   large chicken breast halves, skinned, boned
2   canned pineapple rings, halved
¼   cup unsweetened shredded coconut
1   teaspoon salt
2   tablespoons reduced calorie margarine, melted

1. Preheat oven to 350°F. Place chicken between waxed paper and pound to ¼ inch thickness.

2. Place a pineapple half toward one end of chicken. Sprinkle with 1 tablespoon coconut. Fold sides over and roll up to enclose filling. Secure with wooden toothpicks.

3. Combine salt and bread crumbs. Brush chicken with melted margarine and coat with bread crumbs. Place on sprayed baking sheet. Bake 35 to 45 minutes or until golden and cooked through, brushing with margarine if chicken appears dry.

Per serving: 217 Cal, 10g Fat, 5g Sat F, 72mg Chol, 674mg Sod, 27g Pro, 2g Sug, 4g Carb, 1g Fib

Exchanges   Net Carbs

Fat 1-1/2   3
Very Lean Meat 3-1/2

Chicken Divine Casserole

This is a favorite casserole in our family. Serve with a tossed salad and fresh fruit.

4   chicken breast halves, skinned, boned, cooked
2   cups broccoli florets
1   (8-oz) package light cream cheese, softened
1   cup nonfat milk
¾   teaspoon garlic salt
¾   cup grated Parmesan cheese

1. Preheat oven to 350°F. Cut chicken into ¼ inch slices. Place in a sprayed 8x8-inch baking dish. Top with broccoli.

2. Beat cream cheese until smooth. Gradually add milk to cream cheese.

3. Spoon into a saucepan; add garlic salt and Parmesan. Cook, over low heat, until thickened. Pour over broccoli and bake 35 to 40 minutes.

Per serving: 368 Cal, 18g Fat, 10g Sat F, 118mg Chol, 6825mg Sod, 41g Pro, 3g Sug, 9g Carb, 1g Fib

Exchanges   Net Carbs

Fat 2-1/2   8
Meat 1-1/2
Very Lean Meat 3-1/2
Vegetable 1/2

Baked Chicken Curry

MAKES 6 SERVINGS

Add curry to taste.

6   chicken breast halves, skinned, boned
¼   cup reduced calorie margarine,
     melted
1   teaspoon fresh lemon juice
1   garlic cloves, minced
1   teaspoon salt
1   teaspoon curry powder

1. Preheat oven to 350°F. Place chicken, skin-side down, in a sprayed 13x9-inch baking dish.
2. Combine remaining ingredients. Brush chicken with some of the sauce. Bake 30 minutes, basting once.
3. Turn chicken, bake 20 minutes or until cooked through, basting every 10 minutes.

Per serving: 192 Cal, 9g Fat, 2g Sat F, 72mg Chol, 497mg Sod, 26g Pro, 0g Sug, <1g Carb, 0g Fib

Exchanges   Net Carbs
      Fat 1-1/2   <1
Very Lean Meat 3-1/2

Butterflied Grilled Chicken

MAKES 4 SERVINGS

Butterflying the chicken speeds up the cooking time.

1   (2½ to 3-lb) chicken
¼   cup reduced calorie margarine,
     melted
1   tablespoon lemon juice
     Salt and pepper

1. Split chicken lengthwise all the way through the back. With 2 long metal skewers, skewer chicken diagonally to keep chicken flat.
2. Combine margarine and lemon juice; baste chicken. Sprinkle with salt and pepper.
3. Place, skin-side up, on grill over medium coals. Cover and cook 45 to 60 minutes or until cooked through, basting with the margarine mixture. Discard skin before serving.

Per 3oz serving (average white & dark meat): 170 Cal, 7g Fat, 2g Sat F, 78mg Chol, 80mg Sod, 25g Pro, 0g Sug, 0g Carb, 0g Fib

Exchanges   Net Carbs
      Fat 1   0
Very Lean Meat 3-1/2

Roquefort Chicken

Serve with Asparagus & Almonds, page 237.

6   chicken breast halves, skinned, boned
    Salt and pepper
¼   cup reduced calorie margarine
4   ounces Roquefort cheese
1   garlic clove, minced
1   cup nonfat sour cream

1. Preheat oven to 350°F. Sprinkle chicken with salt and pepper. Heat margarine in a large heavy skillet and lightly brown chicken. Place in a sprayed 13x9-inch baking dish.

2. Add remaining ingredients to skillet. Heat, but do not boil; pour over chicken. Bake 30 to 40 minutes or until cooked through.

Per serving (with 2T sauce): 205 Cal, 8g Fat, 4g Sat F, 87mg Chol, 273mg Sod, 29g Pro, 0g Sug, 3g Carb, 0g Fib

Exchanges	Net Carbs
Fat 1	3
Meat 1/2	
Very Lean Meat 3-1/2	

Chinese Browned Chicken

MAKES 4 SERVINGS

Lots of flavor for so few ingredients.

4   chicken breast halves, skinned, boned
1   tablespoon reduced calorie
    margarine, melted
1   tablespoons Worcestershire sauce
1   tablespoon low sodium soy sauce

1. Preheat oven to 350°F. Line a shallow baking pan with foil for easier cleaning. Place chicken on foil, skin-side up.

2. Combine remaining ingredients. Brush chicken and bake 30 to 40 minutes, basting occasionally.

Per serving: 162 Cal, 5g Fat, 1g Sat F, 72mg Chol, 211mg Sod, 27g Pro, <1g Sug, 1g Carb, 0g Fib

Exchanges	Net Carbs
Fat 1/2	1
Very Lean Meat 3-1/2	

Chicken Monterey

MAKES 4 SERVINGS

Picture perfect. A dish you will enjoy.

4   chicken breast halves, skinned, boned
    Lemon pepper
4   slices reduced fat Monterey Jack
    cheese
½   cup diced tomatoes
3   tablespoons sliced green onions

1. Preheat oven to 350°F. Place chicken in a sprayed 8x8-inch baking dish. Sprinkle lightly with lemon pepper. Bake 20 to 30 minutes or until cooked through.

2. Top with cheese. Return to oven to melt cheese. Place on serving plates and top with tomato and onion.

Per serving: 226 Cal, 9g Fat, 5g Sat F, 92mg Chol, 305mg Sod, 34g Pro, 1g Sug, 2g Carb, <1g Fib

Exchanges   Net Carbs
Fat 1   2
Meat 1
Very Lean Meat 3-1/2

Swiss-Artichoke Chicken

MAKES 4 SERVINGS

Serve with Lemon Broccoli, page 243.

4   chicken breast halves, skinned, boned
1   tablespoon oil
1   (6.5-oz) jar marinated artichoke
    hearts, drained
4   slices reduced fat Swiss cheese

1. Heat oil in a large skillet. Add chicken and cook 6 to 8 minutes or until cooked through, turning once.

2. Cut artichokes if too large and place on chicken. Top with cheese, trimming if necessary. Cover skillet and cook to melt cheese.

Per serving: 308 Cal, 16g Fat, 6g Sat F, 98mg Chol, 242mg Sod, 35g Pro, 0g Sug, 5g Carb, 1g Fib

Exchanges   Net Carbs
Fat 2   4
Meat 1
Very Lean Meat 3-1/2
Vegetable 1

Johnny's Chicken

MAKES 6 SERVINGS

I call this Johnny's Chicken because the seasoning is produced by a popular local restaurant by that name.

4   chicken breast halves, skinned, boned
2   tablespoons reduced calorie margarine, melted
     Johnny's Garlic Spread & Seasoning

1. Preheat oven to 400°F. Place chicken pieces, skin-side up, in a 13x9-inch baking dish. Brush with margarine. Sprinkle lightly with seasoning. Bake 45 to 60 minutes, basting occassionally.

note: The seasoning can usually be found in discount warehouse stores.

Per serving: 165Cal, 6g Fat, 1g Sat F, 72mg Chol, 346mg Sod, 26g Pro, 0g Sug, 0g Carb, 0g Fib

Exchanges   Net Carbs
   Fat 1   0
Very Lean Meat 3-1/2

Chicken Delight

MAKES 4 SERVINGS

4   chicken breast halves, skinned, boned
1   tablespoon oil
4   small slices deli ham
8   asparagus spears, cooked
2   slices reduced fat Swiss cheese

1. In a medium skillet, cook chicken in heated oil, turning once.

2. Place a slice of ham on chicken. Top each with 2 asparagus spears. Cut cheese in half diagonally and place over asparagus. Cover skillet and cook to melt the cheese.

Per serving: 222 Cal, 7g Fat, 2g Sat F, 87mg Chol, 409mg Sod, 35g Pro, 1g Sug, 2g Carb, 0g Fib

Exchanges   Net Carbs
   Fat 1   2
Very Lean Meat 5

Cook's Tip

If you want to take the time to pound boneless chicken to an even thickness, the cooking will be more even and less dry. To do this, place chicken between plastic wrap and pound to 1/4 inch thickness.

Chicken Bundles

A great company dish.

10   chicken breast halves, skinned, boned
2   cups nonfat sour cream
1   tablespoon Worcestershire sauce
2   teaspoons salt
1¼   teaspoons paprika
1½   cups low-fat dry white bread crumbs

1. Place chicken in a 13x9-inch baking dish. Combine next 4 ingredients and pour over chicken. Turn pieces to coat. Cover. Refrigerate overnight.

2. Drop chicken into bread crumbs to coat. Tuck ends under to make a nice round fillet. Place in sprayed shallow baking pan. Cover. Chill at least 1½ hours.

3. Bake 45 to 60 minutes or until golden and cooked through. If coating appears dry, brush with melted margarine.

Per serving: 237 Cal, 4g Fat, 1g Sat F, 76mg Chol, 722mg Sod, 30g Pro, 1g Sug, 19g Carb, 1g Fib

Exchanges   Net Carbs

Starch 1   18
Very Lean Meat 3-1/2

Skillet Chicken with Sage

A very impressive dish.

4   chicken breast halves, skinned, boned
4   slices prosciutto
4   fresh sage leaves
3   tablespoons flour
1   tablespoon olive oil
½   cup dry white wine

1. Pound chicken to ¼-inch thickness. Place prosciutto on chicken, folding to fit. Place a sage leaf in center and secure with wooden toothpicks. Coat with flour; shaking off excess.

2. Heat oil in a large skillet. Cook chicken, sage-side down, 2 to 3 minutes per side, turning once. Chicken should be slightly undercooked. Remove and set aside.

3. Add wine to skillet and stir into drippings. Return chicken; turn to coat both sides and cook about 2 minutes.

Per serving: 274 Cal, 10g Fat, 3g Sat F, 98mg Chol, 611mg Sod, 35g Pro, 0g Sug, 5g Carb, <1g Fib

Exchanges   Net Carbs

Fat 1   5
Meat 1
Very Lean Meat 3-1/2

Italian Chicken

MAKES 6 SERVINGS

A perfect busy day recipe.

1 chicken, cut up
Nonfat vinaigrette dressing

1. Marinate chicken several hours or overnight in the dressing.
2. Preheat oven to 350°F. Remove chicken from dressing and place in a 13x9-inch baking dish. Bake 50 to 60 minutes or until cooked through, basting frequently with additional dressing. Discard skin before serving.

Per serving: 164 Cal, 6g Fat, 2g Sat F, 76mg Chol, 94mg Sod, 25g Pro, <1g Sug, 1g Carb, 0g Fib

Exchanges   Net Carbs
Fat 1   1
Very Lean Meat 3-1/2

∽ Hint ∽

The secret to tender moist chicken is in not over-cooking. Watch carefully during the last few minutes of cooking time. Leaving the skin on the chicken will also contribute to moist chicken and in some recipes will contribute to more even browning.

Soy Chicken

MAKES 4 SERVINGS

Ready to bake in less than 10 minutes.

4 chicken breast halves, skinned, boned
½ cup brown Sugar Twin®
½ cup low sodium soy sauce
3 tablespoons reduced calorie margarine, melted

1. Preheat oven to 350°F. Place chicken, skin-side down, in a sprayed 13x9-inch baking dish.
2. Combine remaining ingredients and pour over chicken. Bake 30 minutes. Turn chicken and bake 20 to 30 minutes, basting occasionally, until cooked through. Serve sauce with chicken.

Per serving: 178 Cal, 6g Fat, 1g Sat F, 72mg Chol, 626mg Sod, 27g Pro, 1g Sug, 3g Carb, 0g Fib

Exchanges   Net Carbs
Fat 1   3
Very Lean Meat 3-1/2

Ben's Chicken Parmesan

MAKES 4 SERVINGS

Use remaining sauce in jar to serve over pasta.

4   chicken breast halves, skinned, boned
3   tablespoons grated Parmesan cheese
1¼ cups low-fat spaghetti sauce
1   cup (4-oz) reduced fat Mozzarella
    cheese, shredded
    Parsley

1. Preheat oven to 350°F. Place chicken in a sprayed 11x7-inch baking dish.

2. Combine Parmesan and spaghetti sauce; pour over chicken. Cover. Bake 30 minutes or until cooked through.

3. Top with cheese and a sprinkle of parsley. Bake 5 minutes to melt cheese.

Per serving: 284 Cal, 9g Fat, 4g Sat F, 86mg Chol, 697mg Sod, 37g Pro, 3g Sug, 10g Carb, <1g Fib

Exchanges	Net Carbs
Fat 1	10
Meat 1-1/2	
Very Lean Meat 3-1/2	

Maple Sauce Chicken

MAKES 6 SERVINGS

This is a family favorite.

6   chicken breast halves, skinned, boned
1   small onion, sliced
½   cup no-carb maple syrup
½   cup low-carb ketchup
¼   cup white vinegar
2   tablespoons Mild & Creamy Dijon
    mustard

1. Preheat oven to 350°F. Clean chicken and pat dry.

2. Place onion in a sprayed 13x9-inch baking dish. Arrange chicken on top.

3. Combine remaining ingredients and spoon over chicken. Bake 50 to 60 minutes or until nicely glazed and cooked through, basting frequently.

Per serving: 171 Cal, 3g Fat, 1g Sat F, 72mg Chol, 223mg Sod, 27g Pro, <1g Sug, 4g Carb, 0g Fib

Exchanges	Net Carbs
Very Lean Meat 3-1/2	4

Chicken Quesadillas

Serve these as a light lunch, or as appetizers, served with additional salsa and/or sour cream, if desired.

1½ cups chopped cooked chicken
1 cup (4-oz) reduced fat Cheddar cheese, shredded
¾ cup thick and chunky salsa
8 (7-inch) low-carb tortillas

1. Combine chicken, cheese and salsa. Place each tortilla in a sprayed heated skillet or griddle. Spread each with 1/4 of the chicken mixture. Top with a tortilla and cook until heated through, turning once. Cut in half and serve.

Per serving: 111 Cal, 4g Fat, 1g Sat F, 18mg Chol, 406mg Sod, 14g Pro, 1g Sug, 13g Carb, 8g Fib

Exchanges   Net Carbs
Very Lean Meat 1-1/2   5

Roast Cornish Hens

Just the right size for a serving.

4 Cornish hens
1 teaspoon seasoning salt
¼ teaspoon garlic powder
¼ teaspoon paprika

1. Preheat oven to 400°F. Combine seasoning salt, garlic powder and paprika. Sprinkle over hens. Place, breast-side down, in a sprayed shallow pan. Bake 30 minutes.
2. Turn, breast-side up, and bake 30 to 40 minutes or until cooked through, basting with drippings. Cut in half, discard skin and serve.

Per serving: 167 Cal, 5g Fat, 1g Sat F, 132mg Chol, 78mg Sod, 29g Pro, 0g Sug, <1g Carb, 0g Fib

Exchanges   Net Carbs
Fat 1/2   <1
Very Lean Meat 4

Paulina's Turkey Meatballs

MAKES 24 SMALL MEATBALLS

These are great to have on hand in the freezer. Just pull out the number you need for a variety of dishes or for between meal snacks.

1   **pound ground turkey**
¼   **cup low-fat soft white bread crumbs**
¼   **cup egg substitute**
2   **tablespoons finely chopped onions**
½   **teaspoon prepared horseradish**
½   **teaspoon salt**

1. Preheat oven to 400°F. Combine ingredients, mixing lightly.
2. Shape into walnut-size meatballs. Place in a sprayed shallow baking pan and bake 18 to 20 minutes or until cooked through.

tip: You'll reach 1 gram of carbohydrates when you've eaten 8 meatballs.

Per 4 meatballs: 141 Cal, 7g Fat, 2g Sat F, 55mg Chol, 284mg Sod, 16g Pro, <1g Sug, 1g Carb, 0g Fib

Exchanges   Net Carbs
Meat 2   1

Teriyaki Turkey Burgers

MAKES 6 PATTIES

A delicious burger, even without the bun.

1   **pound ground turkey**
3   **tablespoons reduced sodium soy sauce**
1   **tablespoon pineapple juice**
¼   **cup low-fat white bread crumbs**
⅛   **teaspoon ground ginger**

1. Gently combine all ingredients; form into 6 patties. Cook in a sprayed nonstick skillet, grill or broiler until browned and cooked through.

Per serving: 151 Cal, 7g Fat, 2g Sat F, 55mg Chol, 357mg Sod, 16g Pro, 1g Sug, 4g Carb, <1g Fib

Exchanges   Net Carbs
Meat 2   4

Taco Burger Patties

MAKES 8 PATTIES

This is a great recipe if you are also watching your fat intake.

1½ pounds ground turkey
1 (1.25-oz) package taco seasoning mix
⅓ cup low-fat soft white bread crumbs
¼ cup egg substitute

1. Gently combine the ingredients and shape into 8 patties, about ¼ inch thick. Shaping will be easier if you wet your hands with a little water.
2. Cook in a sprayed nonstick skillet, turning once. Cook 3 to 4 minutes on each side or until lightly browned and cooked through.

Per serving: 166 Cal, 8g Fat, 2g Sat F, 62mg Chol, 326mg Sod, 18g Pro, 0g Sug, 4g Carb, 0g Fib

Exchanges   Net Carbs
Meat 2-1/2   4

Cook's Tip
For safety reasons, wear plastic gloves when mixing ground meat by hand. Actually you only need one, because you can mix it with one hand. Check your discount warehouse stores for the best prices.

Turkey-Bacon Burgers

MAKES 6 SERVINGS

The bacon keeps the patties moist and adds flavor.

1 pound ground turkey
⅓ cup low-fat soft white bread crumbs
¼ cup egg substitute
1 tablespoon Worcestershire sauce
   Salt and pepper to taste
6 slices of bacon

1. Gently mix the first 5 ingredients (this is easier to do with your hands). Form into 6 patties. Carefully wrap a slice of bacon around outer edge of each patty and secure with a wooden toothpick.
2. Cook patties in a large nonstick skillet, or broil or grill until cooked through, turning once. Remove bacon and discard.

Per serving: 143 Cal, 7g Fat, 2g Sat F, 55mg Chol, 104mg Sod, 17g Pro, <1g Sug, 1g Carb, <1g Fib

Exchanges   Net Carbs
Meat 2   1

Orange Glazed Turkey Breast

SERVINGS ARE 4 OUNCES

A wonderful marmalade glaze and black pepper add a nice touch to the finished dish.

1   **(6-lb) whole turkey breast,**
2   **teaspoons oil**
⅓   **cup sugar-free orange marmalade**
1   **tablespoon prepared mustard**
2   **teaspoons Worcestershire sauce**
½   **teaspoon cracked pepper**

1. Preheat oven to 350°F. Place turkey breast, breast-side up, on a rack in a roasting pan. Brush with oil. Cover with foil or pan lid and bake 1½ to 2 hours.

2. Combine remaining ingredients and brush over turkey. Cook 30 to 40 minutes or until temperature reaches 160°, basting frequently with the pan drippings. Cover and let stand 15 minutes before slicing. Remove skin before serving.

Per serving: 167 Cal, 1g Fat, <1g Sat F, 94mg Chol, 65mg Sod, 34g Pro, 0g Sug, 1g Carb, 0g Fib

Exchanges   Net Carbs
Very Lean Meat 4-1/2   1

Roasted Turkey

SERVES 12-15 WITH LEFTOVERS

This is one of the simplest and best ways to cook that Thanksgiving turkey.

1   **(16-lb) turkey**
2   **tablespoons oil**

1. Preheat oven to 325°F. Place turkey, breast-side up, on rack in a deep roasting pan. Insert thermometer into thickest part of thigh. Brush oil over skin. Bake about 3½ to 4 hours or to 170°. Cover loosely with foil if skin is browning too quickly. Let stand 20 to 30 minutes before carving. Remove skin before serving.

Per 4 oz serving of white meat:
167 Cal, 1g Fat, <1g Sat F, 94mg Chol, 65mg Sod, 25g Pro, 0g Sug, <1g Carb, 0g Fib

Exchanges   Net Carbs
Very Lean Meat 4-1/2   <1

Per 4 oz serving of dark meat:
212Cal, 8g Fat, 3g Sat F, 96mg Chol, 90mg Sod, 32g Pro, 0g Sug, 0g Carb, 0g Fib

Exchanges   Net Carbs
Fat 1   0
Very Lean Meat 4-1/2

Pasta

Pasta

Dreamfields makes a delicious pasta that is low in fat and very low in net carbohydrates, since they deduct their specific fiber blend from the total carbs. If you have any questions call them at 800-250-1917 and they can give you up-to-date information.

Sample Label

Per 2 ounce serving

Calories	190
Fat	1g
S. Fat	0g
Chol	0mg
Sodium	0mg
Fiber	4g
Sugars	1g
Protein	7g
Net Carbs	5

Chicken Pasta Soup

MAKES 6 SERVINGS

A light refreshing soup.

6 cups chicken broth
½ cup diced cooked chicken
3 ounces spaghetti, 1 inch pieces
½ cup green onion, 1 inch slices

1. Combine broth and chicken in a large saucepan. Bring to a boil; add spaghetti and cook about 7 minutes or until almost done.
2. Add onion and cook until pasta is tender.

Per serving: 69 Cal, 1g Fat, 0g Sat F, 6mg Chol, 498mg Sod, 5g Pro, 1g Sug, 11g Carb, 1g Fib

Exchanges   Net Carbs
Starch 1/2   10
Very Lean Meat 1/2

Chicken Noodle Soup

Your mom is right, chicken soup is good for you.

4   ounces linguine
7   cups chicken broth
1   small carrot, shredded
½   cup sliced celery
1   cup cubed cooked chicken
¼   cup frozen peas

1. Break pasta into 2-inch lengths and cook according to package directions. Drain and rinse.

2. In a large pot, combine broth, carrots and celery. Bring to a boil, reduce heat and simmer until vegetables are tender, about 5 to 6 minutes. Add peas, chicken and pasta. Cook until heated through.

Per serving: 62 Cal, <1g Fat,<1g Sat F, 7mg Chol, 361mg Sod, 5g Pro, <1g Sug, 9g Carb, 1g Fib

Exchanges   Net Carbs
Starch 1/2   8
Very Lean Meat 1/2

Chicken Cheese Salad

Just a small amount of pepperoni is all you need.

8   ounces penne
⅓   cup nonfat vinaigrette dressing
1   cup cooked, cubed chicken
1   cup (4-oz) reduced fat Mozzarella
     cheese, cubed
⅓   cup sliced green onions, green part
¼   cup grated Parmesan cheese

1. Cook pasta according to package directions. Rinse to cool, then drain. Place in a large bowl and toss with about 3 tablespoons of the dressing. Add chicken, cheese cubes and green onion. Cover and chill at least 2 hours.

2. Just before serving, toss with additional dressing, if needed, and the Parmesan cheese.

Per serving: 230 Cal, 4 Fat, 2g Sat F, 22mg Chol, 307mg Sod, 15g Pro, 2g Sug, 30g Carb, 2g Fib

Exchanges   Net Carbs
Meat 1   28
Starch 1-1/2
Very Lean Meat 1/2

Broccoli Pasta Salad

MAKES 8 SERVINGS

For a main course, add leftover chicken, ham, or shrimp.

2   **cups elbow macaroni**
2½ **cups broccoli florets**
½   **cup cherry tomatoes, halved**
½   **cup (2-oz) reduced fat Monterey Jack cheese, diced**
½   **cup nonfat vinaigrette dressing**

1. Cook pasta according to package directions. Rinse to cool, then drain.
2. Combine ingredients in a large bowl, using just enough dressing to lightly coat. Cover and chill about 2 hours.

Per serving: 108 Cal, 2g Fat, 1g Sat F, 5mg Chol, 192mg Sod, 5g Pro, 2g Sug, 18g Carb, 2g Fib

Exchanges
Meat 1/2
Starch 1
Vegetable 1/2

Net Carbs
16

Buttered Cheesy Pasta

MAKES 6 SERVINGS

Great side dish with your favorite meats.

12 **ounces spaghetti**
⅓   **cup reduced calorie margarine**
⅓   **cup grated Parmesan cheese**
      Freshly ground black pepper, to taste

1. Cook pasta according to package directions. Quickly rinse, drain and return to pot.
2. Add margarine and toss to melt. Add Parmesan and pepper and toss until cheese is melted.

Per serving: 302 Cal, 12g Fat, 3g Sat F, 4mg Chol, 150mg Sod, 8g Pro, 1g Sug, 40g Carb, 2g Fib

Exchanges
Fat 2
Starch 2-1/2

Net Carbs
38

Asparagus Pasta Dish

At the first sign of fresh asparagus, try this quick and flavorful vegetable dish.

8   ounces penne
1   pound asparagus, trimmed, sliced
¼   cup finely chopped oil-packed sun-dried tomatoes, drained
3   tablespoons oil
    Salt and pepper to taste

1. Cook pasta according to package directions. Rinse and drain.

2. Meanwhile, microwave or steam asparagus until just crisp-tender.

3. In a large skillet, heat sun-dried tomatoes in the oil, 2 to 3 minutes. Watch carefully to prevent burning. Add pasta and asparagus, tossing to coat.

Per serving: 161 Cal, 6g Fat, 1g Sat F, 0mg Chol, 11mg Sod, 5g Pro, 1g Sug, 23g Carb, 3g Fib

Exchanges
Fat 1
Starch 1
Vegetable 1/2

Net Carbs
20

Broccoli-Tomato Pasta Dish

A delicious and colorful way to use up leftover broccoli, asparagus or zucchini.

8   ounces linguine
2   tablespoons oil
1½   cups broccoli florets, cooked crisp-tender
    Freshly ground black pepper to taste
⅓   cup plus 1 tablespoon grated Parmesan cheese
2   small Plum tomatoes

1. Cook pasta according to package directions. Rinse, drain and return to pot.

2. Meanwhile, heat oil in a medium skillet. Add broccoli and cook quickly to heat through. Pour over pasta and toss to coat. Add pepper and the ⅓ cup of Parmesan cheese; toss to melt cheese. Spoon onto a large serving platter.

3. Cut tomatoes crosswise into narrow slices and place around outer edge of pasta. Sprinkle with remaining cheese.

Per serving: 151 Cal, 5g Fat, 1g Sat F, 3mg Chol, 65mg Sod, 5g Pro, 1g Sug, 21g Carb, 2g Fib

Exchanges
Fat 1
Starch 1
Vegetable 1/2

Net Carbs
19

Colorful Red Pepper Pasta

MAKES 6 SERVINGS

Can be made in less than 20 minutes.

8 ounces penne
3 tablespoons reduced calorie margarine
1 small red bell pepper, julienned
¼ cup coarsely chopped pecans

1. Cook pasta according to package directions. Rinse and drain.
2. Meanwhile, during last five minutes of cooking time for pasta, melt the margarine in a medium skillet. Add peppers and pecans and quickly sauté until peppers are just crisp-tender (this doesn't take long). Add pasta and mix well.

Per serving: 209 Cal, 9g Fat, 1g Sat F, 0mg Chol, 40mg Sod, 5g Pro, 1g Sug, 28g Carb, 2g Fib

Exchanges
Fat 1-1/2
Starch 1-1/2

Net Carbs
26

Cauliflower Pasta Dish

MAKES 6 SERVINGS

Not a lot of color so I suggest serving it with a colorful salad and vegetable.

6 ounces penne
2 teaspoons dried rosemary
2 cups small cauliflower florets
¼ cup slivered almonds, toasted
2 teaspoons oil
Salt and pepper to taste

1. Cook pasta according to package directions, adding rosemary to the water. Add cauliflower during last 4 minutes of cooking time. Cook until pasta tests done and cauliflower is tender. Rinse and drain well. Return to pot.
2. Add almonds, oil, salt and pepper.
note: It is easy to overcook the cauliflower. If desired, steam or microwave instead of cooking with the pasta.

Per serving: 146 Cal, 4g Fat, <1g Sat F, 0mg Chol, 6mg Sod, 5g Pro, 1g Sug, 22g Carb, 3g Fib

Exchanges
Fat 1/2
Starch 1
Vegetable 1/2

Net Carbs
19

Zucchini Linguine Pasta

A colorful vegetable pasta dish.

12 ounces linguine
2   tablespoons oil
2   medium garlic cloves, minced
2   medium-small zucchini, julienned
½   cup diced red bell pepper
½   cup grated Parmesan cheese

1. Cook pasta according to package directions. Rinse, drain and return to pot.

2. Meanwhile, heat oil and garlic in a large skillet. Add zucchini and pepper and cook about 4 minutes or until just crisp-tender. Add to pasta and mix well. Pour onto a serving platter and sprinkle with Parmesan cheese.

Per serving: 202 Cal, 6g Fat, 1g Sat F, 4mg Chol, 78mg Sod, 7g Pro, 1g Sug, 31g Carb, 2g Fib

Exchanges   Net Carbs

Fat 1   29
Meat 1/2
Starch

Swiss Noodles with Pecans

Serve on your most attractive serving dish.

12 ounces linguine
6   tablespoons reduced calorie margarine, melted
2   cups (8-oz) reduced fat Swiss cheese, shredded
    Ground black pepper to taste
1   tablespoon finely chopped pecans
1   tablespoon chopped parsley

1. Cook pasta according to package directions. Rinse, drain and return to pot. Add margarine and gradually stir in the cheese. Add pepper to taste.

2. Spoon pasta onto a serving platter. Sprinkle with pecans, then parsley.

Per serving: 329 Cal, 12g Fat, 3g Sat F, 10mg Chol, 145mg Sod, 15g Pro, 1g Sug, 41g Carb, 2g Fib

Exchanges   Net Carbs

Fat 2   39
Starch 2-1/2
Very Lean Meat 1

Penne with Broccoli & Mushrooms

MAKES 6 SERVINGS

Using a nonstick skillet is important in this recipe. Otherwise, you will be scrubbing cheese off the pan until kingdom come.

5   ounces penne
2   cups coarsely chopped broccoli
4   ounces mushrooms, sliced
½   cup reduced calorie margarine, divided
½   cup grated Parmesan cheese

1. Cook pasta according to package directions. Rinse, drain and return to pot.
2. Meanwhile, cook broccoli in a small amount of water until just crisp-tender. Drain and add to pasta.
3. In a large nonstick skillet, sauté the mushrooms in 3 tablespoons of the margarine, cooking until tender. Add pasta, the remaining margarine and the Parmesan cheese. Return to burner and heat just long enough to melt the butter and cheese.

Per serving: 228 Cal, 14g Fat, 3g Sat F, 6mg Chol, 211mg Sod, 7g Pro, 1g Sug, 19g Carb, 2g Fib

Exchanges   Net Carbs
Fat 2-1/2   17
Meat 1/2
Starch 1
Vegetable 1/2

Herbed-Tomato Spaghetti

MAKES 6 SERVINGS

A refreshing pasta dish.

8   ounces spaghetti
¼   cup oil
2   tablespoons slivered almonds
1   tablespoon chopped fresh basil
2   Plum tomatoes, coarsely chopped
6   tablespoons grated Parmesan cheese

1. Cook pasta according to package directions. Rinse, drain and return to pot.
2. Meanwhile, heat oil and almonds until nuts are lightly toasted. Add to pasta along with basil and tomatoes. This is somewhat hard to mix and you may have to re-arrange some of the tomatoes on the serving plates so that everyone gets their share. Sprinkle each serving with 1 tablespoon Parmesan cheese.

Per serving: 234 Cal, 11g Fat, 2g Sat F, 1mg Chol, 28mg Sod, 6g Pro, 1g Sug, 27g Carb, 2g Fib

Exchanges   Net Carbs
Fat 2   25
Starch 1-1/2

Noodles & Ham Casserole

MAKES 4 SERVINGS

This is somewhat on the dry side, but a nice change from our much-loved cream pastas.

6 ounces penne
⅓ cup green onions, sliced
1 teaspoon oil
1 cup (4-oz) diced ham
2 tablespoons sliced almonds
½ cup plus 2 tablespoons grated Parmesan cheese

1. Cook pasta according to package directions. Rinse and drain.

2. Preheat oven to 350°F. Toss onion with oil in a large skillet and cook until soft. Add ham and almonds; heat through. Add pasta and ½ cup of Parmesan. Pour into a sprayed 1½-quart deep casserole. Sprinkle with remaining cheese. Bake about 15 minutes or until heated through.

Per serving: 264 Cal, 8g Fat, 3g Sat F, 23mg Chol, 476mg Sod, 16g Pro, 1g Sug, 31g Carb, 2g Fib

Exchanges	Net Carbs
Fat 1	29
Meat 1	
Starch 1	
Very Lean Meat 1	

Light Dinner Pasta

MAKES 6 SERVINGS

Delicious served as a meatless dish for a light lunch or dinner.

8 ounces linguine
¼ cup oil-packed sun-dried tomatoes, plus 3 tablespoons of the oil
2 small garlic cloves, minced
¼ teaspoon crushed red pepper flakes
⅓ cup grated Parmesan cheese
2 tablespoons slivered almonds

1. Cook pasta according to package directions. Drain, rinse and return to pot.

2. Meanwhile, coarsely chop the sun-dried tomatoes. Heat the oil in a small skillet. Add tomatoes, garlic and red pepper and sauté about 2 minutes or until garlic is just soft. Add to pasta and mix well. Add Parmesan cheese and nuts.

note: If you have continued to add olive oil to the jar to keep the sun-dried tomatoes covered, you should have 4 tablespoons oil. If not, you will need to add additional oil to the recipe.

Per serving: 233 Cal, 10g Fat, 2g Sat F, 4mg Chol, 81mg Sod, 7g Pro, 1g Sug, 28g Carb, 2g Fib

Exchanges	Net Carbs
1-1/2	26
Meat 1/2	
Starch 1-1/2	

Chicken & Pasta Stir-Fry

A colorful pasta dish.

12 ounces spaghetti, broken into thirds
 3 chicken breast halves, skinned, boned
 ¼ cup low sodium soy sauce
 ½ small red and green bell pepper, julienned
    Freshly ground black pepper

1. Cook pasta according to package directions. Rinse and drain.

2. Meanwhile cut chicken crosswise into narrow strips. Cook in a sprayed nonstick skillet over medium-high heat until cooked through, stirring frequently.

3. Add soy sauce and peppers. Cook until vegetables are just crisp-tender. Season with pepper to taste. Toss with pasta.

Per serving: 272 Cal, 2g Fat, 1g Sat F, 36mg Chol, 300mg Sod, 20g Pro, 1g Sug, 41g Carb, 3g Fib

Exchanges   Net Carbs
Starch 2-1/2   38
Very Lean Meat 2

Cornish Hens & Pasta

MAKES 4 SERVINGS

The pasta is served as a side dish with the Cornish hens.

2 Cornish hens, halved
2 tablespoons oil, divided
½ teaspoon dried rosemary, crushed
¼ teaspoon paprika
8 ounces linguine

1. Preheat oven to 350°F. Place Cornish hens, cut-side down, in a sprayed shallow baking pan. Combine 1 tablespoon of the oil with the rosemary and paprika and brush over hens. Bake 45 to 60 minutes or until cooked through.

2. Meanwhile, cook pasta according to package directions. Rinse and drain. Toss with the remaining 1 tablespoon oil. Spoon onto a serving platter and top with Cornish hens. Remove skin before eating.

Per serving: 393 Cal, 9g Fat, 2g Sat F, 132mg Chol, 80mg Sod, 36g Pro, 1g Sug, 39g Carb, 2g Fib

Exchanges   Net Carbs
Fat 1   37
Starch 2-1/2
Very Lean Meat 4

Stove-Top Ground Beef & Pasta

MAKES 8 SERVINGS

I love this recipe. It is quick, easy and filling.

8 ounces penne
¾ pound extra lean ground beef
1 cup thick & chunky salsa
1 cup (4-oz) reduced fat Cheddar cheese, shredded

1. Cook pasta according to package directions. Rinse and drain well.

2. Meanwhile, brown ground beef in a large skillet; drain. Add salsa and simmer about 5 minutes or until some of the liquid is reduced. Add pasta and mix well. Cook until heated through. Sprinkle cheese over top. Cover and cook briefly to melt the cheese.

Per serving: 211 Cal, 6g Fat, 2g Sat F, 34mg Chol, 227mg Sod, 16g Pro, 2g Sug, 22g Carb, 1g Fib

Exchanges   Net Carbs

Fat 1   21
Starch 1
Very Lean Meat 2

Penne & Sun-Dried Tomatoes

MAKES 6 SIDE-DISH SERVINGS

This pasta dish should be served immediately or serve chilled as a delicious pasta salad. Not as good reheated.

8 ounces penne
¼ cup oil-packed sun-dried tomatoes, plus 1 tablespoon of the oil
1 (6.5-oz) jar marinated artichoke hearts, drained

1. Cook pasta according to package directions. Rinse, drain and return to pot.

2. Chop tomatoes and coarsely chop the artichokes. Add to pasta along with the oil.

Per serving: 178 Cal, 5g Fat, <1g Sat F, 0mg Chol, 91mg Sod, 5g Pro, <1g Sug, 29g Carb, 3g Fib

Exchanges   Net Carbs

Fat 1   26
Starch 1-1/2
Vegetable 1/2

Ham-Noodle Casserole

MAKES 8 SERVINGS

A quick economical meal.

8   ounces penne
½   cup sliced green onions
2   large eggs, lightly beaten
1   cup nonfat sour cream
¾   cup (3-oz) reduced fat Swiss cheese, shredded
1½ cups cubed ham

1. Cook pasta according to package directions. Rinse and drain.

2. Preheat oven to 350°F. Cook onion in a small sprayed skillet until just tender.

3. Combine eggs and sour cream. Add onion, cheese and ham. Add pasta and mix well. Pour into a sprayed 2-quart casserole. Cover and bake 30 minutes. Uncover and bake 10 to 15 minutes or until heated through.

Per serving: 204 Cal, 4g Fat, 1g Sat F, 76mg Chol, 465mg Sod, 16g Pro, 4g Sug, 25g Carb, 1g Fib

Exchanges   Net Carbs

Fat 1/2   24
Starch 1
Very Lean Meat 1-1/2

Sausage-Pasta Casserole

MAKES 8 SERVINGS

A great tasting casserole that can be ready to eat in less than an hour.

6   ounces penne
1   (12-oz) package lowfat turkey sausage
4   ounces fresh mushrooms, sliced
1   cup marinara spaghetti sauce
1   cup (4-oz) reduced fat Mozzarella cheese, shredded

1. Preheat oven to 350°F. Cook pasta according to directions. Rinse and drain.

2. Meanwhile, brown the sausage in a large skillet. Add mushrooms toward the end of cooking time and cook 2 or 3 more minutes; drain.

3. Add spaghetti sauce and bring to a boil. Reduce heat and simmer about 5 minutes. Add pasta and mix well. Pour into a sprayed 8x8-inch baking dish and sprinkle with cheese. Bake 15 to 20 minutes or until cheese is lightly browned.

Per serving: 180 Cal, 6g Fat, 2g Sat F, 30mg Chol, 411mg Sod, 12g Pro, 1g Sug, 18g Carb, 2g Fib

Exchanges   Net Carbs

Fat 1/2   16
Meat 1-1/2
Starch 1

Pesto Pasta Frittata

MAKES 6 SERVINGS

This recipe reminds me of a good quiche, but made with pasta. Serve as a brunch, lunch or supper dish.

- 6 ounces spaghetti
- 6 large eggs, lightly beaten
- 1 tablespoons pesto, or to taste
- 1 cup (4-oz) reduced fat Mozzarella cheese, shredded
- ¼ cup grated Parmesan cheese

1. Preheat oven to 350°F. Cook pasta according to package directions. Rinse, drain and spoon into a sprayed 10 inch quiche dish or pie dish.

2. Combine eggs, pesto, and Mozzarella cheese; pour over pasta. Sprinkle with Parmesan and bake 20 minutes or until set.

Per serving: 245Cal, 10g Fat, 4g Sat F, 221mg Chol, 352mg Sod, 17g Pro, 1g Sug, 21g Carb, 1g Fib

Exchanges
Fat 1
Meat 2
Starch 1

Net Carbs
20

Slow Cooker Carbonara

MAKES 6 SERVINGS

By cooking the final stages of this recipe in a slow cooker, you can rest assured the eggs will be cooked through.

- 12 ounces spaghetti
- 6 slices bacon, cooked, crumbled
- ½ cup reduced calorie margarine
- 2 large eggs, lightly beaten
- ¼ cup egg substitute
- ⅔ cup grated Parmesan cheese

1. Cook pasta according to package directions. Rinse and drain, but save ½ cup of the liquid. Place pasta in a sprayed slow cooker.

2. Add remaining ingredients and mix well. If mixture seems a little dry, add some of the reserved pasta water. Cover. Cook on LOW to finish cooking the eggs and to keep the pasta hot, about 1 hour.

Per serving: 407 Cal, 20g Fat, 5g Sat F, 85mg Chol, 448mg Sod, 16g Pro, 1g Sug, 40g Carb, 2g Fib

Exchanges
Fat 3
Meat 1
Starch 2-1/2

Net Carbs
38

Slow Cooker Spaghetti & Chicken

MAKES 8 SERVINGS

There's only one thing to say about this recipe. Delicious! You use the slow cooker to keep the pasta hot until ready to serve.

16	ounces spaghetti
3	chicken breast halves, skinned, boned
⅓	cup oil, divided
2	large garlic cloves, minced
¼	cup chopped parsley
½	cup grated Parmesan cheese

1. Cook pasta according to package directions. Rinse, drain and place in a sprayed slow cooker.

2. Meanwhile, cut chicken into ½ inch slices. Toss with 1 tablespoon oil. Heat remaining oil in a large skillet. Sauté chicken over medium-high heat, stirring almost constantly. Do in 2 batches. Just before chicken is cooked through, add the garlic and parsley. When cooked, pour into slow cooker. (Also, include oil from chicken.)

3. Add cheese and mix well. If mixture seems somewhat dry, add a little oil. Cover and keep hot on LOW until ready to serve. Should be able to keep at least an hour.

Per serving: 350 Cal, 12g Fat, 3g Sat F, 32mg Chol, 103mg Sod, 19g Pro, 1g Sug, 40g Carb, 2g Fib

Exchanges	Net Carbs
Fat 2	38
Meat 1/2	
Starch 2-1/2	
Very Lean Meat 1-1/2	

Casserole Dish or Baking Dish Do you know the difference?

A **Casserole Dish** is usually a round, square or oval deep dish and is referred to in quart sizes such as a 2-quart casserole dish.

A **Baking Dish** is usually rectangle, square or oval and is a shallow dish no more than 2 to 3 inches deep. They are usually referred to in measurements such as a 13x9-inch baking dish or pan.

Slow Cooker Ham & Pasta

MAKES 6 SERVINGS

The most time consuming part of this recipe is cooking the pasta. The rest is easy.

12   ounces linguine
¼   cup reduced calorie margarine
½   cup fat free half & half
⅓   cup sliced green onions, green part
1   cup diced ham
½   cup grated Parmesan cheese

1. Cook pasta according to package directions. Rinse and drain. Add pasta and margarine to sprayed slow cooker and toss to melt the margarine. Add remaining ingredients along with ½-cup water.

2. Cover. Cook on LOW until heated through but probably no longer than an hour, or it will tend to get a little dry. If this should happen, stir in additional half & half.

Per serving: 323 Cal, 10g Fat, 3g Sat F, 20mg Chol, 488mg Sod, 16g Pro, 2g Sug, 42g Carb, 3g Fib

Exchanges   Net Carbs

Fat 1-1/2   39
Meat 1/2
Starch 2-1/2
Very Lean Meat 1

Slow Cooker Broccoli Pasta

MAKES 6 SERVINGS

Serve recipe as a side dish.

8   ounces penne
4   cups frozen broccoli florets, do not thaw
3   tablespoons olive oil
1   small garlic clove, minced
¼   teaspoon crushed red pepper
½   cup grated Parmesan cheese

1. Add pasta and broccoli to boiling water and cook pasta according to package directions. Rinse and drain. Place in a sprayed slow cooker along with the oil, garlic, red pepper and the Parmesan cheese. Cover. Cook on LOW, at the most, 2 hours.

Per serving: 233 Cal, 10g Fat, 2g Sat F, 6mg Chol, 116mg Sod, 8g Pro, 1g Sug, 29g Carb, 3g Fib

Exchanges   Net Carbs

Fat 1-1/2   26
Meat 1/2
Starch 1-1/2
Vegetable 1/2

Slow Cooker

- Beverages
- Appetizers
- Chili & Soups
- Beef
- Pork
- Chicken
- Turkey
- Fish
- Vegetables

Slow Cooker Tips

One thing I have learned about slow cookers is that each one has its own personality. I have 4 slow cookers and each one cooks at a different temperature, even identical models made by the same company. Today's slow cookers cook much faster than the models of the 70's and 80's. If you have purchased a new slow cooker, check the temperature and if it cooks too hot, return it and try another one.

You can check your slow cooker by using the water method. Fill with 2 quarts of water. Cover and heat on LOW for 8 hours. Then use on accurate thermometer to check the temperature. The ranges of my slow cookers are 185° to 218° with the 185° slow cooker being the one I like best. If you are happy with your slow cooker, use the recipes here as a guideline. When you make a recipe for the first time, jot down the cooking time. This will be very helpful the next time you make the recipe.

Since slow cookers come in various sizes, you have to be the judge as to what size best fits your needs. Most of these recipes were done in a 4-quart or a 5-quart slow cooker. They weren't always full so some recipes could accommodate a smaller size. If you haven't yet purchased a slow cooker or are thinking of buying a new one, I would suggest a 5-quart oval-shaped slow cooker. That size will cover most of your cooking needs and the recipes in this book.

Remember

1 hour on HIGH = 2 hours on LOW

Don't peek! We are curious creatures, but valuable heat is lost each time we lift the lid, extending the cooking time by about 20 minutes.

Beefy-Cheese Dip

MAKES 4 CUPS

This is good, too!

1   pound extra lean ground beef
1   teaspoon chili powder
1   teaspoon Worcestershire sauce
½   cup chopped green onion
1   (16-oz) package reduced fat Ameri-
      can cheese, shredded
1   (10-oz) can diced tomatoes & green
      chilies

1. Brown ground beef; drain. In slow
cooker stir beef, chili powder and
Worcestershire sauce.

2. Stir in remaining ingredients. Cover.
Cook on LOW 2 to 2½ hours. Do not allow
to get too thick.

Per 1/4 cup: 124 Cal, 7g Fat, 4g Sat F,
34mg Chol 525mg Sod, 13g Pro,
 3g Sug, 4g Carb, <1g Fib

Exchanges	Net Carbs
Fat 1	4
Meat 1	
Very Lean Meat 1	

Ground Beef & Vegetable Soup

MAKES 12 CUPS

My favorite ground beef soup.

¾   pound extra lean ground beef
½   cup chopped onion
2   (14.5-oz) cans Italian stewed tomatoes
2   cups frozen low-carb vegetables
      Salt and pepper to taste

1. Brown ground beef and onion; drain.
Add to slow cooker along with remaining
ingredients and 2½ cups water. Cover. Cook
on LOW 3 to 4 hours to blend flavors.

Per cup: 82 Cal, 3g Fat, 1g Sat F,
20mg Chol, 174mg Sod, 8g Pro,
4g Sug, 6g Carb, 2g Fib

Exchanges	Net Carbs
Fat 1/2	4
Very Lean Meat 1	
Vegetable 1	

MENU
Ground Beef & Vegetable Soup
Corn Bread Sticks
Lemon Fruit Salad

Ground Beef & CabbageSoup

MAKES 10 CUPS

Don't forget to make your favorite soups in a slow cooker.

¾ **pound extra lean ground beef**
½ **cup chopped onion**
2 **(14.5-oz) cans diced stewed tomatoes**
½ **small cabbage, thinly sliced**
 Salt and pepper to taste

1. Brown ground beef and onion; drain. Add to slow cooker along with remaining ingredients and enough water to cover, or to a soup consistency. Cover. Cook on LOW 7 to 8 hours or until cabbage is tender. Add salt and pepper.

Per cup: 98 Cal, 3g Fat, 1g Sat F, 25mg Chol, 175mg Sod, 9g Pro, 6g Sug, 9g Carb, 2g Fib

Exchanges   Net Carbs

Fat 1/2   7
Very Lean Meat 1
Vegetable 1

Italian Sausage Soup

MAKES 7 CUPS

Chock full of meat and vegetables.

1 **pound lowfat sausage**
⅓ **cup chopped onion**
1 **small green pepper, diced**
1 **(14.5-oz) can diced tomatoes**
2 **(14-oz) cans beef broth**
1 **cup frozen green beans**

1. Brown sausage, onion and pepper; drain. Place in slow cooker along with tomatoes and broth. Last hour of cooking time, add green beans. Cover. Cook on LOW 7 to 8 hours.

Per cup: 97 Cal, 5g Fat, 2g Sat F, 38mg Chol, 667mg Sod, 9g Pro, 1g Sug, 3g Carb, 1g Fib

Exchanges   Net Carbs

Fat 1/2   2
Meat 1
Vegetable 1/2

Barbecue Ribs

MAKES 4 SERVINGS

Ribs are tender, moist and delicious.

1½ **racks of baby back ribs**
¾   **cup low-carb Barbecue Sauce, see**
    page 204

1. Cut ribs into 2-rib sections. Brush with barbecue sauce and place as many of the ribs as you can, meaty-side out, around the pot. Place remaining ribs in the center. Cover. Cook on LOW 8 to 9 hours Serve with sauce, if desired.

Per serving: 301 Cal, 23g Fat, 9g Sat F, 92mg Chol, 193mg Sod, 19g Pro, 1g Sug, 2g Carb, 0g Fib

Exchanges   Net Carbs
Fat 3   2
Meat 2-1/2

Barbecued Pot Roast

MAKES 8 SERVINGS

A nice slow-cooking roast.

1   **(3-lb) beef chuck roast**
1   **cup low-carb ketchup**
½   **cup chopped onion**
2   **teaspoons Worcestershire sauce**
2   **tablespoons brown Sugar Twin®**

1. Trim roast of excess fat and place in slow cooker.
2. Combine remaining ingredients with ½-cup water and pour over roast. Cover. Cook on LOW 10 to 12 hours.

Per 3 oz serving: 274 Cal, 17g Fat,7g Sat F, 86mg Chol, 54mg Sod, 26g Pro, <1g Sug, 1g Carb, 0g Fib

Exchanges   Net Carbs
Fat 1-1/2   1
Meat 3-1/2

Slow Cooker Swiss Steak

Nice for a casual dinner.

1   (3-lb) round steak
1   cup chopped onion
1   (14.5-oz) can diced tomatoes
½   green pepper, cubed
1   teaspoon salt
½   teaspoon Worcestershire sauce

1. Trim meat of excess fat and cut into 6 serving size pieces. Add meat along with remaining ingredients to slow cooker. Cover. Cook on LOW 8 to 10 hours.

Per 3 oz serving: 214 Cal, 8g Fat, 3g Sat F, 90mg Chol, 131mg Sod, 31g Pro, 1g Sug, 3g Carb, <1g Fib

Exchanges   Net Carbs

Meat 4-1/2   3
Vegetable 1/2

Dilly Pot Roast

MAKES 8 SERVINGS

Save money and make broth from bouillon.

1   (3-lb) beef chuck roast
1   teaspoon garlic salt
1   teaspoon paprika
½   teaspoon dill weed
¼   cup low sodium beef broth
1   small onion, sliced

1. Trim roast of excess fat and place in slow cooker. Sprinkle with seasonings. Add broth. Scatter onion around sides of roast. Cover. Cook on LOW 9 to 10 hours.

Per 3 oz serving: 341 Cal, 22g Fat, 9g Sat F, 108mg Chol, 68mg Sod, 30g Pro, <1g Sug, 1g Carb, <1g Fib

Exchanges   Net Carbs

Fat 1-1/2   1
Meat 4-1/2

Medium-Rare Roast Beef

Yes, you can cook a medium-rare roast in a slow cooker. Don't pour wine over meat or baste with drippings. Why? The top of the meat will turn an odd off-white color. This may not happen with all wines, but will with a merlot-type wine.

1   (3-lb) sirloin tip roast
½   cup coarsely chopped onion
1   garlic clove, chopped
½   cup dry red wine
    Salt and pepper

1. Rinse roast and pat dry. Add onion, garlic and wine to slow cooker.

2. Add roast and sprinkle with salt and pepper. Cover. Cook on LOW 7 to 8 hours or to 140°F. Remove and cover lightly with foil. Let stand 10 to 15 minutes before slicing.

Per 4 oz serving: 246 Cal, 11g Fat, 4g Sat F, 83mg Chol, 70mg Sod, 33g Pro, <1g Sug, 1g Carb, <1g Fib

Exchanges   Net Carbs

Meat 4-1/2   1

Slow Cooker Tri-Tip Roast

A popular roast whether cooked in the slow cooker or in the oven.

1   (2½-lb) Tri-Tip roast
    Salt and pepper
1   medium onion, sliced
¼   cup beef broth

1. Trim roast of excess fat and place in slow cooker. Sprinkle with salt and pepper. Add onion and broth. Cover. Cook on LOW 8 to 9 hours or until very tender.

Per 4 oz serving: 212 Cal, 9g Fat, 4g Sat F, 59mg Chol, 65mg Sod, 30g Pro, <1g Sug, 1g Carb, <1g Fib

Exchanges   Net Carbs

Meat 4-1/2   1

MENU

Busy Day Roast
Steamed Green Beans
Club Salad

Beef Round Tip Roast

MAKES ABOUT 10 SERVINGS

This recipe can be in the slow cooker in less than 10 minutes.

1   (3½-lb) beef round tip roast
1   (0.7-oz) package Italian dressing mix
1   (1.1-oz) package Au Jus mix
1   (14-oz) can low sodium beef broth

1. Place roast in slow cooker.
2. Combine remaining ingredients and add to slow cooker. Cover. Cook on LOW 9 to 10 hours or until meat is tender.
note: If desired, the broth can be thickened with a little cornstarch.

Per 4 oz erving: 199 Cal, 7g Fat,
3g Sat F, 100mg Chol, 103mg Sod,
31g Pro, <1g Sug, 0g Carb, 0g Fib

Exchanges   Net Carbs
Meat 4-1/2   0

Busy Day Roast

MAKES 8 SERVINGS

If desired, strain the broth and use it for French Dip sandwiches.

1   (3½-lb) beef bottom round roast
1   cup chopped onion
½   cup dry white wine
1   (1.1 oz) package Au Jus mix
2   cups low sodium beef broth

1. Trim fat from roast. Place in slow cooker and add onion.
2. Combine wine, Au Jus mix and broth. Pour over meat. Cover. Cook on LOW 9 to 10 hours or until meat is tender.

Per serving: 216 Cal, 8g Fat,
3g Sat F, 101mg Chol, 91mg Sod,
31g Pro, 1g Sug, 2g Carb, <1g Fib

Exchanges   Net Carbs
Meat 4-1/2   2
Vegetable 1/2

Meatloaf Dijon

Meat must be cooked to 160°.

1½   **pounds extra lean ground beef**
⅓   **cup low-fat soft white bread crumbs**
½   **cup finely chopped onion**
⅓   **cup low-carb ketchup**
1   **tablespoon Mild & Creamy Dijon mustard**
¼   **cup egg substitute**

1. Gently combine all ingredients until well mixed. Place in slow cooker and form into a loaf about the size of bottom of pot. Cook on LOW 5 to 6 hours or until meat reaches 160°.

Per serving: 237 Cal, 12g Fat, 5g Sat F, 82mg Chol, 172mg Sod, 27g Pro, 1g Sug, 4g Carb, 1g Fib

Exchanges   Net Carbs

Fat 2   3
Very Lean Meat 3-1/2

Soft Taco Casserole

Instead of baking in the oven you can bake in the slow cooker. Cooking time is short.

1   **pound extra lean ground beef**
1   **small green pepper, cubed**
½   **cup thick and chunky salsa**
8   **(7-inch) low-carb white tortillas**
½   **cup nonfat sour cream**
1½   **cups (6-oz) reduced fat Cheddar cheese, shredded**

1. Brown ground beef and green pepper in a medium skillet; drain. Add salsa.

2. Spread each tortilla with 1 tablespoon sour cream. Spoon 2 tablespoons meat mixture on each tortilla and roll to secure filling. Place, seam-side down, in slow cooker.

3. Spoon remaining meat mixture over tortillas. Sprinkle with cheese making sure tortillas are completely covered. Cover. Cook on LOW 1½ to 2 hours or until heated through.

Per serving: 205 Cal, 9g Fat, 3g Sat F, 47mg Chol, 402mg Sod, 23g Pro, <1g Sug, 14g Carb, 8g Fib

Exchanges   Net Carbs

Fat 1   6
Very Lean Meat 2-1/2

Beef Stroganoff

MAKES 4 SERVINGS

We can now have stroganoff served over delicious low-carb pasta.

1 (1-lb) top sirloin steak
1 cup chopped onion
1 (14-oz) can low sodium beef broth
1 cup sliced mushrooms
¼ teaspoon pepper
1 cup nonfat sour cream

1. Cut meat crosswise into slightly less than ¼-inch slices. If slices are too long, cut in half. Place in slow cooker along with onion, broth, mushrooms and pepper. Cover. Cook on HIGH 3½ to 4 hours or until meat is tender. Watch carefully last half hour of cooking time.
2. Add sour cream and cook until heated through.

Per serving: 248 Cal, 9g Fat, 4g Sat F, 70mg Chol, 153mg Sod, 28g Pro, 2g Sug, 13g Carb, 1g Fib

Exchanges   Net Carbs
Fat 1   12
Very Lean Meat 3-1/2

Sweet-Sour Meatballs

MAKES 60 MEATBALLS

In order for the sauce to thicken, this recipe must be cooked on HIGH.

2 pounds extra lean ground beef
2 cups low-carb ketchup
1 cup brown Sugar Twin®
1 tablespoon prepared mustard
2 teaspoons Worcestershire sauce
2 teaspoons soy sauce

1. Preheat oven to 425°F. Shape meat into 1-inch balls and place in a shallow baking pan. Bake 15 minutes or until lightly browned. Drain on paper towels and place in slow cooker.
2. Combine remaining ingredients and pour over meatballs. Cover. Cook on HIGH 1½ to 2 hours or until sauce has thickened.

Per 4 meatballs: 130 Cal, 6 g Fat, 2g Sat F, 44mg Chol, 203mg Sod, 14g Pro, 1g Sug, 4g Carb, 0g Fib

Exchanges   Net Carbs
Fat 1   4
Very Lean Meat 2

Ham & Cheese Casserole

MAKES 8 SERVINGS

Serve for brunch or dinner.

- 2   cups cubed ham
- ¼   cup sliced green onions
- 1   cup (4-oz) reduced fat Monterey Jack cheese, shredded
- 12   large eggs, lightly beaten
- 1   cup nonfat milk

1. Place ham, onion and cheese in slow cooker. Combine eggs, milk and 1 cup water. Pour over cheese. Cover. Cook on HIGH 2½ to 3 hours or until center is set.

Per serving: 217 Cal, 12g Fat, 5g Sat F, 346mg Chol, 822mg Sod, 23g Pro, 2g Sug, 3g Carb, <1g Fib

Exchanges   Net Carbs

Fat 1-1/2   3
Meat 2
Very Lean Meat 1

Pork & Sauerkraut

MAKES 6 SERVINGS

For a milder sauerkraut flavor, rinse well and drain.

- 1   (3-lb) boneless pork loin
       Salt and pepper
- 1   (32-oz) jar sauerkraut, well drained
- 1½   teaspoons caraway seeds
- 1½   cups (6-oz) reduced fat Swiss cheese, shredded

1. Remove fat and silver skin from pork. Sprinkle with salt and pepper. Place in slow cooker and add ½ cup water. Cover. Cook on LOW 4 hours. Remove meat and discard liquid.

2. Combine remaining ingredients. Add all but 1 cup to slow cooker. Add pork and spoon remaining mixture over top of meat. Cover. Cook on LOW 1 to 2 hours or until meat reaches 140°. It should be tender at this point, and not overcooked.

Per 4 oz serving: 260 Cal, 7g Fat, 3g Sat F, 100mg Chol, 887mg Sod, 41g Pro, 2g Sug, 6g Carb, 3g Fib

Exchanges   Net Carbs

Fat 1   3
Very Lean Meat 5-1/2

Slow Cooked Ham

MAKES ABOUT 8-10 SERVINGS

If you can't get the lid on, cover slowcooker with heavy-duty foil, pressing around edges to seal.

1   (5 to 6-lb) ham
½   cup brown Sugar Twin®
½   teaspoon dry mustard
2   tablespoons orange juice

1. Place ham, cut-side down, in slow cooker. Cover. Cook on LOW 4 to 5 hours or until temperature reaches 130°F.
2. Combine remaining ingredients and brush over ham. Cover. Cook on HIGH 20 to 30 minutes or until meat reaches 140°.

Per 4 oz serving: 178Cal, 6g Fat, 2g Sat F, 62mg Chol, 1500mg Sod, 28g Pro, <1g Sug, 1g Carb, 0g Fib

Exchanges   Net Carbs

Fat 1   1
Very Lean Meat 4

Barbecued Pork Chops

MAKES 4 SERVINGS

Easy!

4   (½-inch thick) center loin pork chops
½   cup Barbecue Sauce, page 209

1. Place pork chops in slow cooker. Pour sauce over top. Cover. Cook on LOW 6 to 7 hours.

Per serving: 172 Cal, 7g Fat, 2g Sat F, 65mg Chol, 162mg Sod, 24g Pro, 1g Sug, 2g Carb, 0g Fib

Exchanges   Net Carbs

Fat 1   2
Very Lean Meat 3-1/2

MENU

Slow Cooked Ham
Lemon Broccoli
Crisp Green Salad
Baked Apples

Paprika Drumsticks

MAKES 8 SERVINGS

Drumsticks are great between meal snacks.

8 chicken legs, skinned
1 medium onion, sliced
2 teaspoons oil
1 teaspoon salt
½ teaspoon pepper
2 teaspoons paprika

1. Add onion to slow cooker. Top with chicken legs, in one layer as much as possible.

2. Combine remaining ingredients with 1 teaspoon water and brush on chicken. Cover. Cook on LOW 7 to 8 hours.

Per leg: 126 Cal, 6g Fat, 1g Sat F, 53mg Chol, 343mg Sod, 16g Pro, 1g Sug, 2g Carb, <1g Fib

Exchanges   Net Carbs

Fat 1   2
Very Lean Meat 2

Busy Day Chicken Legs

MAKES 8 SERVINGS

If desired, substitute 8 chicken thighs.

8 chicken legs, skinned
   Paprika
   Garlic salt
   Lemon pepper

1. Place chicken in slow cooker in one layer as much as possible. Sprinkle with seasonings (do not add liquid). Cover. Cook on LOW 7 to 8 hours. The chicken should be nicely browned.

Per serving: 108 Cal, 5g Fat, 1g Sat F, 53mg Chol, 92mg Sod, 15g Pro, 0g Sug, 0g Carb, 0g Fib

Exchanges   Net Carbs

Fat 1/2   0
Very Lean Meat 2

Purchase Tip

Chicken at the supermarket has usually been frozen at least once and sometimes twice. If we freeze it again, we may be looking at one tough chicken. The trick is to find packages with the least amount of liquid in the tray. The more they have been frozen and thawed the more liquid.

Roast Chicken Pesto

I think pesto goes with almost anything.

1   (4-lb) chicken
½   cup pesto
    Salt and Pepper

1. Carefully loosen skin covering breast and leg area.
2. Spread pesto under skin. If desired, tie legs with kitchen string. Place chicken in slow cooker and sprinkle with salt and pepper. Cover. Cook on LOW 7 to 8 hours or until thigh temperature reaches 170°. Remove skin before serving.

Per 3 oz serving (average of white & dark meat): 203 Cal, 12g Fat, 3g Sat F, 75mg Chol, 70mg Sod, 23g Pro, 0g Sug, 0g Carb, 0g Fib

Exchanges   Net Carbs
Fat 1/2   0
Meat 3-1/2

Slow Cooker Chicken

MAKES 6 SERVINGS

If desired, substitute chicken parts for the whole chicken.

1   (4-lb) chicken
⅔   cup coarsely chopped onion
½   cup coarsely chopped celery
½   cup sliced carrots
    Salt and pepper

1. Place chicken in slow cooker. Add 1 cup water. Place vegetables around chicken. Sprinkle with salt and pepper.
2. Cover. Cook on LOW 7 to 8 hours or until thigh temperature reaches 170°. Remove skin before serving.

Per 3 oz serving (average of white & dark meat): 214 Cal, 12g Fat, 2g Sat F, 94mg Chol, 96mg Sod, 31g Pro, 1g Sug, 3g Carb, 1g Fib

Exchanges   Net Carbs
Fat 1   2
Very Lean Meat 4-1/2
Vegetable 1/2

Roast Chicken

1   (5-lb) chicken
1   teaspoon oil
1   teaspoon Italian herbs
¼   teaspoon pepper

1. Brush chicken with oil. Sprinkle with herbs and pepper. Place in slow cooker and add ¼ cup water. Cover. Cook on LOW 8 to 10 hours or until thigh temperature reaches 170°. Remove skin before serving.

Per 4 oz serving (average white & dark meat): 201 Cal, 8g Fat, 2g Sat F, 94mg Chol, 79mg Sod, 31g Pro, 0g Sug, 0g Carb, 0g Fib

Exchanges   Net Carbs

Fat 1   0
Very Lean Meat 4-1/2

Tarragon Chicken

MAKES 4 SERVINGS

Basil or oregano could also be used.

4   chicken breast halves, skinned, boned
⅓   cup chopped onion
4   Plum tomatoes, chopped
1   large garlic clove, minced
½   teaspoon dried tarragon
½   teaspoon salt

1. Place chicken in slow cooker. Add remaining ingredients. Cover. Cook on LOW 3 to 4 hours.

Per serving: 159 Cal, 3g Fat, 1g Sat F, 72mg Chol, 357mg Sod, 27g Pro, 2g Sug, 4g Carb, 1g Fib

Exchanges   Net Carbs

Very Lean Meat 3-1/2   3
Vegetable 1/2

Barbecue Chicken Legs

MAKES 8 SERVINGS

Flavorful and must be eaten with a fork.

8   chicken legs, skinned
½   cup brown Sugar Twin®
½   cup low-carb ketchup
1   tablespoon Worcestershire sauce
1½   teaspoons prepared mustard
2   tablespoons lemon juice

1. Place chicken in one layer, if possible, in slow cooker. Combine remaining ingredients. Remove ⅓ cup of the mixture and brush over chicken. Save remaining sauce to serve with chicken. Cover. Cook on LOW 7 to 8 hours.

Per leg: 115 Cal, 5g Fat, 1g Sat F, 53mg Chol, 96mg Sod,, 15g Pro, 1g Sug, 1g Carb, 0g Fib

Exchanges   Net Carbs
Fat 1/2   1
Very Lean Meat 2

Italian Chicken Legs

MAKES 8 SERVINGS

The brown sugar reduces the acid in the tomato sauce.

8   chicken legs, skinned
1   teaspoon Italian seasoning
1   tablespoon brown Sugar Twin®
1   (8-oz) can tomato sauce
½   cup coarsely chopped onion

1. Place chicken in slow cooker. Add remaining ingredients. Cover. Cook on LOW 7 to 8 hours.

Per leg: 123 Cal, 5g Fat, 1g Sat F, 53mg Chol, 209mg Sod, 16g Pro, 2g Sug, 3g Carb, 1g Fib

Exchanges   Net Carbs
Fat 1/2   2
Very Lean Meat 2
Vegetable 1/2

MENU

Italian Chicken Legs
Brussels Sprouts Saute
Supper Cheese Bread
Baked Cinnamon Pears

Ginger Chicken

MAKES 4 SERVINGS

So easy!

4   chicken breast, skinned, boned
½   cup low sodium soy sauce
15 packets Splenda
¼   teaspoon ground ginger
½   teaspoon hot pepper sauce

1. Place chicken in slow cooker. Combine remaining ingredients and pour over top. Cover. Cook on LOW 3½ to 4 hours. If possible, baste 2 or 3 times while cooking. This will make for more even browning.

Per serving: 170 Cal, 3g Fat, 1g Sat F, 72mg Chol, 782mg Sod, 29g Pro, <1g Sug, 5g Carb, 0g Fib

Exchanges   Net Carbs

Other Carbs 1/2   5
Very Lean Meat 3-1/2

Sherried Chicken

MAKES 10 SERVINGS

The sherry adds a lot of flavor.

4   chicken breasts, skinned, boned
½   medium onion, sliced
4   ounces fresh mushrooms, sliced
⅓   cup dry sherry
1   teaspoon Italian seasoning

1. Place onion and mushrooms in slow cooker. Top with chicken; add sherry and sprinkle with seasoning. Cover. Cook on LOW 3 to 4 hours.

Per serving: 170 Cal, 3g Fat, 1g Sat F, 72mg Chol, 82mg Sod, 27g Pro, 1g Sug, 3g Carb, <1g Fib

Exchanges   Net Carbs

Very Lean Meat 3-1/2   3
Vegetable 1/2

Teriyaki Chicken Thighs

MAKES 8 SERVINGS

A nice change from chicken legs.

8 large chicken thighs, skinned
½ cup low sodium soy sauce
¼ cup brown Sugar Twin®
1 tablespoon grated fresh ginger
2 medium garlic cloves, minced

1. Place chicken in slow cooker. Combine remaining ingredients and pour over chicken. Cover. Cook on LOW 7 to 8 hours. Remove skin before serving. Strain broth and spoon over top of chicken.

Per serving: 116 Cal, 6g Fat, 2g Sat F, 49mg Chol, 314mg Sod, 14g Pro, 0g Sug, 1g Carb, 0g Fib

Exchanges   Net Carbs
Very Lean Meat 2   1

Curried Chicken Legs

MAKES 8 SERVINGS

The marmalade spread can be found in most supermarkets.

8 chicken legs, skinned
¾ cup chopped onion
½ teaspoon curry powder
1 tablespoon reduced calorie margarine, melted
¼ cup sugar free apricot preserves

1. Place chicken in one layer, if possible, in slow cooker. Sprinkle onion over top.
2. Combine remaining ingredients and spoon over chicken. Cover. Cook on LOW 7 to 8 hours.

Per serving: 123 Cal, 6g Fat, 2g Sat F, 53mg Chol, 61mg Sod, 15g Pro, 0g Sug, 3g Carb, 0g Fib

Exchanges   Net Carbs
Fat 1   3
Very Lean Meat 2

Sweet-Hot Chicken Thighs

MAKES 8 SERVINGS

Hopefully, more supermarkets will soon be carrying low-carb ketchup.

8   **large chicken thighs, skinned**
½   **cup sugar free apricot preserves**
¼   **cup low-carb ketchup**
2   **tablespoons low sodium soy sauce**
½   **teaspoon hot sauce**

1. Place chicken in one layer, in slow cooker.
2. Combine remaining ingredients and spoon over chicken. Cover. Cook on LOW 7 to 8 hours.

Per serving: 116 Cal, 6g Fat, 2g Sat F, 49mg Chol, 131mg Sod, 14g Pro, 0g Sug, 3g Carb, 0g Fib

Exchanges   Net Carbs
Very Lean Meat 2   3

Saucy Chicken Thighs

MAKES 4 SERVINGS

A flavorful slow cooker recipe.

4   **large chicken thighs, skinned**
1   **large garlic clove, minced**
⅓   **cup low sodium soy sauce**
1½   **tablespoons low-carb ketchup**

1. Place chicken in slow cooker. Combine remaining ingredients and pour over top. Cover. Cook on LOW 7 to 8 hours. If possible, baste chicken twice during cooking time.

Per serving: 164 Cal, 8g Fat, 2g Sat F, 66mg Chol, 788mg Sod, 21g Pro, 0g Sug, 2g Carb, 0g Fib

Exchanges   Net Carbs
Very Lean Meat 2-1/2   2

MENU
Apricot Turkey Breast
Asparagus & Red Peppers
Sweet-Sour Spinach Salad
Blueberry Drop Biscuits

Apricot Turkey Breast

MAKES 8 SERVINGS

*The apricot spread adds few calories,
but a lot of flavor.*

1   **(2½-lb) turkey breast half**
½   **cup sugar-free apricot preserves**
1   **tablespoon prepared mustard**
2   **teaspoons Worcestershire sauce**
¼   **teaspoon ground pepper**

1. Place turkey breast, skin-side up, in slow cooker.
2. Combine remaining ingredients and spread over turkey. Cover. Cook on LOW 8 to 9 hours or until temperature reaches 160°. Remove skin before serving.

Per 4 oz serving: 160 Cal, 1g Fat, 0g Sat F, 94mg Chol, 68mg Sod, 34g Pro, 0g Sug, 3g Carb, 0g Fib

Exchanges   Net Carbs
Very Lean Meat 4-1/2   3

Slow Cooker Turkey Thighs

MAKES 6 SERVINGS

If you can't find the turkey thighs, use turkey legs. Use the meat for sandwiches and soups or serve with vegetables and a salad for an easy dinner meal.

3   **pounds turkey thighs, skinned**
    Salt and Pepper

1. Place turkey in slow cooker. Sprinkle with salt and pepper. Cover. Cook on LOW heat 7 to 8 hours.

Per 3 oz serving: 160 Cal, 6g Fat, 2g Sat F, 72mg Chol, 222mg Sod, 24g Pro, 0g Sug, 0g Carb, 0g Fib

Exchanges   Net Carbs
Fat 1   0
Very Lean Meat 3-1/2

Turkey Meatloaf

You can't fool everyone, but some don't
even realize this is ground turkey.

2   **pounds ground turkey**
⅓   **cup finely chopped celery**
½   **cup finely chopped onion**
6   **tablespoons chopped Plum tomatoes**
¼   **cup egg substitute**
½   **teaspoon dried Italian herbs**

1. Combine ingredients until blended. Add to slow cooker and form into an 8-inch loaf. Cover. Cook on LOW 5½ to 6 hours or until firm.

Per serving: 204 Cal, 11g Fat, 3g Sat F, 82mg Chol, 109mg Sod, 23g Pro, 1g Sug, 2g Carb, <1g Fib

Exchanges
Fat 1/2
Meat 3
Vegetable 1/2

Net Carbs
2

Halibut with Roasted Peppers

1   **(1-lb) halibut fillet**
½   **cup canned roasted red peppers, drained**
1   **tablespoon oil**
3   **to 4 dashes hot pepper sauce**
2   **tablespoons chopped fresh basil**
⅓   **cup grated Parmesan cheese**

1. Place halibut in slow cooker.
2. Place roasted peppers, oil and pepper sauce in a blender and blend until almost smooth (it's nice to have a few small bits of pepper.) Spoon over halibut.
3. Combine basil and Parmesan; sprinkle on top. You may or may not use all the mixture. Cover. Cook on LOW 1-1/2 to 2 hours.

Per serving: 224 Cal, 8g Fat, 2g Sat F, 44mg Chol, 457mg Sod, 28g Pro, 0g Sug, 5g Carb, 0g Fib

Exchanges
Fat 1-1/2
Meat 1/2
Very Lean Meat 3
Vegetable 1-1/2

Net Carbs
5

Company Salmon Pesto

MAKES 4 SERVINGS

Here's that pesto again, but it teams well with salmon.

4 (4-oz) salmon fillets
4 teaspoons pesto

1. Place fillets in slow cooker and brush with pesto. Cover. Cook on LOW 1-1/2 to 2 hours.

Per serving: 183 Cal, 7g Fat, 2g Sat F, 64mg Chol, 105mg Sod, 28g Pro, 0g Sug, <1g Carb, <1g Fib

Exchanges   Net Carbs
Fat 1   <1
Very Lean Meat 4

❧ Hint ❧

Fish cooks rather quickly in a slow cooker. The advantage of this method of cooking is that it eliminates last minute watching, freeing you to do other things. Fish that is a thicker cut, and somewhat firm, works best in a slow cooker.

Salmon in a Pot

MAKES 6 SERVINGS

Cook in a slow cooker while you are preparing the rest of the meal.

1 (1½ to 2-lb) salmon fillet
¼ cup dry white wine
2 tablespoons reduced calorie margarine, melted
2 tablespoons fresh lemon juice
1 teaspoon low sodium soy sauce

1. Check for bones before placing salmon in a slow cooker. Combine remaining ingredients and pour over fish. Cover. Cook on LOW 1½ to 2 hours. After first hour of cooking time, watch carefully so as not to overcook.
note: If you don't want to use wine, omit and add 1 minced garlic clove and 2 tablespoons finely chopped fresh basil.

Per serving: 172 Cal, 7g Fat, 2g Sat F, 53mg Chol, 114mg Sod, 23g Pro, <1g Sug, <1g Carb, <1g Fib

Exchanges   Net Carbs
Fat 1   <1
Very Lean Meat 3

Florentine Salmon

Fancy enough for company.

4   (4-oz) salmon fillets
1   tablespoon reduced calorie
    margarine
¾   cup sliced mushrooms
⅓   cup sliced green onions
½   bunch fresh spinach
⅓   cup dry white wine

1. Cut a long slit in top of each fillet and spread slightly.

2. Heat margarine in a large skillet and quickly cook mushrooms and onion. Add spinach and cook until spinach is just slightly wilted.

3. Fill fillets with spinach mixture. Place in slow cooker and add wine. Cover. Cook on LOW 1½ to 2 hours.

Per serving: 183 Cal, 7g Fat, 1g Sat F, 53mg Chol, 112mg Sod, 24g Pro, 1g Sug, 3g Carb, 1g Fib

Exchanges   Net Carbs

Fat 1   2
Very Lean Meat 3
Vegetable 1/2

Fillet of Sole

Lots of flavor from the mushrooms and cheese.

4   sole fillets, about 1 pound
1   medium onion, sliced
2   tablespoons reduced calorie
    margarine
8   ounces mushrooms, sliced
1   cup (4-oz) reduced fat Swiss cheese,
    shredded

1. Cook onion in margarine until just soft. Add mushrooms and cook until soft. Place half the mixture in slow cooker. Sprinkle with half the cheese.

2. Fold fillets in half or thirds and place over cheese. Top with remaining vegetables and cheese. Cover. Cook on LOW 2 to 2½ hours.

Per serving: 211 Cal, 8g Fat, 2g Sat F, 63mg Chol, 201mg Sod, 29g Pro, 3g Sug, 6g Carb, 1g Fib

Exchanges   Net Carbs

Fat 1   5
Very Lean Meat 4
Vegetable 1

Orange Roughy

This is a mild white fish similar to cod.

4   (4-oz) Orange Roughy fillets
3   tablespoons fresh lemon juice
1   medium garlic clove, minced
½   teaspoon dried dill weed
    Salt and pepper to taste

1. Place fish in one layer in slow cooker. Combine lemon juice, garlic and dill weed; brush over fish. Lightly sprinkle with salt and pepper. Cover. Cook on LOW 1 hour.
note: If using fresh dill weed, sprinkle over fish during last half hour of cooking time.

Per serving: 87 Cal, 1g Fat, 0g Sat F, 24mg Chol, 76mg Sod, 17g Pro, <1g Sug, 1g Carb, 0g Fib

Exchanges   Net Carbs
Very Lean Meat 2-1/2   1

Fajita Vegetables

MAKES 6 SERVINGS

Add beef or chicken and serve in tortillas. Also good served over grilled steaks and hamburgers or as a vegetable tortilla wrap.

2   medium peppers, 1 red & 1 green, julienned
2   medium onions, thinly sliced
2   tablespoons oil
½   teaspoon paprika
    Salt and pepper to taste

1. Combine ingredients in slow cooker. Cover. Cook on HIGH 3½ to 4 hours or until vegetables are crisp tender.

Per serving: 65 Cal, 5g Fat, 1g Sat F< 0mg Chol, 2mg Sod, 1g Pro, 2g Sug, 6g Carb, 1g Fib

Exchanges   Net Carbs
Fat 1   5
Vegetable 1

Green Bean Dish

This dish can also be baked in the oven.

3 (14.5-oz) cans green beans, drained
¼ cup finely chopped onion
3 tablespoons reduced calorie
    margarine, melted
4 teaspoons prepared mustard
2 teaspoons prepared horseradish
3 tablespoons brown Sugar Twin®

1. Place green beans in slow cooker.
2. Heat remaining ingredients in small saucepan cooking just until onion is soft. Pour over beans. Cover. Cook on LOW 2½ to 3 hours.
note: My family doesn't like tomatoes added to this dish, but I like to top the beans with 3 to 4 tomato slices and then the sauce.

Per serving: 64 Cal, 4g Fat, 1g Sat F, 0mg Chol, 381mg Sod, 2g Pro, 2g Sug, 7g Carb, 3g Fib

Exchanges   Net Carbs
Fat 1   4
Vegetable 1

Zucchini Casserole

Watch carefully to avoid overcooking.

4 medium zucchini
    Salt and pepper
1   medium onion, sliced
1 medium green pepper, sliced
6 Plum tomatoes, sliced
1 cup (4-oz) reduced fat Monterey Jack
    cheese

1. Cut zucchini into ½ inch slices. Place in slow cooker. Sprinkle with salt and pepper.
2. Layer onion, green pepper and then tomatoes, sprinkling each layer lightly with salt and pepper. Cover. Cook on LOW 5 to 6 hours or until almost tender.
3. Sprinkle with cheese. Cover and cook until vegetables are tender and cheese is melted, about 30 minutes.

Per serving: 44 Cal, 1g Fat, 1g Sat F, 5mg Chol, 40mg Sod, 5g Pro, 2g Sug, 5g Carb, 1g Fib

Exchanges   Net Carbs
Very Lean Meat 1/2   4
Vegetable 1

Salads, Dressings & Sauces

- Green Salads
- Spinach Salads
- Chicken Salads
- Jell-O Salads
- Dressings
- Sauces
- Gravies
- Marinades

Artichoke-Olive Salad

Artichokes are a nice addition to most salads.

8   cups mixed greens
1   (6.5-oz) jar marinated artichokes, drained
¾   cup sliced fresh mushrooms
½   cup sliced ripe olives
⅓   cup nonfat vinaigrette dressing

1. Combine first 4 ingredients in large bowl. (cut artichokes if too large). Toss with just enough dressing to lightly coat.

Per serving: 90 Cal, 4g Fat, <1g Sat F, 0mg Chol, 465mg Sod, 4g Pro, 3g Sug, 13g Carb, 4g Fib

Exchanges

Fat 1/2
Othe Carbs 1/2
Vegetable 1-1/2

Net Carbs

9

Asparagus-Tomato Salad

Simple but good.

4   cups romaine, torn
2   small Plum tomatoes, sliced crosswise
1   pound asparagus, cooked, chilled
½   cup nonfat vinaigrette dressing

1. Place romaine on 4 salad plates. Place asparagus spears on top. Garnish with tomatoes. Drizzle with dressing.

Per serving: 64 Cal, <1g Fat, 0g Sat F, 0mg Chol, 270mg Sod, 3g Pro, 5g Sug, 14g Carb, 4g Fib

Exchanges

Other Carbs 1/2
Vegetable 1-1/2

Net Carbs

10

Ice Cold Salad Greens

Line a large bowl with several layers of paper towels. Place clean dry greens in bowl. Cover greens with 3 to 4 layers of paper towels. Cover paper towels with one layer of ice cubes. Chill at least 8 hours or overnight. Before serving, if paper towels get too wet, replace with new ones and add additional ice cubes.

Asparagus Salad

MAKES 4 SERVINGS

Three vegetables all in one salad.

8   medium romaine leaves
8   thin tomato slices
8   ounces asparagus, cooked, chilled
2   hard-boiled eggs, quartered
4   tablespoons nonfat vinaigrette

1. Arrange romaine and tomato slices on salad plates. Top with asparagus and eggs and drizzle each with 1 tablespoon vinaigrette.

Per serving: 68 Cal, 3 Fat, 1g Sat F, 106mg Chol, 207mg Sod, 4g Pro, 3g Sug, 7g Carb, 1g Fib

Exchanges   Net Carbs

Meat 1   6
Vegetable 1/2

Mixed Green Salad

MAKES 4 SERVINGS

Jicama adds a nice crunch to almost any salad.

8   cups mixed greens
2   tablespoons sliced almonds
½   cup julienned jicama
⅓   cup nonfat vinaigrette dressing

1. Preheat oven to 350°F. Combine greens and almonds in a large mixing bowl. Toss with just enough dressing to lightly coat.

Per serving: 61 Cal, 2g Fat, <1g Sat F, 0mg Chol, 194mg Sod, 3 Pro, 3g Sug, 10g Carb, 4g Fib

Exchanges   Net Carbs

Other Carbs 1/2   6
Vegetable 1

Tomato-Tarragon Salad

MAKES 4 SERVINGS

Use a light hand with tarragon.

2 medium tomatoes, sliced
1 tablespoon oil
¼ cup tarragon wine vinegar
2 teaspoons chopped fresh tarragon
Freshly ground black pepper

1. Place tomatoes in an 11x7-inch baking dish. Combine oil, vinegar and tarragon and pour over tomatoes. Sprinkle with pepper. Cover. Refrigerate at least 2 hours to blend flavors.

Per serving: 48 Cal, 4g Fat, <1g Sat F, 0mg Chol, 3mg Sod, 1g Pro, 2g Sug, 4g Carb, 1g Fib

Exchanges   Net Carbs
Fat 1/2   3
Vegetable 1/2

Romaine Salad

MAKES 6 SERVINGS

There are times when what you really want is a rather simple, but tasty salad. This one will go with almost any meal.

2 bunches romaine
5 tablespoons oil
2 tablespoons apple cider vinegar
1 garlic clove, thinly sliced
½ teaspoon salt
⅛ teaspoon pepper

1. Tear romaine into bite-size pieces; you should have about 8 cups. Cover and chill.
2. Combine remaining ingredients; let stand at room temperature 1 to 2 hours to blend flavors.
3. Remove garlic and toss romaine with just enough dressing to lightly coat.

Per serving: 113 Cal, 11g Fat, 2g Sat F, 0mg Chol, 200mg Sod, 1g Pro, 1g Sug, 3g Carb, 2g Fib

Exchanges   Net Carbs
Fat 1   1
Vegetable 1/2

Romaine-Artichoke Salad

A perfect salad with almost any meal.

8   cups romaine
1   (6.5-oz) jar marinated artichoke hearts, drained
6   tablespoons oil
2   tablespoons garlic red wine vinegar
2   tablespoons grated Parmesan cheese, divided
8   cherry tomatoes, halved

1. Place romaine in a large salad bowl. Cut artichokes into smaller pieces and add to bowl.
2. Combine oil, vinegar and 2 tablespoons of the Parmesan. Toss salad with just enough dressing to lightly coat. Serve on salad plates. Sprinkle with remaining Parmesan and garnish with tomatoes.

Per serving: 122 Cal, 12g Fat, 2g Sat F, 1mg Chol, 87mg Sod, 2g Pro, 1g Sug, 4g Carb, 2g Fib

Exchanges   Net Carbs
Fat 2   2
Vegetable 1

Mini Chef Salad

MAKES 1 SALAD

This is a nice recipe to take to work.

3   cups assorted greens
¼   cup sliced mushrooms
1   slice deli ham, julienned
¼   cup (1-oz) reduced fat Cheddar cheese, shredded
¼   cup nonfat Thousand Island dressing

1. Place greens on a dinner plate. Top with ingredients in order given.

Per salad: 245 Cal, 12g Fat, 2g Sat F, 39mg Chol, 1280mg Sod, 15g Pro, 12g Sug, 21g Carb, 4g Fib

Exchanges   Net Carbs
Fat 2   17
Other Carb 1
Very Lean Meat 1-1/2
Vegetable 1

Spring Shrimp Salad

A nice and filling low-carb salad.

6   cups spring greens
4   ounces cooked small shrimp
½   small red onion, thinly sliced
½   cup sugar snap peas
⅓   cup nonfat vinaigrette dressing

1. Combine first 4 ingredients in a salad bowl. Toss with just enough dressing to lightly coat.

Per serving: 70 Cal, <1g Fat, 0g Sat F, 60mg Chol, 539mg Sod, 7g Pro, 4g Sug, 9g Carb, 2g Fib

Exchanges   Net Carbs

Other Carb 1/2   7
Very Lean Meat 1/2
    Vegetable 1/2

Italian Tuna Salad

MAKES 4 SERVINGS

Can substitute other vegetables, if desired.

8   cups mixed greens
½   small cucumber, thinly sliced
1   cup small cauliflower florets
1   (6-oz) can tuna in water, drained
½   cup nonfat vinaigrette dressing

1. Place first 4 ingredients in a large salad bowl and toss with just enough dressing to lightly coat.

Per serving: 102 Cal, 1g Fat, <1g Sat F, 15mg Chol, 416mg Sod, 11g Pro, 4g Sug, 12g Carb, 3g Fib

Exchanges   Net Carbs

Other Carb 1/2   9
Very Lean Meat 1-1/2
    Vegetable 1

Tuna-Pineapple Salad

This makes a nice salad or sandwich.

2 (6-oz) cans tuna, drained
1 (8-oz) can crushed pineapple, drained
½ cup finely chopped celery
2 large hard-boiled eggs, chopped
⅓ cup light mayonnaise

1. Combine first 4 ingredients and toss with just enough mayonnaise to lightly coat. Cover and chill before serving.

Per serving: 184 Cal, 7g Fat, 2g Sat F, 136mg Chol, 483mg Sod, 20g Pro, 7g Sug, 8g Carb, <1g Fib

Exchanges   Net Carbs

Fat 1   8
Meat 1/2
Very Lean Meat 1-1/2
Fruit 1/2

Taco Salad

A quick easy way to serve a salad.

¾ pound extra lean ground beef
1 cup thick and chunky salsa
8 cups shredded lettuce
1 cup (4-oz) reduced fat Cheddar
    cheese, shredded
¼ cup Plum tomatoes, chopped

1. Brown ground beef in medium skillet; drain. Add the salsa. Bring to a boil, reduce heat and simmer 5 to 10 minutes, or until liquid is absorbed.
2. Place meat mixture, lettuce, cheese and tomatoes in a mixing bowl. Toss lightly and serve with a dollop of sour cream.

Per serving: 247 Cal, 11g Fat, 5g Sat F, 68mg Chol, 512mg Sod, 27g Pro, 2g Sug, 7g Carb, 2g Fib

Exchanges   Net Carbs

Fat 1-1/2   5
Very Lean Meat 3-1/2
Vegetable 1

Crisp Green Salad

A very vegetable salad.

4 cups assorted salad greens
8 cherry tomatoes, halved
1 cup small cauliflower florets
½ small green pepper, sliced
½ small cucumber, sliced
¼ cup nonfat vinaigrette dressing

1. Combine first 5 ingredients with just enough dressing to lightly coat.

Per serving: 27 Cal, <1g Fat, 0g Sat F, 0mg Chol, 99mg Sod, 1g Pro, 3g Sug, 5g Carb, 1g Fib

Exchanges   Net Carbs
Vegetable 1/2   4

Caesar Salad

MAKES 6 SERVINGS

Homemade is almost always better, but if using a purchased dressing, watch the fat count.

2 bunches romaine (about 8 cups)
½ cup jicama, julienned
½ cup nonfat Caesar Salad Dressing
3 tablespoons grated Parmesan cheese

1. Tear romaine into bite-size pieces. Place romaine and jicama in a large salad bowl. Toss with just enough dressing to lightly coat. Spoon onto salad plates and sprinkle with cheese.

Per serving: 44 Cal, 1g Fat, <1g Sat F, 2mg Chol, 366mg Sod, 3g Pro, 3g Sug, 6g Carb, 2g Fib

Exchanges   Net Carbs
Vegetable 1/2   4

Caesar Salads

Although not exactly traditional, you can enhance these wonderful salads by adding your choice of the following items: chicken, turkey, salmon, shrimp, fried oysters, bacon, sun-dried tomatoes, and low-carb penne pasta.

Tossed Salad with Mushrooms

MAKES 6 SERVINGS

There is a lot of crunch in this salad.

6   cups mixed greens
8   slices bacon, cooked, crumbled
½   cup cubed jicama
½   cup sliced mushrooms
½   cup nonfat vinaigrette dressing
2   tablespoons grated Parmesan cheese

1. Combine first 4 ingredients in a large bowl. Toss with just enough dressing to lightly coat. Arrange on salad plates and sprinkle lightly with Parmesan.

Per serving: 65 Cal, 2g Fat, 1g Sat F, 6mg Chol, 304mg Sod, 3g Pro, 3g Sug, 8g Carb, 2g Fib

Exchanges   Net Carbs

Meat 1/2   6
Other Carb 1/2
Vegetable 1/2

Ham Salad

MAKES 4 SERVINGS

Serve as salad or a sandwich spread.

2   cups (8-oz) cooked ham, ground
1   teaspoon prepared mustard
3   tablespoons finely chopped dill pickles
½   cup (2-oz) reduced fat Cheddar cheese, diced
½   cup light mayonnaise (approximately)

1. Combine first 4 ingredients with just enough mayonnaise to lightly moisten.

Per serving: 167 Cal, 8g Fat, 3g Sat F, 34mg Chol, 1188mg Sod, 18g Pro, 2g Sug, 5g Carb, 0g Fib

Exchanges   Net Carbs

Fat 1   5
Very Lean Meat 2-1/2

Raspberry-Spinach Salad

MAKES 4 SERVINGS

The dressing must be chilled before serving.

- **4 cups fresh spinach**
- **1 cup fresh raspberries**
- **2 cup chopped almonds**
- **⅓ cup nonfat raspberry vinaigrette**

1. Combine ingredients in salad bowl and toss with just enough dressing to lightly coat.

Per serving: 121 Cal, 7g Fat, 1g Sat F, 0mg Chol, 189mg Sod, 4g Pro, 4g Sug, 12g Carb, 4g Fib

Exchanges
Fat 1
Other Carb 1/2
Meat 1/2

Net Carbs
8

Sweet-Sour Spinach Salad

MAKES 4 SERVINGS

Dressing can be made ahead and chilled. For variety add sliced fresh mushrooms.

- **8 cups fresh spinach**
- **4 slices bacon, cooked, crumbled**
- **½ of a small red onion, sliced**
- **½ cup light mayonnaise**
- **2 packets Splenda®**
- **2 tablespoons white vinegar**

1. Place spinach, bacon and onion in a large salad bowl. Combine remaining ingredients and toss salad with just enough dressing to lightly coat. You may not need all the dressing. Do not allow to stand too long before serving.

Per serving: 106 Cal, 7g Fat, 2g Sat F, 7mg Chol, 454mg Sod, 4g Pro, 3g Sug, 8g Carb, 1g Fib

Exchanges
Fat 1
Meat 1/2
Othe Carb 1/2
Vegetable 1/2

Net Carbs
7

Spinach-Tomato Salad

If desired, the eggs can be omitted.

8　cups fresh spinach
2　hard-boiled eggs, chopped
12　cherry tomatoes, halved
4　bacon slices, cooked, crumbled
½　cup nonfat Ranch dressing

1. Place first 4 ingredients in a salad bowl and toss with just enough dressing to lightly coat.

Per serving: 95 Cal, 4g Fat, 1g Sat F, 75mg Chol, 416mg Sod, 5g Pro, 3g Sug, 10g Carb, 1g Fib

Exchanges　　　Net Carbs

Fat 1/2　　　　　9
Meat 1/2
Other Carb 1/2
Vegetable 1/2

Spinach-Orange Salad

The orange peel adds a lot of flavor.

8　cups fresh spinach
½　cup jicama, julienned
¼　cup toasted chopped pecans
2　teaspoons grated orange peel
⅓　cup nonfat vinaigrette dressing

1. Place first 4 ingredients in a large bowl. Toss with just enough dressing to lightly coat.

Per serving: 58 Cal, 3g Fat, <1Sat F, 0mg Chol, 142mg Sod, 2g Pro, 2g Sug, 6g Carb, 2g Fib

Exchanges　　　Net Carbs

Fat 1　　　　　4
Vegetable 1/2

Almond-Spinach Salad

MAKES 4 SERVINGS

Don't tell kids there is spinach in this salad and you won't have any problems getting them to eat it.

8   cups fresh spinach
2   tablespoons sliced or slivered almonds, toasted
4   slices bacon, cooked, crumbled
½   small red onion, thinly sliced
⅓   cup nonfat vinaigrette dressing

1. Combine first 4 ingredients with just enough dressing to lightly coat.

Per serving: 91 Cal, 5g Fat, 1g Sat F, 7mg Chol, 359mg Sod, 8g Pro, 1g Sug, 9g Carb, 2g Fib

Exchanges   Net Carbs

Fat 1/2   7
Other Carb 1/2
Meat 1/2
Vegetable 1/2

Coconut Chicken Salad

MAKES 5 SERVINGS

If you can afford the carbs, add 1/2 cup drained crushed pineapple.

4   cups diced cooked chicken
½   cup thinly sliced celery
½   cup unsweetened shredded coconut
½   teaspoon curry, or to taste
1   cup light mayonnaise

1. Combine first 3 ingredients in mixing bowl.
2. Combine curry and mayonnaise. Add just enough mayonnaise to chicken to lightly moisten.

Per serving: 293 Cal, 16g Fat, 8g Sat F, 77mg Chol, 497mg Sod, 29g Pro, 4g Sug, 9g Carb, 2g Fib

Exchanges   Net Carbs

Fat 2-1/2   7
Very Lean Meat 4
Other Carb 1/2

Spinach Salad with Chicken

For variety, add shredded cheese or sliced mushrooms.

8 cups spinach
1 cup cubed cooked chicken
2 hard-boiled eggs, chopped
2 tablespoons sliced almonds
½ cup nonfat Vinaigrette

1. Combine first 4 ingredients with just enough dressing to lightly coat.

Per serving: 133 Cal, 5g Fat, 1g Sat F, 124mg Chol, 387mg Sod, 12g Pro, 4g Sug, 10g Carb, 2g Fib

Exchanges   Net Carbs

Fat 1/2   8
Meat 1/2
Other Carb 1/2
Very Lean Meat 1
Vegetable 1/2

Chicken-Jicama Salad

Chicken and cabbage combine well to make this delicious salad. For variety, add an 8-oz can crushed pineapple, drained.

1 cup cubed cooked chicken
2 cups shredded cabbage
½ cup cubed jicama
¼ cup coarsely chopped pecans
⅓ cup chopped celery
⅔ cup light mayonnaise

1. Combine first 5 ingredients with enough mayonnaise to lightly coat. Cover and chill at least 1 hour before serving.

Per serving: 169 Cal, 11g Fat, 2g Sat F, 18mg Chol, 374mg Sod, 8g Pro, 3g Sug, 20g Carb, 2g Fib

Exchanges   Net Carbs

Fat 2   18
Other Carb 1/2
Very Lean Meat 1/2
Vegetable 1/2

Cook's Tip
Leftover cooked chicken can be used for salads, soups, casseroles and sandwiches.

Grilled Chicken Salad

MAKES 4 SERVINGS

Ranch is a nice versatile dressing.

4   chicken breast halves, skinned, boned
8   cups romaine lettuce
½   yellow pepper, cut into strips
½   cup jicama, julienned
½   cup nonfat Ranch dressing

1. Grill or broil chicken until cooked through.
2. Meanwhile, place lettuce, pepper strips and jicama in a large bowl. Toss with just enough dressing to lightly coat. Place on individual salad plates and top with chicken breasts sliced on the diagonal.

Per serving: 218 Cal, 4g Fat, 1g Sat F, 73mg Chol, 427mg Sod, 28g Pro, 4g Sug, 17g Carb, 5g Fib

Exchanges   Net Carbs

Other Carb 1/2   12
Very Lean Meat 3-1/2
   Vegetable 1

Club Salad

MAKES 4 SERVINGS

If desired, add green pepper and mushrooms.

1½   cups cubed cooked chicken, white meat
6   cups mixed salad greens
3   Plum tomatoes, chopped
⅓   cup nonfat vinaigrette dressing
2   hard-boiled eggs, halved

1. Place first 3 ingredients in a large salad bowl. Toss with just enough dressing to lightly coat. Garnish with eggs.

Per serving: 139 Cal, 4g Fat, 1g Sat F, 136mg Chol, 246mg Sod, 16g Pro, 4g Sug, 9g Carb, 2g Fib

Exchanges   Net Carbs

   Fat 1/2   7
   Meat 1/2
Other Carb 1/2
Very Lean Meat 1-1/2

Cashew Chicken Salad

The cashews add flavor as well as crunch.

2½   cups cubed cooked chicken
¼   cup cashews, chopped
⅓   cup thinly sliced celery
2   tablespoons finely chopped onion
     Salt and pepper to taste
⅓   cup light mayonnaise

1. Combine ingredients, stirring gently to mix. Cover and chill before serving.

Per serving: 177 Cal, 9g Fat, 2g Sat F, 48mg Chol, 247mg Sod, 19g Pro, 2g Sug, 6g Carb, <1g Fib

Exchanges   Net Carbs

     Fat 1-1/2   6
Very Lean Meat 2-1/2

Romaine-Hazelnut Salad

MAKES 4 SERVINGS

A nice luncheon salad

1   bunch romaine, bite-size pieces
½   cup cubed cooked chicken
4   slices bacon, cooked, crumbled
¼   cup coarsely chopped hazelnuts
⅓   cup nonfat vinaigrette dressing

1. Combine first 4 ingredients with just enough dressing to lightly coat.

Per serving: 132 Cal, 8g Fat, 1g Sat F, 19mg Chol, 326mg Sod, 9g Pro, 3g Sug, 8g Carb, 2g Fib

Exchanges   Net Carbs

     Fat 1   6
     Meat 1/2
   Other Carb 1/2
 Very Lean Meat 1/2
  Vegetable 1/2

Cobb Salad

You could omit the bacon and add chopped ham or Canadian Bacon.

8 **cups shredded lettuce**
2 **cups cubed cooked chicken**
1 **medium tomato, chopped**
2 **hard-boiled eggs, chopped**
4 **slices bacon, cooked, crumbled**
½ **cup nonfat Ranch dressing**

1. Arrange lettuce on four plates. Divide rows of chicken, tomato and egg on plates. Sprinkle with bacon and drizzle with dressing.

Per serving: 220 Cal, 7g Fat, 2g Sat F, 149mg Chol, 577mg Sod, 21g Pro, 6g Sug, 17g Carb, 2g Fib

Exchanges   Net Carbs

Fat 1   15
Meat 1
Other Carb 1/2
Very Lean Meat 2
Vegetable 1

Waldorf Chicken Salad

MAKES 6 SERVINGS

Jicama is a very good substitute for the apples traditionally found in Waldorf salads.

3 **cups cubed cooked chicken**
⅓ **cup chopped celery**
¾ **cup chopped jicama**
⅓ **cup chopped walnuts**
½ **cup light mayonnaise**

1. Combine first 4 ingredients with just enough mayonnaise to moisten. Cover and chill before serving.

Per serving: 153 Cal, 8g Fat, 1g Sat F, 36mg Chol, 211mg Sod, 15g Pro, 2g Sug, 5g Carb, 1g Fib

Exchanges   Net Carbs

Fat 1   4
Very Lean Meat 2
Vegetable 1/2

Mixed Vegetable Salad

*I used broccoli, red onion and red peppers
but you can choose your own vegetables.*

8 cups mixed greens
2 cups mixed fresh vegetables
1½ cups cubed cooked chicken
1 cup (4-oz) reduced fat Monterey Jack
  cheese, cubed
⅓ cup nonfat Ranch dressing

1. Combine first 4 ingredients in a large
mixing bowl. Toss with just enough dressing
to lightly coat.

Per serving: 159 Cal, 5g Fat, 3g Sat F,
38mg Chol, 418mg Sod, 16g Pro,
3g Sug, 15g Carb, 3g Fib

Exchanges   Net Carbs

Fat 1/2   12
Meat 1/2
Other Carb 1/2
Very Lean Meat 1
Vegetable 1

Lemon Fruit Salad

*The celery adds a nice crunch,
but can be omitted.*

1 (0.6-oz) package sugar-free lemon
  gelatin
2 cups diet lemon-lime soda
½ cup raspberries
½ cup sliced strawberries
⅓ cup thinly sliced celery

1. Thoroughly dissolve gelatin in 1 cup
boiling water. Add soda. Chill until consistency of unbeaten egg white.
2. Fold in fruit and celery. Pour into an
11x7-inch baking dish. Chill until set.

Per serving: 15 Cal, 0g Fat, 0mg Sat F,
0mg Chol, 62mg Sod, 1g Pro, 1g Sug,
2g Carb, 1g Fib

Exchanges   Net Carbs

Free   1

Strawberry Fruit Salad

Use as a dessert or salad.

1 (0.6-oz) package sugar free strawberry gelatin
1 cup low-fat sour cream, room temperature
1 cup chopped strawberries

1. Thoroughly dissolve gelatin in 1 cup boiling water.
2. Add sour cream and whisk until smooth.
3. Add strawberries and pour into an 8x8-inch baking dish. Chill until set.

note: The sour cream may be difficult to blend in. If so, use a rotary beater or mixer on low speed.

Per serving: 74 Cal, 5g Fat, 3g Sat F, 16mg Chol, 73mg Sod,, 3g Pro, 1g Sug, 4g Carb, 1g Fib

Exchanges   Net Carbs
Fat 1   5

Berry-Berry Fruit Salad

MAKES 8 SERVINGS

Serve as a salad or light dessert.

1 (0.6-oz) package sugar free strawberry gelatin
1 cup sliced strawberries
1 cup raspberries

1. Prepare gelatin as directed on package. Pour into an 11x7-inch baking dish. Chill until consistency of unbeaten egg whites.
2. Gently fold in berries. Pour into a mold or keep in dish. Chill until set.

Per serving: 23 Cal, <1g Fat, 0g Sat F, 0mg Chol, 42mg Sod, 1g Pro, 2g Sug, 3g Carb, 1g Fib

Exchanges   Net Carbs
0   2

Lemon-Mayonnaise Dressing

MAKES 1/2 CUP

This is wonderful on a salad of romaine, mushrooms, croutons, and Parmesan cheese.

¼ cup light mayonnaise
¼ cup nonfat sour cream
1 teaspoon fresh lemon juice
1½ teaspoons Dijon mustard
½ teaspoon dried dill weed

1. Combine ingredients, cover and chill to blend flavors. If too thick, thin with a small amount of nonfat milk.

Per 1 tablespoon: 18 Cal, 1g Fat, <1g Sat F, 1mg Chol, 90mg Sod, <1g Pro, 1g Sug, 2g Carb, 0g Fib

Exchanges	Net Carbs
0	2

Sweet Onion Dressing

MAKES 1 CUP

Especially good on spinach salads and has an added bonus of keeping several days in the refrigerator.

½ cup oil
¼ cup cider vinegar
¼ cup finely chopped onion
½ teaspoon prepared mustard
½ teaspoon salt
2 packets Splenda®

1. Combine ingredients, mixing well to blend. Chill until ready to use.

Per 1 tablespoon: 62 Cal, 7g Fat, 1g Sat F, 0mg Chol, 73mg Sod, 0g Pro, <1g Sug, 1g Carb, 0g Fib

Exchanges	Net Carbs
Fat 1-1/2	1

Salad Dressings

A good home-made salad dressing is so much better than most purchased dressings. Commit yourself to making at least one new salad dressing a week, then choose your favorite dressings to make again and again.

Dijon Vinaigrette

MAKES 1-3/4 CUPS

Will keep about a week in the refrigerator.

1¼   cups oil
⅓   cup Dijon mustard
⅓   cup garlic red wine vinegar
¼   teaspoon ground black pepper

1. Combine ingredients and mix well.

Per 1 tablespoon: 89 Cal, 10g Fat, 1g Sat F,
0mg Chol, 72mg Sod, <1g Pro,
0g Sug, <1g Carb, 0g Fib

Exchanges   Net Carbs
Fat 2   <1

Creamy Caesar Dressing

MAKES 1-1/2 CUPS

My favorite Caesar salad dressing.

1   medium garlic clove
¼   cup fresh lemon juice
1   tablespoon Dijon mustard
1   teaspoon Worcestershire sauce
½   cup grated Parmesan cheese
1   cup light mayonnaise

1. Combine first 4 ingredients in a blender or small food processor, blending until smooth (you can do this by hand if you mince the garlic first).
2. Add cheese and mayonnaise and briefly blend. Chill at least one hour to allow flavors to blend.

Per 1 tablespoon: 26 Cal, 2g Fat, 1g Sat F,
1mg Chol, 130mg Sod, 1g Pro,
1g Sug, 2g Carb, 0g Fib

Exchanges   Net Carbs
Fat 1/2   2

Raspberry Vinaigrette

MAKES 1/2 CUP

A sweet-tart vinaigrette. Can be made in minutes and chilled until ready to serve.

3   packets Splenda®
¼   teaspoon salt
1   teaspoon Dijon mustard
3   tablespoons raspberry wine vinegar
⅓   cup oil

1. Combine ingredients and mix well.

Per 1 tablespoon: 81 Cal, 2g Fat, 1g Sat F,
0mg Chol, 89mg Sod, 0g Pro,
0g Sug, 1g Carb, 0g Fib

Exchanges	Net Carbs
Fat 2	1

Quick Roquefort Dressing

MAKES 1 CUP

This is for those of us who prefer a milder Roquefort dressing.

½   cup purchased low-fat Roquefort dressing
½   cup nonfat sour cream

1. Combine ingredients and mix well.

Per 2 tablespoons: 23 Cal, <1g Fat, 0g Sat F,
3mg Chol, 276mg Sod, 1g Pro,
1g Sug, 4g Carb, 0g Fib

Exchanges	Net Carbs
0	4

Not Just Luck

Don't necessarily subscribe to the notion that you can just throw together a hodgepodge of ingredients in a bowl and call it a salad. Sometimes this works, but usually only after some cooking experience, and perhaps a bit of luck.

Creamy Italian Dressing

MAKES 1-1/4 CUPS

Serve over salads or as a dip with fresh vegetables.

- ¾ **cup nonfat sour cream**
- ⅓ **cup light mayonnaise**
- 1 **tablespoon nonfat milk**
- 1 **(0.6-oz) package Italian dressing mix**
- 2 **packets Splenda®**
- ⅛ **teaspoon salt**

1. Combine ingredients with 3 tablespoons water and mix thoroughly. Chill to blend flavors.

Per 1 tablespoon: 50 Cal, 1g Fat, <1g Sat F, 1mg Chol, 60mg Sod, <1g Pro, 1g Sug, 2g Carb, 0g Fib

Exchanges   Net Carbs
0   2

Coleslaw Dressing

MAKES 1-1/4 CUPS

Very good in almost any type of coleslaw.

- 1 **cup light mayonnaise**
- 12 **packets Splenda®**
- ¼ **cup cider vinegar**

1. Combine ingredients. Cover and chill to blend flavors.

Per 1 tablespoon: 23 Cal, 2g Fat, 0g Sat F, 0mg Chol, 104mg Sod, 0g Pro, 1g Sug, 2g Carb, 0g Fib

Exchanges   Net Carbs
0   2

Spinach Salad Dressing

MAKES 2/3 CUP

Goes well with almost any spinach salad.

2 tablespoons Splenda®
2 tablespoons white vinegar
½ cup light mayonnaise

1. Combine ingredients and mix well. Chill to blend flavors.

Per 2 tablespoons: 44 Cal, 3g Fat, 1g Sat F, 0mg Chol, 208mg Sod, 0g Pro, 2g Sug, 4g Carb, 0g Fib

Exchanges   Net Carbs
Fat 1/2   4

Raspberry Dressing

MAKES 1/2 CUP

A little different, but very good.

2 tablespoons raspberry vinegar
2 tablespoons sugar free raspberry
   spread
⅓ cup oil

1. Combine vinegar and raspberry spread in a small bowl.
2. Gradually whisk in oil until blended. Cover. Chill at least 1 hour.

Per 1 tablespoon: 81 Cal, 9g Fat, 1g Sat F, 0mg Chol, 0mg Sod, 0g Pro, 0g Sug, 1g Carb, 0g Fib

Exchanges   Net Carbs
Fat 1-1/2   1

Orange Spread

MAKES 1/2 CUP

*Serve on low-carb French toast,
pancakes or muffins.*

$\frac{1}{2}$ **cup soft reduced calorie
      margarine, softened**
1   **tablespoon fresh orange zest**

1. Beat ingredients until well blended.

Per tablespoon: 102 Cal, 11g Fat, 2g Sat F,
0mg Chol, 153mg Sod, <1g Pro,
0g Sug,<1g Carb, 0g Fib

Exchanges   Net Carbs
Fat 1/2   9

Hints

Instant Soft Butter

Forget to soften the butter? Place the
unwrapped butter in a resealable plastic
bag and flatten with a rolling pin.

Egg Whites

Egg whites will have a higher volume if
beaten at room temperature. However,
they are more easily separated from the
yolk if done when the eggs are cold.

Cranberry Sauce

MAKES ABOUT 2 CUPS

Our traditional holiday cranberry sauce.

8   **ounces fresh cranberries**
1   **cup Splenda**
$\frac{1}{4}$ **cup sugar free apricot preserves**
2   **tablespoons fresh lemon juice**

1. Wash cranberries and discard the bad
ones.
2. In medium saucepan, combine Splenda
and 6 tablespoons water. Bring to a boil and
cook 3 to 4 minutes. Add cranberries and
cook 8 to 10 minutes or until cranberries
make a popping sound and become transparent.
3. Remove from heat and stir in apricot
preserves and lemon juice. Cover and chill
before serving.

Per 1/4-cup: 46 Cal, 0g Fat, 0g Sat F,
0mg Chol, 1mg Sod, 0g Pro,
 3g Sug, 8g Carb, 1g Fib

Exchanges   Net Carbs
Fat 1/2   7

Blueberry Sauce

MAKES 2-1/2 CUPS

*This is a wonderful sauce on
cheesecake and ice cream.*

1   cup Splenda
1½ tablespoons cornstarch
1   teaspoon grated lemon zest
3   cups fresh or frozen blueberries

1. Combine Splenda, cornstarch and lemon
zest in a medium saucepan. Gradually stir in
1 cup water. Cook over medium heat until
thickened, stirring frequently.
2. Add blueberries. Bring to a boil then
remove from heat. Cover and chill.

Per 2 tablespoons: 39 Cal, 0g Fat, 0g Sat
F, 0mg Chol, 0mg Sod, <1g Pro, 2g Sug,
4g Carb, 1g Fib

Exchanges   Net Carbs
Fat 1/2   9

Pesto Mayonnaise

MAKES 1 CUP

*Keep on hand as a spread for sandwiches and
wraps and as a topping for hamburgers.*

1   cup light mayonnaise
1   tablespoon pesto, or to taste

1. Combine ingredients. Cover and store in
the refrigerator.

Per tablespoon: 28 Cal, 2g Fat, 1g Sat F,
0mg Chol, 130mg Sod, <1g Pro,
1g Sug, 2g Carb, 0g Fib

Exchanges   Net Carbs
Fat 1/2   2

Cook's Tip
There are several
brands of pesto on the market.
Experiment to find the one you
like best or better yet, make your
own.

Onion-Mushroom Topping

MAKES 4 SERVINGS

A nice topping for hamburgers and meatloaf.

1 medium onion, sliced, separated into rings
1 cup sliced mushrooms
1 tablespoon reduced calorie margarine
½ teaspoon Worcestershire sauce

1. Cook onion and mushrooms in margarine in a medium nonstick skillet, until just tender. Add Worcestershire sauce and 1 tablespoon water; stir to blend.

Per serving: 41 Cal, 3g Fat, 1g Sat F, 0mg Chol, 33mg Sod, 1g Pro, 2g Sug, 3g Carb, <1g Fib

Exchanges   Net Carbs
Fat 1/2   9

Tartar Sauce

MAKES 1 CUP

Make ahead and allow time to chill.

¾ cup light mayonnaise
1 teaspoon finely chopped onion
1 tablespoon finely chopped parsley
1 tablespoon finely chopped dill pickle

1. Combine ingredients and mix well. Chill at least one hour to blend flavors.

Per tablespoon: 19 Cal, 2g Fat, <1g Sat F, 0mg Chol, 105mg Sod, 0g Pro, 1g Sug, 2g Carb, 0g Fib

Exchanges   Net Carbs
Fat 1/2   9

Horseradish Sauce

MAKES 3/4 CUP

For a Prime Rib dinner, fill large mushroom caps with sauce; then, top with chopped chives. Bake 10 to 15 minutes at 325°F until heated through.

¼   **cup light mayonnaise**
½   **cup nonfat sour cream**
1½ **teaspoons prepared horseradish**
¼   **teaspoon onion salt**
¼   **teaspoon garlic salt**

1. Combine ingredients and mix well. Chill at least one hour to blend flavors.

Per tablespoon: 15 Cal, 1g Fat, 0g Sat F
< 1mg Chol, 93mg Sod, <1g Pro,
<1g Sug, 2g Carb, 0g Fib

Exchanges   Net Carbs
Fat 1/2   2

Tomato-Basil Sauce

MAKES 2-1/2 CUPS

Serve over meat, chicken, seafood or low-carb pasta.

3   **tablespoons oil**
3   **medium garlic cloves, minced**
1   **(28-oz) can diced tomatoes**
    Salt and pepper
1   **tablespoon chopped basil or to taste**

1. Heat oil in saucepan over low heat. Add garlic and cook until soft but not brown.
2. Add tomatoes, salt and pepper to taste. Cook over medium heat, 12 to 15 minutes, or until thickened, stirring frequently.
3. Add basil and cook for about 2 minutes.

note: If diced tomatoes are too large, process in a blender or food processor. This takes only a second.

Per ¼ cup: 53 Cal, 4g Fat, 1g Sat F,
0mg Chol, 230mg Sod, 1g Pro,
2g Sug, 3g Carb, 1g Fib

Exchanges   Net Carbs
Fat 1/2   2

Bordelaise Sauce

MAKES 2 CUPS

Especially good with steaks, beef tenderloin and fondue.

¼ cup minced shallots
4 tablespoons reduced calorie margarine, divided
2 bay leaves, finely crumbled
1 cup Burgundy wine
5 teaspoons cornstarch
1½ cups canned, condensed beef broth, undiluted

1. In a small saucepan, cook shallots in 2 tablespoons of the margarine. They should be tender but not brown.

2. Add bay leaves and wine; simmer over medium heat until reduced to about 1/3 of original volume.

3. Combine cornstarch and 1/4-cup beef broth, mixing to form a smooth paste. Add to wine mixture along with remaining broth. Cook, stirring frequently, until thickened. Add remaining 2 tablespoons margarine.

Per tablespoon: 21 Cal, 1g Fat, <1g Sat F, 0mg Chol, 49mg Sod, 0g Pro, 0g Sug, 1g Carb, 0g Fib

Exchanges
Fat 1/2

Net Carbs
1

Spicy Barbecue Sauce

MAKES 1-1/2 CUPS

Excellent for basting chicken & ribs.

½ cup oil
½ cup fresh lemon juice
2 tablespoons Worcestershire sauce
1½ teaspoons hot sauce
2 tablespoons prepared mustard
¼ cup brown Sugar Twin®

1. Combine ingredients in a small saucepan. Bring to a boil and then remove from heat.

Per tablespoon: 44 Cal, 5g Fat, 1g Sat F, 0mg Chol, 26mg Sod, 0g Pro, 1g Sug, 1g Carb, 0g Fib

Exchanges
Fat 1

Net Carbs
1

Cook's Tip
If using a barbecue sauce with a high sugar content, brush on chicken or meat during last 15 minutes of cooking time.

Barbecue Sauce

MAKES 1-1/2 CUP

You should always have this in your refrigerator.
Use for ribs, hamburger patties, grilled chicken,
pork chops, as a meatloaf topping, etc.

1   **cup low-carb ketchup**
½   **cup brown Sugar Twin®**
1   **tablespoon Worcestershire sauce**
1   **tablespoon prepared mustard**
½   **teaspoon lemon pepper**

1. Combine ingredients and let stand at
least an hour to blend flavors.

Per tablespoon: 6 Cal, 0g Fat, 0g Sat F,
0mg Chol, 57mg Sod, 0g Pro,
<1g Sug, 1g Carb, 0g Fib

Exchanges   Net Carbs
Fat 1/2   1

Pizza Sauce

MAKES ABOUT 1 CUP

An easy but flavorful pizza sauce.

¼   **teaspoon garlic powder**
¼   **teaspoon oregano**
½   **teaspoon basil**
½   **cup grated Parmesan cheese**
1   **(8-oz) can tomato sauce**

1. Combine all the ingredients and mix
well.

Per 2 tablespoons: 31 Cal, 2g Fat, 1g Sat F,
4mg Chol, 225mg Sod, 2g Pro,
1g Sug, 2g Carb, <1g Fib

Exchanges   Net Carbs
Meat 1/2   2
Vegetable 1/2

Company Gravy

MAKES 2-1/2 CUPS

Serve with chicken or pork.

½ **cup finely chopped onion**
2 **tablespoons reduced calorie margarine**
2 **tablespoons flour**
1½ **cups chicken broth**
½ **cup nonfat milk**
¼ **cup dry white wine**

1. In a small saucepan, cook onion in heated margarine until soft. Add flour and cook about 2 minutes, stirring frequently.
2. Remove from heat and gradually stir in broth, milk and wine. Bring to a boil, reduce heat and simmer, stirring frequently until mixture has thickened.

note: For added flavor, if you have a small amount of browned bits from a roast or turkey, stir that into the gravy as it boils.

Per ¼ cup: 39 Cal, 2g Fat, <1g Sat F, <1mg Chol, 98mg Sod, 1g Pro, 1g Sug, 3g Carb, <1g Fib

Exchanges
Fat 1/2

Net Carbs
3

Turkey Gravy

MAKES 4 CUPS

Since this recipe makes a lot, this is the one I use for my daughter's Thanksgiving dinner.

½ **cup fat drippings**
½ **cup flour**
4 **cups turkey broth**
Salt and pepper

1. After turkey is roasted, pour meat juices into a large measuring cup. Remove ½ cup of fat that rises to the top. Discard remaining fat, but reserve the broth.
2. Pour fat into a medium saucepan; heat until hot. Gradually stir in flour (that has been mixed with a little water or broth) and cook over medium heat until lightly browned. Gradually add broth. Cook, stirring frequently, until thickened. Season with salt and pepper.

tip: If you don't have quite 4 cups broth, add water to make up the difference. If the gravy is too thin, add additional flour mixed with a little water. If too thick, thin with additional broth or water.

Per ¼ cup: 74 Cal, 7g Fat, 2g Sat F, 7mg Chol, 123mg Sod, 1g Pro, <1g Sug, 3g Carb, <1g Fib

Exchanges
Fat 1

Net Carbs
3

Brining

Brining is a simple way to enhance flavor and make meats and poultry more tender and juicy. Although salt is the key ingredient, the meat will not taste salty. We have not included the carbs in the brining solution because the amount absorbed into the meat, per serving, is negligible.

Brining Solution

MAKES 4 QUARTS

This very simple brining solution can be used for meats, chicken, turkey, etc.

4   quarts water
⅔   cup kosher salt

1. Combine ingredients, stirring until salt is dissolved.

note: Amount of solution needed may vary with each recipe depending on the size of the poultry or meat. There should be enough to cover completely.

Maple Flavored Brine

MAKES 6-1/2 CUPS

There should be enough brine to cover the meat you are cooking.

6   cups water
¼   cup brown Sugar Twin®
½   cup kosher salt
½   cup no-carb maple syrup

Combine ingredients, stirring until salt is dissolved.

We have not included the nutritional analysis in these marinade recipes because the amount of marinade absorbed into the meat, per serving, is negligible.

Ginger Marinade

MAKES 1 CUP

A good marinade for beef or chicken.

⅓ cup low sodium soy sauce
⅓ cup brown Sugar Twin®
2 tablespoons white vinegar
1½ tablespoons Worcestershire sauce
1 tablespoon oil
3 slices fresh ginger

1. Combine ingredients and pour over meat. Cover and chill at least 2 hours or overnight.

Red Wine Marinade

MAKES 1 CUP

An excellent marinade for beef.

1 cup dry red wine
¼ cup chopped onion
1 medium garlic, minced
½ teaspoon dried thyme
¼ teaspoon black pepper
¼ teaspoon salt

1. Combine ingredients in a small saucepan. Bring to a boil, reduce heat and simmer 2 to 3 minutes. Cover and chill. Will keep about a week in the refrigerator.

We have not included the nutritional analysis in these marinade recipes because the amount of marinade absorbed into the meat, per serving, is negligible.

Easy Beef Marinade

MAKES 1/2 CUP

Use to marinate sirloin, chuck and flank steak.

¼ cup low sodium soy sauce
¼ cup oil
2 tablespoons fresh lemon juice
1 tablespoon brown Sugar Twin®
¼ teaspoon garlic salt
⅛ teaspoon oregano

1. Combine ingredients; pour over meat and marinate in refrigerator several hours or overnight, turning occasionally.

Herb Marinade

MAKES 1/2 CUP

A good marinade for fish, chicken and meats.

¼ cup oil
2 tablespoons lemon juice
1½ tablespoons dry red wine
1 teaspoon dried thyme
1 medium garlic clove, minced
¼ teaspoon pepper

1. Combine ingredients until blended.

Soups, Sandwiches, Pizza & Wraps

♜ Soups
♜ Sandwiches
♜ Pizza
♜ Wraps

Oriental Soup

MAKES 4 CUPS

The next time you prepare a large flank steak, remove a 4 ounce portion to save for this quick and flavorful soup.

4   **ounces flank steak**
1   **teaspoon cornstarch**
1   **packet Splenda®**
2   **teaspoons low sodium soy sauce**
2   **cups low sodium beef broth**
2   **cups Bok Choy, sliced thin**
     (both green and white parts)

1. Cut beef lengthwise (with the grain) into 1½ to 2-inch strips. Cut each strip across the grain into ⅛-inch slices.

2. Combine cornstarch, Splenda and soy sauce. Add meat; cover and marinate 30 minutes.

3. In medium saucepan, bring broth to a boil. Add Bok Choy; cook 1½ to 2 minutes until just crisp-tender. Add meat and cook about 1 minute.

Per cup: 71 Cal, 3g Fat, 1g Sat F, 11mg Chol, 148mg Sod, 9g Pro, 1g Sug, 2g Carb, <1g Fib

Exchanges   Net Carbs
Fat 1-1/2   2
Meat 1/2
Very Lean Meat 1

Egg Drop Soup

MAKES 3 CUPS

A nice light prelude to a meal.

3   **cups chicken broth**
2   **large eggs, beaten**
⅓   **cup snow peas, julienned**
     Salt and pepper to taste

1. In medium saucepan, bring broth to a boil. Gradually add eggs, stirring briskly after each addition.

2. Add snow peas and cook 1 to 2 minutes. Season with salt and pepper.

Per cup: 77 Cal, 5g Fat, 1g Sat F, 141mg Chol, 962mg Sod, 6g Pro, 1g Sug, 3g Carb, 1g Fib

Exchanges   Net Carbs
Fat 1/2   2
Meat 1
Vegetable 1/2

Company Egg Soup

As you can see, this is low-carb as well as low-fat and low calories.

3   cups chicken broth
2   large eggs, beaten
⅓   cup chopped green onions
¾   cup sliced mushrooms
¼   cup chopped water chestnuts
1   tablespoon low sodium soy sauce

1. In a large saucepan, bring broth to a boil. Gradually add the eggs, stirring briskly after each addition.
2. Add remaining ingredients and cook until mushrooms are tender.

Per cup: 68 Cal, 4g Fat, 1g Sat F, 106mg Chol, 858mg Sod, 5g Pro, 1g Sug, 4g Carb, 1g Fib

Exchanges   Net Carbs

Meat 1/2   3
Vegetable 1/2

Shrimp & Mushroom Soup

MAKES 4 CUPS

A small amount of carrots adds just a bit of color.

4   cups chicken broth
¼   cup shredded carrots
2   cups coarsely chopped Bok Choy
    (both white and green part)
¼   cup finely chopped water chestnuts
2   ounces sliced mushrooms
2   ounces tiny cooked shrimp

1. In large saucepan, bring broth to a boil. Add carrots, Bok Choy, water chestnuts and mushrooms. Bring to a boil; reduce heat and simmer 3 to 4 minutes or until Bok Choy is just crisp tender.
2. Add shrimp and heat through.

Per cup: 50 Cal, 2g Fat, 0g Sat F, 30mg Chol, 1106mg Sod, 5g Pro, 1g Sug, 5g Carb, 1g Fib

Exchanges   Net Carbs
Very Lean Meat 1/2   4
Vegetable 1/2

Grilled Cheese Sandwiches

MAKES 2 SERVINGS

Add a large green salad and you will have a very satisfying meal.

2   slices lowfat white bread
1   tablespoon sugar free raspberry jam
1   tablespoon finely chopped pecans
1   slice reduced fat Monterey Jack cheese
1   tablespoons reduced calorie margarine

1. Spread 1 slice bread with jam. Sprinkle with pecans and top with cheese. Top with bread.

2. Spread each side with margarine and cook in sprayed nonstick skillet until toasted, turning once. Slice diagonally.

Per serving: 208 Cal, 12g Fat, 3g Sat F, 10mg Chol, 361mg Sod, 7g Pro, <1g Sug, 20g Carb, 1g Fib

Exchanges   Net Carbs

Fat 2   19
Meat 1/2
Starch 1

Bacon-Cheese Melt

MAKES 4 SERVINGS

Kids love these. Serve with a green salad or Baked Tortilla Chips, page 22.

6   slices bacon, cooked, crumbled
2   tablespoons chopped Plum tomatoes
4   slices low-fat white bread
¾   cup (3-oz) reduced fat Cheddar cheese, shredded

1. Lightly toast bread on one side.

2. Sprinkle bacon and tomatoes on untoasted side. Top with cheese. Broil until cheese is melted and hot.

Per serving: 177 Cal, 6g Fat, 2g Sat F, 15mg Chol, 545mg Sod, 12g Pro, <1g Sug, 27g Carb, 2g Fib

Exchanges   Net Carbs

Fat 1   25
Meat 1/2
Starch 1

Asparagus-Tuna Melt

My kids grew up on tuna melts.

1   (6-oz) can tuna, drained
2   tablespoons chopped onion
⅓   cup light mayonnaise
4   slices low-fat white bread
4   cooked asparagus spears, halved
4   slices reduced fat Swiss cheese

1. Preheat oven to 350°F. Combine tuna and onion with just enough mayonnaise to moisten.

2. Spread bread with tuna mixture. Top each with 2 asparagus halves. Top with a cheese slice. Carefully place on oven rack and bake 6 to 8 minutes or until hot.

Per serving: 213 Cal, 6g Fat, 2g Sat F, 22mg Chol, 549mg Sod, 18g Pro, 2g Sug, 21g Carb, 1g Fib

Exchanges   Net Carbs

Fat 1/2   19
Starch 1
Very Lean Meat 2

Artichoke-Cheese Melts

A convenient topping to have on hand when needed.

3   large hard-boiled eggs, shredded
1½ cups (6-oz) reduced fat Cheddar cheese, shredded
1   (14-oz) can artichoke hearts, chopped
¼   cup light mayonnaise
1   tablespoon Mild & Creamy Dijon mustard
9   slices low-fat white bread, toasted

1. Preheat oven to 350°F. Combine ingredients. Spread ⅓ cup on desired number of bread slices, spreading all the way to the edges. Place on baking pan and bake 6 to 8 minutes or until golden. Makes enough spread for 9 slices of bread.

Per slice: 171 Cal, 5g Fat, 2g Sat F, 75mg Chol, 491mg Sod, 10g Pro, 1g Sug, 20g Carb, 3g Fib

Exchanges   Net Carbs

Fat 1/2   17
Meat 1/2
Starch 1
Very Lean Meat 1/2
Vegetable 1/2

Sloppy Joes

MAKES 10 SANDWICHES

You can prepare filling ahead, but do not assemble sandwiches until ready to serve.

2 pounds extra lean ground beef
1 cup chopped onion
¾ cup low-carb ketchup
3 tablespoons prepared mustard
2 teaspoons chili powder

1. In large skillet, brown ground beef and onion; drain. Add remaining ingredients along with ½ cup water. Bring to a boil, reduce heat and simmer 15 to 20 minutes or until liquid is absorbed. Serve as a sandwich using low-carb tortillas or bread.
note: Nutritional analysis is based on filling only.

Per serving: 189 Cal, 10g Fat, 4g Sat F, 66mg Chol, 139mg Sod, 20g Pro, 1g Sug, 3g Carb, <1g Fib

Exchanges   Net Carbs
Fat 1-1/2   3
Very Lean Meat 3
Vegetable 1/2

Open-Face Cheese Sandwich

MAKES 4 SERVINGS

A nice cool weather sandwich.

4 slices bacon, halved
4 slices low-fat white bread
2 tablespoons light mayonnaise
4 thin tomato slices
4 thin onion slices
4 slices reduced fat Cheddar cheese

1. Cook bacon until cooked through. Drain.
2. Spread bread with mayonnaise. Top with tomato, onion, bacon and cheese. Broil to melt cheese.

Per serving: 190 Cal, 7g Fat, 3g Sat F, 13mg Chol, 581mg Sod, 12g Pro, 2g Sug, 20g Carb, 1g Fib

Exchanges   Net Carbs
Fat 1   19
Meat 1/2
Starch 1
Very Lean Meat 1
Vegetable 1/2

Pizza Toppings

Pizza Sauce Creations

Be sure to use a reduced fat Mozzarella.

- Barbecue sauce, Mozzarella cheese, cooked chicken, chopped red onion

- Pizza sauce, Mozzarella cheese, cooked chicken, chopped tomatoes, green onion

- Pizza sauce, Mozzarella cheese, ham, pineapple tidbits (just a few)

- Pizza sauce, Mozzarella cheese and/or Cheddar cheese & cooked sausage, onion, green pepper, red pepper

- Pizza sauce, Mozzarella cheese, chopped Plum tomatoes, fresh basil, Parmesan cheese

- Stewed tomatoes, drained, basil, olive oil

- Pizza sauce, Mozzarella cheese, pepperoni, cooked sausage, mushrooms

- Pizza sauce, Mozzarella cheese, artichoke hearts, coarsely chopped onion, green peppers

- Pizza sauce, Mozzarella cheese, red pepper, basil

- Pizza sauce, Mozzarella and Cheddar cheese, artichoke hearts, pepper strips, sliced ripe olives

Classy Little Pizzas

Some of my favorite pizzas use no sauce at all. Just the cheese.

Some favorite toppings are:

- Cheese, arugula, Prosciutto, shaved Parmesan cheese, fresh rosemary, olive oil.

- Cheese, pancetta strips, roasted garlic, rosemary, hot pepper flakes.

- Cheese, artichokes, red pepper strips, asparagus, basil, goat cheese.

- Cheese, sliced pancetta, sliced radicchio, hot pepper flakes, parsley.

Artichoke Cheese Pizza

MAKES 4 SERVINGS

A flavorful, not so traditional, pizza.

1   tablespoon oil
4   (7-inch) low-carb tortillas
¾   small onion, sliced
1   cup (4-oz) reduced fat Mozzarella
    cheese, shredded
1   (9-oz) can artichoke hearts, drained

1. Preheat oven to 400°F. Heat oil in medium skillet. Cook onion until soft, stirring frequently. Drain.

2. Place tortillas on a baking sheet and bake 4 to 5 minutes until lightly toasted. Turn over and sprinkle with cheese. Top with onion and artichokes. Cut artichokes if too large. Bake 8 to 10 minutes or until cheese melts.

Per serving: 173 Cal, 8g Fat, 2g Sat F, 10mg Chol, 536mg Sod, 14g Pro, 1g Sug, 16g Carb, 8g Fib

Exchanges   Net Carbs

Fat 1   8
Meat 1
Vegetable 1

Barbecue Chicken Pizza

MAKES 2 SERVINGS

A nice after school snack.

2   (7-inch) low-carb tortillas
2   tablespoons Barbecue Sauce,
     page 205
1   cup cubed cooked chicken
¾   cup (3-oz) reduced fat Cheddar
     cheese, shredded
1½   tablespoons chopped green onion

1. Preheat oven to 425°F. Place tortillas on baking sheet and bake 4 minutes. Turn over.

2. Spread with barbecue sauce. Top with remaining ingredients. Bake 8 to 10 minutes or until cheese has melted.

Per serving: 202 Cal, 7g Fat, 2g Sat F, 45mg Chol, 570mg Sod, 29g Pro, 1g Sug, 13g Carb, 8g Fib

Exchanges   Net Carbs

Fat 1/2   5
Very Lean Meat 3-1/2

Chicken Pesto Pizza

MAKES 4 SERVINGS

One of our favorite pizzas.

4   (7-inch) low-carb tortillas
2   tablespoons pesto
1½ cups (6-oz) reduced fat Mozzarella
    cheese, shredded
1½ cups cubed cooked chicken
¼   cup Plum tomatoes, chopped
4   asparagus stems

1. Preheat oven to 400°F. Place tortillas on
baking sheet. Layer ingredients in order
listed to within 1 inch of edge. Bake 8 to 10
minutes or until golden and heated through.

Per serving: 268 Cal, 12g Fat, 4g Sat F,
54mg Chol, 613mg Sod, 32g Pro,
<1g Sug, 14g Carb, 9g Fib

Exchanges   Net Carbs
Fat 1   5
Meat 2
Very Lean Meat 2
Vegetable 1/2

Mushroom Pizza

MAKES 2 SERVINGS

*Remember to keep the cheese 1 inch
from the edge.*

1   (10-inch) low-carb tortilla
⅓   cup chopped Plum tomatoes
½   cup (2-oz) reduced fat Mozzarella
    cheese, shredded
1   tablespoon grated Parmesan cheese
    Dash oregano
¼   cup sliced mushrooms

1. Preheat oven to 425°F. Place tortilla on
baking sheet. Layer ingredients in order
listed to within 1 inch of edge. Bake 8 to 10
minutes or until golden and heated through.
Cut in half and serve.

Per serving: 128 Cal, 5g Fat, 2g Sat F,
12mg Chol, 390mg Sod, 13g Pro,
1g Sug, 12g Carb, 7g Fib

Exchanges   Net Carbs
Meat 1   5

∾ Hint ∾

Because most low-carb tortillas are
quite thin, it is best to leave a 1
inch border when sprinkling cheese on
top. This will help prevent cheese
from flowing over the edge.

Sausage-Onion Pizza

MAKES 4 SERVINGS

Make your own pizza sauce and keep on hand for last minute pizzas.

4 (7-inch) low-carb tortillas
2 tablespoons pizza sauce, page 204
4 ounces lowfat turkey sausage, cooked
¾ cup (3-oz) reduced fat Mozzarella cheese, shredded
1 tablespoon chopped green onions

1. Preheat oven to 400°F. Place tortillas on a baking sheet and bake 4 to 5 minutes or until lightly toasted. Turn over and spread with pizza sauce. Top with remaining ingredients and bake 8 to 10 minutes or until cheese is melted.

Per serving: 168 Cal, 8g Fat, 3g Sat F, 33mg Chol, 655mg Sod, 17g Pro, 1g Sug, 13g Carb, 8g Fib

Exchanges	Net Carbs
Fat 1/2	5
Meat 1-1/2	

Turkey Club Wrap

MAKES 1 WRAP

A restaurant favorite.

1 (7-inch) low-carb tortilla
1 teaspoon Mild & Creamy Dijon mustard
2 slices deli turkey
2 slices bacon, cooked, crumbled
½ cup shredded lettuce

1. Spread tortilla with mustard. Layer ingredients in order listed. Roll tightly.

Per serving: 270 Cal, 8g Fat, 32g Sat F, 64mg Chol, 1269mg Sod, 6g Pro, 2g Sug, 16g Carb, 9g Fib

Exchanges	Net Carbs
Fat 1/2	7
Meat 1/2	
Very Lean Meat 3-1/2	
Vegetable 1/2	

Beef & Cheese Roll-ups

MAKES 4 SERVINGS

Try using some of your own favorite ingredients and you might come up with some fantastic sandwich ideas.

4   **(7-inch) low-carb tortillas**
½   **cup fat-free garlic & herb cream cheese spread**
8   **slices deli roast beef**
½   **cup (2-oz) reduced fat Monterey Jack cheese, shredded**
2   **cups shredded lettuce**

1. Spread each tortilla with 2 tablespoons cheese spread. Top with ingredients in order listed. Roll tightly.

Per serving: 170 Cal, 7g Fat, 3g Sat F, 40mg Chol, 793mg Sod, 22g Pro, 1g Sug, 15g Carb, 9g Fib

Exchanges   Net Carbs

Fat 1/2   6
Meat 1/2
Very Lean Meat 2

Veggie Wrap

MAKES 1 SERVING

We seem to think we have to have meat on a sandwich, but this is a nice change and quite delicious.

1   **(7-inch) low-carb tortilla**
2   **tablespoons light cream cheese, softened**
8   **thin slices cucumber**
½   **cup shredded lettuce**
1   **tablespoon Plum tomato, chopped**

1. Spread tortilla with cream cheese. Top with ingredients in order listed. Roll tightly.

Per serving: 134 Cal, 7g Fat, 3g Sat F, 17mg Chol, 314mg Sod, 9g Pro, 2g Sug, 16g Carb, 9g Fib

Exchanges   Net Carbs

Fat 1   7
Meat 1/2
Vegetable 1/2

Turkey-Swiss Wrap

MAKES 1 SERVING

Bacon can be omitted, if desired.

1 (7-inch) low-carb tortilla
1 teaspoon Dijon mustard
2 slices deli turkey
2 slices bacon, cooked, crumbled
¼ cup (1-oz) reduced fat Swiss cheese, shredded
½ cup shredded lettuce

1. Spread tortilla with mustard. Layer remaining ingredients in order listed. Roll tightly.

Per serving: 232 Cal, 5g Fat, 1g Sat F, 60mg Chol, 1103mg Sod, 40g Pro, 1g Sug, 13g Carb, 8g Fib

Exchanges
Fat 1/2
Very Lean Meat 4-1/2

Net Carbs
5

Dijonnaise

If you like both Dijon mustard and light mayonnaise on your sandwiches, make your own Dijonnaise and keep on hand. All you have to do is mix ½-cup mayonnaise with 2 teaspoons Dijon mustard (or to taste).

Bacon & Tomato Wraps

MAKES 4 SERVINGS

To avoid totally crushing everything, cut the sandwiches with a very sharp or serrated knife.

4 (7-inch) low-carb tortillas
2 tablespoons light mayonnaise
4 thin onion slices
4 thin tomato slices
1 cup (4-oz) reduced fat Cheddar cheese, shredded
2 slices bacon, cooked, crumbled

1. Spread tortillas with mayonnaise. Top with remaining ingredients in order listed. Roll tightly.

Per serving: 136 Cal, 6g Fat, 2g Sat F, 9mg Chol, 533mg Sod, 13g Pro, 1g Sug, 14g Carb, 8g Fib

Exchanges
Fat 1/2
Very Lean Meat 1
Vegetable 1/2

Net Carbs
6

Deli Sub Wrap

MAKES 1 SERVING

*A meal in itself, but if really hungry,
add dill pickles, raw vegetable sticks and
1/2 cup fresh raspberries.*

1 **(7-inch) low-carb tortilla**
1 **teaspoon Dijon mustard**
2 **slices deli roast beef**
½ **cup alfalfa sprouts**
2 **thin slices tomato**

1. Spread tortilla with mustard. Top with
remaining ingredients. Roll tightly.

Per serving: 116 Cal, 4g Fat, 1g Sat F,
25mg Chol, 599mg Sod, 15g Pro,
1g Sug, 13g Carb, 9g Fib

Exchanges   Net Carbs

Very Lean Meat 1-1/2   4
Vegetable 1/2

Roast Beef Wrap

MAKES 1 SERVING

*Reduce fat even more by using
low-carb, low-fat tortillas.*

1 **(7-inch) low-carb tortilla**
2 **teaspoons Mild and Creamy Dijon
   Mustard**
2 **slices deli roast beef**
2 **tablespoons (½-oz) reduced fat
   Monterey Jack cheese, shredded**

1. Spread tortilla with mustard. Top with
roast beef and cheese. Roll tightly.

Per serving: 150 Cal, 7g Fat, 3g Sat F,
35mg Chol, 730mg Sod, 18g Pro,
0g Sug, 14g Carb, 8g Fib

Exchanges   Net Carbs

Fat 1/2   6
Meat 1
Very Lean Meat 1-1/2

Tuna Wraps

You can get 2 more wraps by adding 2 hard-boiled eggs, chopped.

1   (6-oz) can tuna, drained
¼   cup finely chopped celery
¼   cup chopped onion
¼   cup chopped dill pickle
⅓   cup light mayonnaise
2   (7-inch) low-carb tortillas

1. Combine first 4 ingredients. Mix with just enough mayonnaise to moisten. Spread on tortillas and roll tightly.

Per serving: 196 Cal, 8g Fat, 1g Sat F, 17mg Chol, 1016mg Sod, 20g Pro, 4g Sug, 20g Carb, 9g Fib

Exchanges   Net Carbs

Fat 1   11
Other Carb 1/2
Very Lean Meat 2
Vegetable 1/2

Guacamole Turkey Wrap

MAKES 1 SERVING

Use prepared or purchased guacamole.

1   (7-inch) low-carb tortilla
1   tablespoon guacamole
2   slices deli turkey
½   cup shredded lettuce

1. Spread tortilla with guacamole. Top with turkey, then lettuce. Roll tightly.

Per serving: 190 Cal, 4g Fat, 0g Sat F, 50mg Chol, 903mg Sod, 31g Pro, <1g Sug, 13g Carb, 9g Fib

Exchanges   Net Carbs

Very Lean Meat 3-1/2   4

Guacamole Spread

MAKES 8 SERVINGS

This makes a nice spread for tortilla wraps .

1   ripe avocado, mashed
1   tablespoon thick and chunky salsa

Combine ingredients and use as a spread on tortillas or sandwiches.

Turkey Wrap

MAKES 1 SERVING

*A little bit of sun-dried tomatoes
is just what this wrap needs.*

1   (7-inch) low-carb tortilla
2   teaspoons Mild & Creamy Dijon
    Mustard
2   slices deli turkey
2   thin slices red onion
¼   cup (1-oz) reduced fat Mozzerella
    cheese, shredded

1. Spread tortilla with mustard. Layer
ingredients in order given and roll up tightly.

Per serving: 162 Cal, 5g Fat, 2g Sat F,
21mg Chol, 866mg Sod, 17g Pro,
1g Sug, 17g Carb, 8g Fib

Exchanges   Net Carbs
   Fat 1/2   9
   Meat 1
Very Lean Meat 1/2
   Vegetable 1/2

Veggie Tortilla Wrap

MAKES 1 SERVING

Simple but good.

1   (7-inch) low-carb tortilla
1   tablespoon light mayonnaise
¼   cup chopped Plum tomato
¼   cup alfalfa sprouts

1. Spread tortilla with mayonnaise. Top
with tomato and sprinkle lightly with salt.
Top with sprouts and roll tightly.

Per serving: 81 Cal, 4g Fat, 1g Sat F,
0mg Chol, 352mg Sod, 6g Pro,
2g Sug, 14g Carb, 8g Fib

Exchanges   Net Carbs
   Fat 1/2   6

Pesto-Beef Wrap

MAKES 1 SERVING

Monterey Jack is a good substitute for the Provolone.

1 (7-inch) low-carb tortilla
1 teaspoon pesto
2 slices deli roast beef
½ Plum tomato, chopped
½ cup shredded lettuce

1. Spread tortilla with pesto. Layer with remaining ingredients. Roll tightly.

Per serving: 136 Cal, 6g Fat, 1g Sat F, 27mg Chol, 519mg Sod, 16g Pro, 1g Sug, 13g Carb, 9g Fib

Exchanges   Net Carbs

Fat 1/2   4
Very Lean Meat 1-1/2
Vegetable 1/2

Pastrami Wrap

MAKES 1 SERVING

Pastrami is a nice change from roast beef.

1 (7-inch) low-carb tortilla
1 tablespoon light mayonnaise
2 slices deli pastrami
1 tablespoon chopped Plum tomato
1 slice (1-oz) reduced fat Cheddar cheese, julienned
½ cup shredded lettuce

1. Spread tortilla with mayonnaise. Top with pastrami slices, tomato, and cheese. Microwave to heat through and melt cheese.
2. Sprinkle with lettuce and roll tightly.

Per serving: 179 Cal, 7g Fat, 2g Sat F, 29mg Chol, 874mg Sod, 20g Pro, 2g Sug, 15g Carb, 9g Fib

Exchanges   Net Carbs

Fat 1   6
Very Lean Meat 2
Vegetable 1/2

Easy Beef Wrap

You can use any flavored cream cheese here.

1 (7-inch) low-carb tortilla
2 tablespoons light garlic cream cheese spread
2 slices deli roast beef
1 thin onion slice, separated

1. Spread tortilla with cheese spread. Top with roast beef and onion. Roll tightly.

Per serving: 174 Cal, 9g Fat, 4g Sat F, 40mg Chol, 650mg Sod, 17g Pro, 2g Sug, 14g Carb, 8g Fib

Exchanges   Net Carbs
Fat 1   6
Very Lean Meat 1-1/2

Pastrami & Onion Wrap

MAKES 1 SERVING

Feel free to substitute any meat for the pastrami.

1 (10-inch) low-carb tortilla
2 teaspoons Mild & Creamy Dijon mustard
3 slices deli pastrami
1 thin slice red onion
½ cup shredded lettuce

1. Spread tortilla with mustard and layer with remaining ingredients. Roll tightly.

Per serving: 169 Cal, 5g Fat, 1g Sat F, 35mg Chol, 964mg Sod, 20g Pro, 1g Sug, 23g Carb, 15g Fib

Exchanges   Net Carbs
Very Lean Meat 1-1/2   8
Vegetable 1/2

Turkey Deli Wrap

MAKES 1 SERVING

If desired, onion can be substituted for the pepper slices.

1 (7-inch) low-carb tortilla
1 tablespoon light mayonnaise
2 slices deli turkey
1 tablespoon chopped Plum tomato
3 small slices yellow pepper
½ cup shredded lettuce

1. Spread tortilla with mayonnaise. Top with remaining ingredients and roll tightly.

Per serving: 112 Cal, 5g Fat, 1g Sat F, 11mg Chol, 659mg Sod, 10g Pro, 3g Sug, 16g Carb, 9g Fib

Exchanges   Net Carbs

Fat 1/2   7
Very Lean Meat 1/2
Vegetable 1/2

Beef-Tomato Wrap

MAKES 1 SERVING

Can omit cheese spread and use mayo.

1 (7-inch) low-carb tortilla
2 tablespoons light garlic herb cream cheese spread
3 slices deli roast beef
1 small Plum tomato, chopped
½ cup shredded lettuce

1. Spread tortilla with cheese spread. Layer with remaining ingredients. Roll tightly.

Per serving: 210 Cal, 9g Fat, 4g Sat F, 52mg Chol, 786mg Sod, 29g Pro, 4g Sug, 16g Carb, 9g Fib

Exchanges   Net Carbs

Fat 1   7
Very Lean Meat 2-1/2
Vegetable 1/2

Chicken Caesar Wraps

MAKES 4 SERVINGS

Tastes just like a Caesar salad.

- 4   cups romaine
- 2   tablespoons grated Parmesan
- ¼   cup nonfat Caesar Salad Dressing
- 1   cup cubed cooked chicken
- 4   (7-inch) low-carb tortillas

1. Combine romaine and Parmesan with just enough dressing to lightly coat. Add chicken and spoon mixture on tortillas. Roll tightly.

Per serving: 118 Cal, 4g Fat, 1g Sat F, 20mg Chol, 518mg Sod, 14g Pro, 2g Sug, 15g Carb, 9g Fib

Exchanges   Net Carbs

Very Lean Meat 1   6
Vegetable 1/2

Chicken-Avocado Wraps

MAKES 4 SERVINGS

A great combination, but if watching your fat closely, omit the bacon and reduce fat by 3 grams and calories by 34.

- 4   (7-inch) low-carb tortillas
- 4   tablespoons light mayonnaise
- 1   ripe avocado, mashed
- 8   slices deli chicken
- 4   slices bacon, cooked, crumbled
- 1   cup shredded lettuce

1. Spread tortilla with mayonnaise and avocado.
2. Top with chicken, bacon and lettuce. Roll tightly.

Per serving: 213 Cal, 13g Fat, 2g Sat F, 20mg Chol, 723mg Sod, 15g Pro, 1g Sug, 18g Carb, 12g Fib

Exchanges   Net Carbs

Fat 2   6
Meat 1/2
Very Lean Meat 1
Fruit 1/2

Chicken-Alfalfa Wrap

MAKES 1 SERVING

Slice on diagonal for more attractive roll-ups.

- 1 (10-inch) low-carb tortilla
- 2 teaspoons Mild & Creamy Dijon mustard
- 3 slices deli chicken
- 2 tablespoons Plum tomato, chopped
- ¼ cup alfalfa sprouts

1. Spread tortilla with mustard. Layer with remaining ingredients. Roll tightly.

Per serving: 147Cal, 4g Fat, 0g Sat F, 20mg Chol, 872mg Sod, 19g Pro, 1g Sug, 23g Carb, 15g Fib

Exchanges   Net Carbs

Very Lean Meat 1-1/2   8

Sausage Wraps

MAKES 4 SERVINGS

- 1 (12-oz) package low-fat turkey sausage
- ⅓ cup chopped onions
- 1 (4-oz) can sliced mushrooms, drained, chopped
- 4 (7-inch) low-carb tortillas

1. Brown sausage and onion; drain. Add mushrooms and heat through. Place ¼ of mixture on each tortilla. Roll tightly.

Per serving: 164 Cal, 9g Fat, 2g Sat F, 50mg Chol, 583mg Sod, 16g Pro, 1g Sug, 14g Carb, 9g Fib

Exchanges   Net Carbs

Fat 1/2   5
Meat 1-1/2
Vegetable 1/2

Beef-Salsa Turnovers

MAKES 6 SERVINGS

Use your favorite salsa in this turnover.

1   pound extra lean ground beef
1   cup thick and chunky salsa
6   (7-inch) low-carb tortillas
1   cup (4-oz) reduced fat Cheddar
    cheese shredded

1. Preheat oven to 400°F. In medium skillet, brown ground beef; drain. Add salsa, bring to a simmer and cook 15 minutes or until liquid is absorbed.

2. Place tortillas on baking sheets. Just off center, place a portion of meat mixture. Sprinkle with cheese.

3. Bake just long enough to melt cheese. Remove from oven and fold tortillas in half like a turnover. Press edge to seal.

Per serving: 242 Cal, 11g Fat, 4g Sat F, 59mg Chol, 700mg Sod, 26g Pro, 3g Sug, 14g Carb, 8g Fib

Exchanges   Net Carbs

Fat 1-1/2   6
Very Lean Meat 3
Vegetable 1/2

Reuben Wrap

MAKES 1 SERVING

Just like from your favorite deli.

1   (7-inch) low-carb tortilla
1   tablespoon mustard
2   slices deli corned beef
¼   cup (1-oz) reduced fat Swiss cheese,
    shredded
½   cup low sodium sauerkraut, drained

1. Preheat oven to 350°F. Spread tortilla with mustard. Top with corned beef, then cheese and sauerkraut. Roll-up and secure with a wooden toothpick.

2. Place on a baking sheet and bake 8 to 10 minutes or until tortilla is somewhat toasted and cheese begins to melt.

Per serving: 202 Cal, 8g Fat, 2g Sat F, 35mg Chol, 1281mg Sod, 21g Pro, 3g Sug, 19g Carb, 12g Fib

Exchanges   Net Carbs

Fat 1   7
Very Lean Meat 2
Vegetable 1

Beef-Sauerkraut Wraps

MAKES 4 SERVINGS

Rinsing sauerkraut may remove even more sodium if necessary.

1 pound extra lean ground beef
½ cup chopped onion
1 (8-oz) can low sodium sauerkraut, drained
1 teaspoon salt
½ teaspoon caraway seeds
4 (7-inch) low-carb tortillas

1. Brown ground beef and onion; drain.
2. Add sauerkraut, salt and caraway seeds and heat through. Place mixture on tortillas and roll to enclose filling.

Per serving: 277 Cal, 13g Fat, 4g Sat F, 82mg Chol, 998mg Sod, 31g Pro, 2g Sug, 15g Carb, 10g Fib

Exchanges   Net Carbs

Fat 2   5
Very Lean Meat 3-1/2
Vegetable 1/2

Pizza Wrap

MAKES 1 SERVING

This one you bake in the oven.

1 (10-inch) low-carb tortilla
½ cup (2-oz) reduced fat Monterey Jack cheese, shredded
1 tablespoon Plum tomato, chopped
1 tablespoon sliced green onions

1. Preheat oven to 350°F. Place tortilla on baking sheet and sprinkle with cheese, then tomato and onion. Roll up rather tightly and bake, seam-side down, 5 to 6 minutes or until cheese is melted.

Per serving: 245Cal, 15g Fat, 8g Sat F, 40mg Chol, 782mg Sod, 22g Pro, 1g Sug, 22g Carb, 14g Fib

Exchanges   Net Carbs

Fat 1   8
Meat 2

Chicken Turnover

MAKES 1 SERVING

These are quick to make for multiple servings.

1   (7-inch) low-carb tortilla
⅓   cup cubed cooked chicken
2   tablespoons salsa, well-drained
¼   cup (1-oz) reduced fat Cheddar
     cheese, shredded

1. Preheat oven to 425°F. Place tortilla on a baking sheet. Arrange chicken over half the tortilla. Top with salsa and sprinkle with cheese.
2. Bake about 1 minute to melt cheese. Fold tortilla over and press to seal.

Per serving: 151 Cal, 5g Fat, 2g Sat F, 30mg Chol, 416mg Sod, 21g Pro, <1g Sug, 13g Carb, 8g Fib

Exchanges   Net Carbs
Fat 1/2   5
Very Lean Meat 2

Chicken Stir-Fry Wraps

MAKES 4 SERVINGS

I like to use the larger tortillas for these since they tend to be a little messy.

3   chicken breast halves, skinned, boned
1   tablespoon oil
½   small onion, sliced
1   small green pepper, sliced
     Salt and pepper to taste
4   (10-inch) low-carb tortillas

1. Cut chicken into narrow strips.
2. Heat oil in a large skillet. Add chicken, onion and green pepper and cook over medium-high heat, stirring frequently. Chicken should be cooked through and vegetables crisp-tender. Add salt and pepper to taste.
3. Divide mixture among tortillas and roll tightly.

Per serving: 220 Cal, 9g Fat, 1g Sat F, 54mg Chol, 348mg Sod, 28g Pro, 1g Sug, 20g Carb, 14g Fib

Exchanges   Net Carbs
Fat 1   6
Very Lean Meat 3

Hot Ham & Cheese Wraps

Makes a nice hot lunch.

4   (7-inch) low-carb tortillas
¼   cup light mayonnaise
4   thin slices deli ham
4   thin slices deli chicken
½   cup (2-oz) reduced fat Swiss cheese, shredded

1. Preheat oven to 325°F. Spread tortillas with mayonnaise. Layer with ham, chicken and cheese. Roll tortillas.

2. Place, seam-side down, on a baking sheet. Bake 4 to 5 minutes or until just heated through.

Per serving: 137 Cal, 5g Fat, 1g Sat F, 22mg Chol, 835mg Sod, 16g Pro, 2g Sug, 14g Carb, 8g Fib

Exchanges   Net Carbs

Fat 1/2   6
Very Lean Meat 1-1/2

Canadian Bacon Wrap

MAKES 1 SERVING

Low-carb tortillas have come to the rescue for low-carb and low-fat diets.

1   (7-inch) low-carb tortilla
1   teaspoon Mild & Creamy Dijon mustard
2   thin slices Canadian bacon, julienned
1   tablespoon chopped Plum tomato
1   (1-oz) slice reduced fat Swiss cheese, julienned

1. Spread tortilla with mustard. Top with Canadian bacon, tomato and cheese. Microwave to heat through and melt cheese. Roll tightly.

Per serving: 149 Cal, 5g Fat, 2g Sat F, 22mg Chol, 717mg Sod, 18g Pro, 1g Sug, 14g Carb, 8g Fib

Exchanges   Net Carbs

Meat 1/2   6
Very Lean Meat 1

Ham Pesto Wrap

MAKES 1 SERVING

To further reduce fat and sodium, use thinly sliced Canadian bacon.

1   (7-inch) low-carb tortilla
1   teaspoon pesto sauce
2   slices deli ham
¼   cup (1-oz) reduced fat Swiss cheese, shredded
½   cup shredded lettuce

1. Spread tortilla with mayonnaise. Layer with remaining ingredients. Roll tightly.

Per serving: 201Cal, 11g Fat, 5g Sat F, 42mg Chol, 1113mg Sod, 21g Pro, 2g Sug, 14g Carb, 8g Fib

Exchanges   Net Carbs

Fat 1   6
Meat 1
Very Lean Meat 1
Vegetable 1/2

Deli Wrap

MAKES 1 SERVING

A nice picnic wrap.

1   (7-inch) low-carb tortilla wrap
1   tablespoon low-carb pizza sauce
2   slices deli ham
¼   cup (1-oz) reduced fat Cheddar cheese, shredded
3   thin green pepper slices

1. Spread tortilla with pizza sauce. Layer with remaining ingredients and roll tightly.

Per serving: 150 Cal, 5g Fat, 1g Sat F, 26mg Chol, 1047mg Sod, 20g Pro, 2g Sug, 15g Carb, 9g Fib

Exchanges   Net Carbs

Fat 1/2   6
Very Lean Meat 2
Vegetable 1/2

Vegetables

- 🍄 Asparagus
- 🍄 Beans
- 🍄 Broccoli
- 🍄 Brussels Sprouts
- 🍄 Cabbage
- 🍄 Cauliflower
- 🍄 Kale
- 🍄 Mixed Vegetables
- 🍄 Mushrooms
- 🍄 Spinach
- 🍄 Squash
- 🍄 Zucchini

Asparagus & Almonds

Can serve with almost any meal.

1¼ pounds asparagus, trimmed
1 tablespoon reduced calorie margarine
1 tablespoon slivered almonds

1. Slice asparagus diagonally into 1½-inch pieces.

2. Cook in a large skillet in ½ cup water, until crisp-tender, about 5 to 7 minutes. Drain. Remove and keep warm.

2. Toast almonds in margarine until golden. Return asparagus to skillet and heat through.

Per serving: 50 Cal, 4g Fat, 1g Sat F, 0mg Chol, 35mg Sod, 2g Pro, 1g Sug, 3g Carb, 2g Fib

Exchanges   Net Carbs
Fat 1/2   1
Vegetable 1/2

Asparagus and Red Peppers

MAKES 4 SERVINGS

A colorful vegetable dish to serve with almost any menu.

1¼ pounds asparagus, trimmed
½ small red pepper, cut into narrow strips
1 tablespoon reduced calorie margarine
  Dash black pepper
1 tablespoon grated Parmesan cheese

1. Place asparagus and pepper strips in a medium skillet and add ¼ cup water. Cover and cook 5 to 7 minutes or until crisp-tender; drain.

2. Add margarine and pepper and toss to coat. Sprinkle with Parmesan.

Per serving: 62 Cal, 4g Fat, 1g Sat F, 1mg Chol, 71mg Sod, 4g Pro, 2g Sug, 6g Carb, 3g Fib

Exchanges   Net Carbs
Fat 1/2   3
Vegetable 1

Family Favorite Asparagus

*Serve with Quiche Lorraine
and a small Caesar salad.*

1   **pound asparagus, trimmed**
1   **tablespoon reduced calorie margarine**
2   **tablespoons chopped hazelnuts**
¼   **teaspoon dried basil**
⅛   **teaspoon ground pepper**
2   **tablespoons grated Parmesan cheese**

1. Heat ¼ cup water in a medium skillet. Add asparagus and cook on medium-high heat 4 to 6 minutes or until just crisp-tender. Drain. Remove and set aside.

2. Add margarine to skillet and sauté hazelnuts until lightly toasted. Return asparagus to skillet; season with basil and pepper and heat through. Place on serving plate and sprinkle with Parmesan.

Per serving: 71 Cal, 6g Fat, 1g Sat F, 2mg Chol, 79mg Sod, 3g Pro, 1g Sug, 3g Carb, 2g Fib

Exchanges   Net Carbs

Fat 1   1
Vegetable 1/2

Asparagus & Bacon

Serve with ham or roast beef.

1   **pound asparagus, trimmed**
2   **tablespoons nonfat vinaigrette dressing**
3   **slices bacon, cooked, crumbled**

1. Trim asparagus and place in a medium skillet. Add enough hot water to cover. Cook, over medium heat, until just crisp-tender. Remove and drain thoroughly.

2. Toss with just enough dressing to lightly coat. Cover and chill no longer than 1 hour.

3. Place on serving dish and sprinkle with bacon.

Per serving: 45 Cal, 2g Fat, 1g Sat F, 5mg Chol, 180mg Sod, 3g Pro, 1g Sug, 4g Carb, 1g Fib

Exchanges   Net Carbs

Vegetable 1/2   3

Green Beans Dijon

Just as good without the almonds.

1 tablespoon reduced calorie margarine
1 tablespoon slivered almonds
2 teaspoons lemon juice
1 teaspoon Dijon mustard
1 pound green beans, cooked

1. Heat margarine in a small skillet. Add almonds and lightly toast. Stir in the lemon juice and mustard. Pour over hot beans and toss gently to coat.

Per serving: 45 Cal, 3g Fat, 0g Sat F, 0mg Chol, 47mg Sod, 2g Pro, 1g Sug, 5g Carb, 2g Fib

Exchanges   Net Carbs

Fat 1/2   3
Vegetable 1

Green Beans & Bacon

MAKES 6 SERVINGS

My mother used to cook her green beans for hours; something unheard of today. Although the flavor was quite different, it was delicious.

1 pound green beans, trimmed
1½ tablespoons reduced calorie margarine
6 slices bacon, cooked, crumbled
   Salt and pepper

1. Cook beans in a large pot of boiling salted water until just crisp-tender, about 4 minutes or so. They will turn a bright green. Drain.

2. Heat margarine in a large skillet; add beans and toss. Add bacon and heat through. Season with salt and pepper.

Per serving: 80 Cal, 6g Fat, 1g Sat F, 7mg Chol, 184mg Sod, 4g Pro, 1g Sug, 5g Carb, 2g Fib

Exchanges   Net Carbs

Fat 1   3
Meat 1/2
Vegetable 1

Deviled Green Beans

The horseradish adds a little zip to the recipe.

⅓ cup finely chopped onion
3 tablespoons reduced calorie margarine
1 tablespoon prepared horseradish
1 tablespoon prepared mustard
1 (14.5-oz) can green beans, drained

1. In a medium skillet, cook onion in margarine until soft. Add horseradish and mustard. Add green beans and heat through.

Per serving: 104 Cal, 9g Fat, 1g Sat F, 0mg Chol, 305mg Sod, 1g Pro, 1g Sug, 5g Carb, 2g Fib

Exchanges   Net Carbs

Fat 2   3
Vegetable 1

Steamed Green Beans

A simple and fresh way to enjoy beans in season.

Desired amount of fresh green beans

1. Rinse beans and snap off ends. Cook in steamer rack over boiling water 10 to 15 minutes until just crisp-tender.
2. Or drop into a large pot of boiling water and cook 4 to 8 minutes or until just crisp-tender.
note: Unless you grow your own green beans, really fresh green beans are hard to find. Don't purchase them unless they feel firm and crisp to the touch.

Per ½ cup: 17 Cal, 0g Fat, 0g Sat F, 0mg Chol, 3mg Sod, 1g Pro, 1g Sug, 4g Carb, 2g Fib

Exchanges   Net Carbs

Vegetable 1/2   2

German Style Green Beans

A nice sweet-sour flavor.

1 pound green beans, cooked
4 slices bacon, cooked, crumbled
1 tablespoon finely chopped onion
2 packages Splenda®
1 tablespoon red wine vinegar

1. Cook onion in 1 tablespoon bacon drippings.
2. Add Splenda and vinegar, then the beans and bacon. Cook until heated through.

Per serving: 68 Cal, 3g Fat, 1g Sat F, 7mg Chol, 152mg Sod, 4g Pro, 2g Sug, 8g Carb, 3g Fib

Exchanges   Net Carbs

Fat 1/2   5
Meat 1/2
Vegetable 1

Broccoli Stir-Fry

MAKES 4 SERVINGS

During the Christmas holidays, add 1/4 cup chopped pimiento.

4 cups broccoli florets
1 tablespoon oil
6 thin slices fresh ginger
1 garlic clove, minced
1 packet Splenda®
½ teaspoon salt

1. Steam broccoli until just crisp-tender.
2. Heat oil in a medium skillet. Add ginger and garlic. Cook 1 minute.
3. Add broccoli, Splenda, salt and 1 tablespoon water. Cook, stirring frequently, until heated through. Remove ginger before serving.

Per serving: 52 Cal, 4g Fat, 0g Sat F, 0mg Chol, 310mg Sod, 2g Pro, 0g Sug, 4g Carb, 2g Fib

Exchanges   Net Carbs

Fat 1/2   2
Vegetable 1

Broccoli-Tomato Dish

This recipe has both eye and taste appeal.

4   cups broccoli florets
1   tablespoon reduced calorie
     margarine, melted
¼   teaspoon oregano
     Salt and pepper to taste
2   medium tomatoes
⅓   cup (1½-oz) reduced fat Mozzarella
     cheese, shredded

1. Preheat oven to 350°F. Cook broccoli until just crisp-tender. Toss with margarine, oregano, salt and pepper. Place in center of a 10-inch oven-proof dish.

2. Cut tomatoes into 16 wedges and arrange around the edge. Sprinkle with cheese. Bake 5 minutes or until tomatoes are heated through and cheese is melted.

Per serving: 89 Cal, 4g Fat, 1g Sat F, 4mg Chol, 130mg Sod, 6g Pro, 2g Sug, 8g Carb, 3g Fib

Exchanges   Net Carbs
Fat 1/2   5
Meat 1/2
Vegetable 1-1/2

Onion & Broccoli Stir-Fry

Can substitute asparagus or zucchini for the broccoli.

4   cups broccoli florets
1   tablespoon oil
1   medium onion, thin wedges
½   cup sliced celery
1½   teaspoons cornstarch
1½   teaspoons low sodium soy sauce

1. Cook broccoli until just partially cooked.

2. Heat oil in a medium skillet or a wok. Add broccoli, onion and celery and cook, over medium-high heat, until crisp-tender.

3. Combine remaining ingredients until smooth. Add to vegetables and cook about 2 minutes, stirring frequently.

Per serving: 46 Cal, 3g Fat, <1g Sat F, 0mg Chol, 66mg Sod, 2g Pro, 1g Sug, 5g Carb, 2g Fib

Exchanges   Net Carbs
Fat 1/2   3
Vegetable 1

Lemon Broccoli

MAKES 4 SERVINGS

Just a touch of lemon adds that extra flavor to please most appetites.

1   **pound broccoli spears**
1½ **tablespoons reduced calorie margarine**
1   **tablespoon fresh lemon juice**
    Dash ground black pepper

1. Place broccoli in a sprayed 11x7-inch baking dish. Add about ¼ cup water. Cover lightly and microwave 4 to 6 minutes or until bright green and just crisp-tender; drain.

2. Combine remaining ingredients and microwave to melt margarine. Pour over broccoli.

Per serving: 72 Cal, 4g Fat, 1g Sat F, 0mg Chol, 88mg Sod, 3g Pro, 2g Sug, 9g Carb, 4g Fib

Exchanges
Fat 1/2
Vegetable 1

Net Carbs
5

Cabbage Stir-Fry

MAKES 4 SERVINGS

For color, add a small shredded carrot.

2   **tablespoons oil**
6   **cups cabbage, 1 to 1½-inch slices**
    Salt and pepper

1. In large skillet, heat oil over medium heat.

2. Add cabbage and ¼ cup water. Cook until just crisp-tender, about 8 to 10 minutes, stirring occasionally. Season with salt and pepper.

Per serving: 85 Cal, 7g Fat, 1g Sat F, 0mg Chol, 19mg Sod, 1g Pro, 0g Sug, 6g Carb, 2g Fib

Exchanges
Fat 1
Vegetable 1

Net Carbs
4

Cauliflower-Broccoli Dish

Simple but tasty.

1 small head cauliflower, cut into florets
1 cup frozen broccoli florets
2 tablespoons reduced calorie margarine
  Salt and pepper

1. In medium saucepan, add cauliflower and ½ cup water. Bring to a boil, cover and cook until almost tender, about 8 minutes.

2. Add broccoli and cook until vegetables are tender. Drain. Add margarine and season with salt and pepper.

Per serving: 48 Cal, 4g Fat, 1g Sat F, 0mg Chol, 60mg Sod, 1g Pro, 1g Sug, 3g Carb, 2g Fib

Exchanges   Net Carbs
Fat 1   1
Vegetable 1/2

Sweet-Sour Brussels Sprouts

Even if you aren't too fond of Brussels sprouts, you just might enjoy this recipe.

¾ pound Brussels sprouts
¼ cup finely chopped onion
1 tablespoon oil
3 tablespoons apple cider vinegar
2 tablespoons Splenda
¼ teaspoon dry mustard

1. Wash and trim Brussels sprouts. Cook onion in heated oil in a medium skillet.

2. Stir in vinegar, Splenda, mustard and then the Brussels sprouts. Bring to a boil, reduce heat. Cover and simmer 10 to 12 minutes or until crisp-tender.

variation: For a special dinner, sprinkle the cooked Brussels sprouts with cooked crumbled bacon.

Per serving: 73 Cal, 4g Fat, 1 Sat F, 0mg Chol, 21mg Sod, 2g Pro, 3g Sug, 9g Carb, 3g Fib

Exchanges   Net Carbs
Fat 1/2   6
Vegetable 1-1/2

Brussels Sprouts Sauté

A taste tester favorite.

1 **pound Brussels sprouts**
¼ **cup reduced calorie margarine**
½ **teaspoon basil**
   Salt and pepper to taste

1. Trim Brussels sprouts and remove outer leaves. Cut each into 3 or 4 slices.
2. Heat margarine in medium skillet. Add remaining ingredients and toss to coat. Cook 8 to 10 minutes or until just crisp-tender.

Per serving: 145Cal, 12g Fat, 2g Sat F, 0mg Chol, 159mg Sod, 3g Pro, 2g Sug, 9g Carb, 3g Fib

Exchanges   Net Carbs

Fat 2   6
Vegetable 2

Eggplant Parmesan

MAKES 12 SLICES

For added color, top with a little marinara or spaghetti sauce.

1 **eggplant, about ¾ pound**
½ **cup low-fat dry white bread crumbs**
3 **tablespoons grated Parmesan cheese**
1 **large egg, lightly beaten**
½ **cup (2-oz) reduced fat Mozzarella cheese, shredded**

1. Preheat oven to 375°F. Cut eggplant into ¼ inch slices (do not peel).
2. Combine bread crumbs and Parmesan. Dip eggplant in egg, then in crumb mixture. Place on sprayed baking sheet. Bake 20 to 25 minutes or until lightly browned and cooked through.
3. Sprinkle cheese on slices and bake just until cheese is melted.

Per serving: 48 Cal, 2g Fat, 1g Sat F, 20mg Chol, 98mg Sod, 3g Pro, 1g Sug, 5g Carb, 1g Fib

Exchanges   Net Carbs

Meat 1/2   4
Vegetable 1/2

Sautéed Kale

There are many reasons to include kale in our diet. It has several disease fighting components and is high in vitamin A as well as calcium and potassium.

1	large bunch kale, about 10 ounces
1½	tablespoons oil
	Salt and pepper
2	teaspoons fresh lemon juice

1. Strip kale leaves from stems. Rinse and drain well.

2. Heat oil in large nonstick skillet. Add kale and cook, covered, for 1 minute. Uncover. Cook, stirring, for 1 minute or until just wilted. Sprinkle with salt, pepper and lemon juice.

Per serving: 66 Cal, 5g Fat, 1g Sat F, 0mg Chol, 27mg Sod, 1g Pro, 1g Sug, 4g Carb, 2g Fib

Exchanges   Net Carbs

Fat 1   2
Vegetable 1

Sautéed Mushrooms

This goes nicely with grilled or broiled steaks.

1	tablespoons reduced calorie margarine
1	tablespoon oil
8	ounces mushrooms, whole or sliced
½	cup coarsely chopped onion
1	garlic clove, minced

1. Heat margarine and oil in a medium skillet. Add remaining ingredients and cook, stirring frequently, 4 to 5 minutes or until cooked through.

Per serving: 72 Cal, 6g Fat, 1g Sat F, 0mg Chol, 21mg Sod, 2g Pro, 2g Sug, 4g Carb, 1g Fib

Exchanges   Net Carbs

Fat 1   3
Vegetable 1/2

Grilled Onions

MAKES 4 SERVINGS

Serve with hamburgers, steaks, pork or chicken.

2   medium onions, sliced 1-inch thick
2   tablespoons reduced calorie
    margarine
    Salt and pepper

1. Brush onion slices with margarine and place on heated grill. Cook until just crisp-tender and lightly browned, turning once. Sprinkle with salt and pepper.

Per serving: 74 Cal, 6g Fat, 1g Sat F, 0mg Chol, 155mg Sod, 1g Pro, 2g Sug, 6g Carb, 1g Fib

Exchanges   Net Carbs
Fat 1   5
Vegetable 1

Spaghetti Squash

PER 1/2 CUP SERVING

Serve as a substitute for pasta.

1   spaghetti squash
2   tablespoons reduced calorie
    margarine

1. Preheat oven to 350°F. Cut squash in half lengthwise. Remove seeds and place, cut-side down, in a shallow pan. Add a small amount of water, about ½ cup, and bake 40 to 50 minutes or until cooked through. With a fork, pull into strands and toss with just enough margarine to lightly coat. Servings depend on the size of the squash.

Per ½ cup: 30 Cal, 1g Fat, <1g Sat F, 0mg Chol, 25mg Sod, 1g Pro, 2g Sug, 5g Carb, 1g Fib

Exchanges   Net Carbs
Vegetable 1   4

Cook's Tip

Spaghetti squash can be used as a vegetable in casseroles or as a substitute for pasta.

Squash & Red Peppers

Colorful as well as good for you.

2   tablespoons oil
½   cup red onion, sliced
1   small red pepper, ¼-inch strips
3   yellow squash, sliced
1   teaspoon dried basil
     Salt and pepper

1. Heat oil in medium skillet. Cook onion for 2 minutes.

2. Add red pepper and cook 5 minutes.

3. Add squash and basil. Cook until crisp-tender, or desired doneness, stirring frequently.

4. Add salt and pepper to taste.

Per serving: 59 Cal, 5g Fat, 1g Sat F,
0mg Chol, 1mg Sod, <1g Pro,
2g Sug, 4g Carb, 1g Fib

Exchanges   Net Carbs
   Fat 1   3
   Vegetable 1/2

Sautéed Spinach

MAKES 4 SERVINGS

The garlic adds a lot of flavor.

1   pound spinach, rinsed, stemmed
1   tablespoon oil
1   medium garlic, finely chopped
1   tablespoon pine nuts
     Shaved Parmesan cheese

1. Heat oil in a large skillet. Add garlic and cook until soft, but not brown. Add spinach and cook, over medium-high heat, 2 to 3 minutes. Stir frequently until slightly wilted.

2. Add pine nuts and toss to coat. Place on serving plate and garnish with Parmesan.

Per serving: 70 Cal, 6g Fat, 1g Sat F,
1mg Chol, 84mg Sod, 3g Pro,
<1g Sug, 4g Carb, 2g Fib

Exchanges   Net Carbs
   Fat 1   2
Vegetable 1/2

Baked Tomato Halves

MAKES 6 SERVINGS

If desired, top with a dab of sour cream just before serving.

3   **medium tomatoes**
1   **cup low-fat soft white bread crumbs**
2   **tablespoons reduced calorie margarine**
¼   **teaspoon dried basil**

1. Preheat oven to 350°F. Cut tomatoes in half cross-wise. Place in a shallow baking dish.
2. Combine remaining ingredients and sprinkle on tomatoes. Bake 15 to 20 minutes or until tomatoes are heated through, but still firm.

Per serving: 61 Cal, 3g Fat, 1g Sat F, 0mg Chol, 84mg Sod, 1g Pro, 3g Sug, 7g Carb, 1g Fib

Exchanges   Net Carbs

Fat 1/2   6
Vegetable 1/2

Zucchini-Tomato Casserole

MAKES 6 SERVINGS

For crisp vegetables, watch the cooking time carefully. If you prefer the vegetables soft and juicy, cook a few minutes longer.

2   **medium zucchini, sliced**
    Salt and pepper
1   **medium onion, thinly sliced**
1   **green pepper, thinly sliced**
2   **medium tomatoes, sliced**
1½   **cups (6-oz) reduced fat Cheddar cheese, shredded**

1. Preheat oven to 350°F. Place zucchini in a sprayed 2-quart deep casserole dish; sprinkle with salt and pepper.
2. Top with onions and then the green pepper and tomatoes. Sprinkle with cheese. Bake 50 to 60 minutes.

Per serving: 72 Cal, 2g Fat, 1g Sat F, 6mg Chol, 176mg Sod, 8g Pro, 3g Sug, 5g Carb, 1g Fib

Exchanges   Net Carbs

Fat 1/2   4
Very Lean Meat 1
Vegetable 1

Zucchini Patties

MAKES 21 PATTIES

This is a great way to use up all that zucchini from the garden that keeps on growing and growing.

1½	pounds zucchini
½	teaspoon salt
½	medium garlic clove, finely chopped
2	large eggs, lightly beaten
⅓	cup grated Parmesan cheese
2	tablespoons oil

1. Wash zucchini and coarsely shred. Combine with salt and let stand 15 minutes. Squeeze with hands to release most of the liquid. Drain on paper towels.

2. Add garlic, eggs and cheese. Heat oil in large nonstick skillet over medium-high heat. Mound heaping tablespoons of zucchini in skillet; flatten slightly if necessary. Fill the skillet, but don't crowd. Cook 6 to 8 minutes, turning once, until golden. Repeat.

Per 2 patties: 53 Cal, 4g Fat, 1g Sat F, 40mg Chol, 171mg Sod, 3g Pro, 1g Sug, 2g Carb, 1g Fib

Exchanges

Fat 1/2
Meat 1/2
Vegetable 1/2

Net Carbs

1

Sautéed Zucchini

MAKES 4 SERVINGS

An easy simple recipe.

3	zucchini, 8 ounces each
1	tablespoon oil
½	teaspoon grated lemon zest
	Salt and pepper

1. Cut zucchini into matchstick size pieces.

2. Heat oil in medium skillet over medium heat. Add zucchini and sauté, stirring frequently, until just tender. Add lemon zest and season with salt and pepper.

Per serving: 51 Cal, 4g Fat, 1g Sat F, 0mg Chol, 5mg Sod, 2g Pro, 2g Sug, 4g Carb, 2g Fib

Exchanges

Fat 1/2
Vegetable 1

Net Carbs

2

Zucchini-Parmesan Dish

MAKES 4 SERVINGS

The Parmesan adds a nice touch.

1   **pound small zucchini, sliced**
2   **teaspoons oil**
½   **teaspoon lemon zest**
¼   **teaspoon ground black pepper**
1   **tablespoon grated Parmesan cheese**

1. Cook zucchini in heated oil about 4 minutes or until just crisp-tender. Drain off any excess oil. Toss lightly with remaining ingredients.

Per serving: 40 Cal, 3g Fat, 1g Sat F, 1mg Chol, 22mg Sod, 2g Pro, 2g Sug, 3g Carb, 1g Fib

Exchanges   Net Carbs
   Fat 1/2   2
   Vegetable 1/2

Three Pepper Stir-Fry

MAKES 4 SERVINGS

This colorful stir-fry compliments almost any main course. Also makes a nice pizza topping.

1   **tablespoon oil**
1   **medium red, yellow and green pepper, sliced into ¼-inch rings**
1   **medium onion, sliced, separated into rings**
    Salt and pepper to taste

1. Heat oil in a large nonstick skillet. Add vegetables and cook, over medium heat, until crisp-tender, stirring occasionally. Season with salt and pepper.

tip: The peppers should remain a bright color; if they've lost their color, you know they have cooked too long.

Per serving: 63 Cal, 4g Fat, 1g Sat F, 0mg Chol, 3mg Sod, 1g Pro, 4g Sug, 8g Carb, 2g Fib

Exchanges   Net Carbs
   Fat 1/2   6
   Vegetable 1-1/2

Steamed Vegetable Mix

You get a little taste of carrots without going over your carb budget for the day.

1 medium onion, thin wedges, separated
1 small carrot, thinly sliced
1 medium red pepper, narrow strips
1 medium-small zucchini, sliced
1 tablespoon reduced calorie margarine
  Salt and pepper to taste

1. Place first 3 ingredients in a large steamer basket. Place over boiling water; cover and cook 6 minutes.

2. Add zucchini; continue cooking 3 to 4 minutes or until vegetables are crisp-tender. Place in a large serving bowl and toss with margarine, salt and pepper.

Per serving: 37 Cal, 2g Fat, <1g Sat F, 0mg Chol, 29mg Sod, <1g Pro, 2g Sug, 4g Carb, 1g Fib

Exchanges	Net Carbs
Fat 1/2	3
Vegetable 1	

Roasted Vegetables

Vegetables can be roasted in the oven or on a grill.

½ pound Brussels sprouts, halved
1 pound fresh green beans, trimmed
¾ cup chopped green onions
1 teaspoon dried basil or rosemary
2 tablespoons oil
  Salt and pepper to taste

1. Preheat oven to 425°F. In a small stock pot, cook Brussels sprouts in 2 inches of water for 3 minutes.

2. Add green beans and cook 4 to 5 minutes or until they turn a bright green--no longer, please. Drain thoroughly.

3. In a sprayed shallow roasting pan, combine vegetables with remaining ingredients. Bake 10 to 12 minutes or until lightly roasted.

Per serving: 61 Cal, 4g Fat, 1g Sat F, 0mg Chol, 12mg Sod, 2g Pro, 2g Sug, 7g Carb, 3g Fib

Exchanges	Net Carbs
Fat 1/2	4
Vegetable 1	

Sautéed Onions and Peppers

MAKES ENOUGH FOR 8 (7-INCH)TORTILLAS

Serve with chicken or beef fajitas.

1   tablespoon of olive oil
¼   teaspoon paprika
½   red and green peppers, julienned
2   medium onions, thin wedges
     Salt and pepper to taste

1. Heat oil in a large skillet. Stir in paprika. Add peppers and onions. Cook until just crisp-tender.

Per serving: 23 Cal, 2g Fat, <1g Sat F, 0mg Chol, 1mg Sod, 0g Pro, 1g Sug, 2g Carb, <1g Fib

Exchanges   Net Carbs

Fat 1/2   2
Vegetable 1/2

Sesame Vegetable Stir-Fry

MAKES 4 SERVINGS

Quick and easy! If you want a little more color, add 1/4 cup chopped red peppers.

1   tablespoon oil
2   cups cauliflower florets
2   cups broccoli florets
1   tablespoon low sodium soy sauce
1   teaspoon toasted sesame seeds

1. Heat oil in a medium skillet over medium-high heat. Add cauliflower and broccoli and cook, stirring frequently, until just crisp-tender. Stir in soy sauce. Sprinkle with sesame seeds.

Per serving: 58 Cal, 4g Fat, 1g Sat F, 0mg Chol, 152mg Sod, 3g Pro, 1g Sug, 4g Carb, 2g Fib

Exchanges   Net Carbs

Fat 1/2   2
Vegetable 1

Sautéed Mixed Vegetables

MAKES 8 SERVINGS

A great accompaniment to steak.

2   tablespoons oil
2   medium onions, thin wedges
½   pound mushrooms, sliced
1   medium green pepper, narrow strips
3   tablespoons dry sherry
½   teaspoon salt (optional)

1. Heat oil in a large skillet. Add vegetables and sherry and cook over medium heat until vegetables are crisp-tender. Sprinkle with salt, if using.

Per serving: 54 Cal, 4g Fat, <1g Sat F, 0mg Chol, 3mg Sod, 1g Pro, 2g Sug, 4g Carb, 1g Fib

Exchanges   Net Carbs
Fat 1/2   3
Vegetable 1

Onion Blossoms

MAKES 4 SERVINGS

These little gems team well with grilled chicken, steaks or fish.

4   small sweet onions
2   tablespoons reduced calorie
     margarine, melted
     Salt and pepper
1   tablespoon chopped parsley

1. Preheat oven to 350°F. Peel onions, but don't cut off the root end, as this is what holds the onion together.

2. Cut onions almost to the root, cutting into 8 wedges. Place in a sprayed 8x8-inch baking dish.

3. Pour margarine over onions and sprinkle with salt and pepper. Cover dish with foil and bake 30 minutes. Remove foil and baste onions with liquid. Bake 10 to 15 minutes or until tender. Remove from oven and sprinkle with parsley. Carefully lift blossoms and place on each serving plate.

Per serving: 50 Cal, 2g Fat, 1g Sat F, 0mg Chol, 24mg Sod, 1g Pro, 5g Sug, 8g Carb, 1g Fib

Exchanges   Net Carbs
Fat 1/2   7
Vegetable 1-1/2

Desserts

✧ Cookies
✧ Candies
✧ Desserts
✧ Pies
✧ Pie Crusts

Chocolate-Coconut Candies

MAKES 24 CANDIES

These get quite hard if refrigerated.

2   (3.5-oz) bars low-carb dark chocolate
1¼ cups unsweetened shredded coconut.
½   teaspoon almond extract

1. Melt chocolate in heavy small saucepan over low heat.

2. Add coconut and extract. Drop by mounded teaspoons onto baking pan. Let stand until set.

Per 2 candies: 124 Cal, 10g Fat, 7g Sat F, 0mg Chol, 8mg Sod, 1g Pro, <1g Sug, 4g Carb, 3g Fib

Exchanges   Net Carbs
Fat 2   1

Macaroons

MAKES 18 MACAROONS

These are best eaten within a few hours of being made.

2 large egg whites
½ teaspoon vanilla extract
9 packets Splenda®
1 cup unsweetened shredded coconut

1. Preheat oven to 300°F. Beat egg whites until foamy. Add vanilla. Gradually add the Splenda and beat until soft peaks form.

2. Fold in coconut. Drop by tablespoons, 2 inches apart on sprayed baking sheet. Bake 20 to 25 minutes or until lightly browned. Cool on rack.

Per 2 macaroons: 63 Cal, 5g Fat, 5g Sat F, 0mg Chol, 15mg Sod, 1g Pro, <1g Sug, 3g Carb, 1g Fib

Exchanges   Net Carbs
Fat 1   2

Peanut Butter Snack Bar

Different, but good.

4 cups Rice Chex cereal
2 cups miniature pretzels, broken in half
¾ cup raisins
5 tablespoons reduced calorie margarine
5 tablespoons low-fat peanut butter
1 (10-oz) package miniature marshmallows.

1. In large mixing bowl, combine cereal, pretzels and raisins. In medium heavy saucepan melt margarine, peanut butter and marshmallows over low heat, stirring occasionally until smooth.

2. Pour over cereal mixture. Toss quickly to coat. Spoon into a sprayed 13x9-inch baking pan. Press evenly into pan. Chill and cut into bars.

Per bar: 115 Cal, 3g Fat, 1g Sat F, 0mg Chol, 135mg Sod, 2g Pro, 11g Sug, 21g Carb, 1g Fib

Exchanges	Net Carbs
Fat 1/2	20
Other Carbs 1	
Fruit 1/2	

Crispy Pizza Treat

MAKES 16 WEDGES

Don't expect any leftovers.

5 tablespoons reduced calorie margarine
1 (10-oz) package large marshmallows
6 cups crispy rice cereal
½ of a 1-oz square unsweetened chocolate, melted

1. Melt margarine in large heavy saucepan over low heat. Add marshmallow; cook until melted, stirring frequently to blend. Stir in cereal to coat.

2. Press evenly into a sprayed 12-inch pizza pan. You need to work quickly. This is easier to do if you lightly butter your hands and use your fingers to press mixture into pan. Drizzle chocolate over top. Cool. Cut into 16 wedges.

Per wedge: 133 Cal, 4g Fat, 1g Sat F, 0mg Chol, 120mg Sod, 1g Pro, 11g Sug, 24g Carb, <1g Fib

Exchanges	Net Carbs
Fat 1/2	24
Other Carbs 1	
Starch 1/2	

Ice Cream Sandwiches

SERVINGS VARY

Don't expect any leftovers.

1   **(9-oz) box chocolate wafer cookies**
½   **gallon nonfat vanilla ice cream**

1. Remove paper container from ice cream. Cut 1 (½-inch) slice off of ice cream. Using a 2-inch cookie cutter, cut small rounds out of slice. Place between 2 cookies. Place on cookie sheet to freeze. Continue with remaining ingredients until desired number is reached. Freeze sandwiches, then place in an air tight container or plastic bag.

Variations: Use different flavors of ice cream and/or graham crackers.

Per sandwich: 96 Cal, 2g Fat, <1g Sat F, 0mg Chol, 101mg Sod, 2g Pro, 11g Sug, 18g Carb, 1g Fib

Exchanges   Net Carbs

Other Carbs 1   17

Ice Cream Balls

MAKES 1 SERVING

With more and more delicious nonfat ice creams on the market, we can now enjoy these once forbidden desserts.

½   **cup nonfat vanilla ice cream**
2   **tablespoons sliced almonds**
¼   **cup sliced strawberries (sweetened with Splenda, if desired)**

1. Form ice cream into a ball. This is easier to do if the ice cream is frozen quite firm. Place in muffin tin; cover and freeze. When ready to serve, place in a wine glass or dessert dish. Spoon strawberries over ice cream.

Per serving: 176 Cal, 6g Fat, <1g Sat F, 0mg Chol, 63mg Sod, 6g Pro, 18g Sug, 26g Carb, 3g Fib

Exchanges   Net Carbs

Fat 1   23
Meat 1/2
Other Carbs 1-1/2

Ice Cream & Amaretto

MAKES 1 SERVING

An elegant but quick and easy dessert.

1   (½-cup) scoop nonfat vanilla ice
    cream
1   teaspoon Amaretto liqueur
1   tablespoon Lite frozen whipped
    topping, thawed
1   teaspoon sliced almonds

1. Spoon ice cream into a wine glass or
small dessert dish. Spoon Amaretto over top.
Top with whipped topping and sprinkle with
almonds.

Per serving: 127 Cal, 2g Fat, 1g Sat F,
63mg Chol, 0mg Sod, 3g Pro,
18g Sug, 24g Carb, 1g Fib

Exchanges   Net Carbs
Fat 1/2   23
Other Carbs 1-1/2

Cook's Tip Small servings of
low-carb berries are now allowed on low-
carb diets--even Atkins. Those lowest are
raspberries, strawberries, blueberries, and
blackberries.

Raspberry Delight

MAKES 5 SERVINGS

If desired, garnish with whipped cream.

1   (0.6-oz) package sugar-free raspberry
    gelatin
1   cup nonfat vanilla ice cream
1   cup raspberries
3   tablespoons chopped pecans

1. Combine gelatin with 1 cup boiling
water, stirring until completely dissolved.
Add ice cream and whisk until blended.
Refrigerate until the thickness of uncooked
egg whites, about 20 minutes.

2. Stir in raspberries and pecans. Spoon
into small serving dishes and refrigerate until
firm.

Per serving: 93 Cal, 3g Fat, <1g Sat F,
0mg Chol, 100mg Sod, 3g Pro,
7g Sug, 11g Carb, 2g Fib

Exchanges   Net Carbs
Fat 1/2   9
Other Carbs 1/2

Creme De Menthe Dessert

An easy dessert for St. Patrick's Day.

½   cup nonfat vanilla ice cream
1   teaspoon Cream De Menthe

1. Spoon ice cream into a small dessert dish. Drizzle Cream De Menthe over top.

Per serving: 106 Cal, 0g Fat, 0g Sat F, 0mg Chol, 63mg Sod, 3g Pro, 17g Sug, 22g Carb, 1g Fib

Exchanges   Net Carbs

Other Carbs 1-1/2   21

What is Coulis?

Coulis is a fruit that has been sweetened, processed in a blender or food processor and then pressed through a sieve to remove the seeds. What you then have is a nice sauce to serve over or under a dessert or to decorate a plate.

Ice Cream Parfait

MAKES 1 SERVING

Fill your most attractive small parfait or wine glasses with ice cream and freeze for a nice frosty look.

2   tablespoons chopped pecans
⅓   cup nonfat chocolate ice cream
⅓   cup nonfat vanilla ice cream

1. Finely crush toffee bar. Fill glass with the chocolate ice cream. Sprinkle with half the toffee. Add vanilla ice cream, then rest of toffee.

Per serving: 223 Cal, 11g Fat, 2g Sat F, 3mg Chol, 75mg Sod, 5g Pro, 20g Sug, 29g Carb, 4g Fib

Exchanges   Net Carbs

Fat 2   25
Other Carbs 1

Nonfat Variations

- Vanilla ice cream, sliced strawberries
- Vanilla ice cream, raspberries
- Vanilla ice cream, blueberries
- Vanilla ice cream, grated low-carb chocolate
- Strawberry ice cream, sliced strawberries

Vanilla Sherbet Dessert

MAKES 6 SERVINGS

A wonderful dessert you can prepare in just a few minutes. Make the dessert just before serving, but toast the coconut ahead of time.

1　pint nonfat vanilla ice cream, softened slightly
1　pint pineapple sherbet
1　teaspoon fresh orange zest
1½　tablespoons Grand Marnier liqueur
⅓　cup toasted unsweetened coconut

1. In large mixer bowl, combine the first four ingredients; beat just until smooth and blended. Spoon into parfait or wine glasses. Sprinkle with toasted coconut.

Per serving: 100 Cal, 3g Fat, 2g Sat F, 0mg Chol, 44mg Sod, 2g Pro, 12g Sug, 16g Carb, 1g Fib

Exchanges　　Net Carbs

Fat 1/2　　　　　　15
Other Carbs 1

Strawberry-Raspberry Dessert

MAKES 4 SERVINGS

A colorful dessert and so few carbs.

2　cups fresh raspberries
¼　cup Splenda
4　½-cup scoops nonfat strawberry ice cream
　　A few thin strips of lemon peel (optional)

1. Puree raspberries and Splenda just briefly in a blender.
2. Place ice cream in small serving dishes and spoon sauce over top. If desired, garnish with lemon strips. If you just happen to have 4 mint leaves hanging around, add those to add a bit more color.

Per serving:　128 Cal, <1g Fat, 0g Sat F, 0mg Chol, 64mg Sod, 4g Pro, 18g Sug, 28g Carb, 5g Fib

Exchanges　　Net Carbs

Other Carbs 1-1/2　　23
Fruit 1/2

Ben's Strawberries

MAKES 48

*My Grandson, Ben, ate about a dozen of these
before I could get them on the serving tray.*

8 ounces Mascarpone cheese, softened
⅓ cup Splenda®
1 tablespoon Grand Marnier
24 medium-small strawberries

1. Combine cheese, Splenda and Grand
Marnier until smooth.

2. Spoon into a pastry bag fitted with a
small star tip. Cut strawberries in half
lengthwise and pipe a small mound of cheese
mixture onto center. Serve as soon as possible. Sprinkle very lightly with a little
Splenda, if desired.

Per half: 25 Cal, 2g Fat, 1g Sat F,
6mg Chol, 3mg Sod, <1g Pro,
<1g Sug, 1g Carb, <1g Fib

Exchanges   Net Carbs
Fat 1/2   1

Serving Suggestion

Serve Ben's Strawberries on a nice
serving tray and garnish with
fresh mint leaves.

Chocolate Covered
Strawberries

MAKES 20 SERVINGS

*We have to have discipline when
eating these, they are so good.*

1 (3.5-oz) bar low-carb dark chocolate
1 teaspoon shortening
20 medium-size strawberries

1. Break chocolate into 1 inch pieces.
Place in heavy small saucepan along with the
shortening. Heat, over low heat, until melted
and smooth.

2. Dip strawberries into chocolate and
place, point-side up on a dish. Place in
refrigerator to set. Serve same day made.

Per strawberry: 28 Cal, 2g Fat, 1g Sat F,
0mg Chol, 2mg Sod, <1g Pro,
1g Sug, 2g Carb, 1g Fib

Exchanges   Net Carbs
Fat 1/2   1

Strawberries Grand Marnier

MAKES 4 SERVINGS

If desired, top with whipped cream or serve with French toast or crepes.

2   cups sliced strawberries
¼   cup Splenda
1   tablespoon Grand Marnier
1   teaspoon fresh orange zest

1. Combine all ingredients. Cover and chill until ready to serve.

Per serving: 45 Cal, <1g Fat, 0g Sat F, 0mg Chol, 1mg Sod, 1g Pro, 5g Sug, 10g Carb, 2g Fib

Exchanges   Net Carbs
   Fruit 1/2   8

Baked Apples

MAKES 1 SERVING

A nice low-fat dessert.

½   Golden Delicious apple
1   tablespoon brown Sugar Twin
10   raisins
½   teaspoon reduced calorie margarine
1   tablespoon water

1. Preheat oven to 350°F. Peel apple. Carefully remove core by cutting a "V" in middle of each apple half. Place, cut side up, in baking dish. Sprinkled with sugar twin. Top with raisins and margarine. Add water.
2. Bake 20 to 25 minutes or until tender, basting 2 or 3 times with the sauce. Serve hot or warm with sauce.

Per serving: 66 Cal, 2g Fat, <1g Sat F, 0mg Chol, 25mg Sod, <1g Pro, 12g Sug, 14g Carb, 2g Fib

Exchanges   Net Carbs
   Fat 1/2   12
   Fruit 1/2

Mandarin Orange Delight

A favorite for everyone.

1 (8-oz) container nonfat, sugar-free Mandarin orange yogurt
1 cup Lite frozen whipped topping, thawed
1 (11-oz) can Mandarin oranges, drained thoroughly

1. In small bowl, combine yogurt and whipped topping. Gently stir in oranges. Cover and chill until ready to serve.

Per serving: 60 Cal, 1g Fat, 1g Sat F, 1mg Chol, 23mg Sod, 2g Pro, 7g Sug, 9g Carb, <1g Fib

Exchanges   Net Carbs

Fat 1/2   9

Pineapple Orange Dessert

A quick light dessert after a hearty meal.

1 medium orange, peeled, cut into 4 slices
4 slices canned pineapple rings
1 tablespoon Cointreau
8 tablespoons Lite frozen whipped topping, thawed
1 teaspoon grated orange peel

1. Place an orange and pineapple slice on each of four small serving plates. Drizzle Cointreau over fruit. Top each serving with 2 tablespoons whipped topping. Sprinkle with grated peel. Makes 4 servings.

Per serving: 71 Cal, 1g Fat, 1g Sat F, 0mg Chol, 1mg Sod, <1g Pro, 11g Sug, 14g Carb, 1g Fib

Exchanges   Net Carbs

Fat 1/2   13
Other Carbs 1/2
Fruit 1/2

Mandarin Orange Dessert

Fresh and light.

1 (6-oz) package sugar-free orange gelatin
1 pint Mandarin orange sorbet
1 (11-oz) can Mandarin oranges, drained thoroughly
1 (16-oz) can crushed pineapple, drained thoroughly
¾ cup miniature marshmallows
1 (8-oz) container Lite frozen whipped topping, thawed

1. In large mixing bowl, combine gelatin with 2 cups boiling water, stirring until completely dissolved. Stir in sorbet until melted. Chill until thickened, about 30 minutes. Add oranges, pineapple and marshmallows. Fold in whipped topping. Pour into a 13x9-inch dish. Cover; chill until set. Cut into squares to serve.

Per serving: 128 Cal, 2g Fat, 2g Sat F, 0mg Chol, 300mg Sod, 5g Pro, 13g Sug, 16g Carb, <1g Fib

Exchanges
Vegetable 1/2

Net Carbs
16

Quick Pear Delight

A great combination.

2 canned pear halves, drained thoroughly
2 tablespoons Lite frozen whipped topping, thawed
1 teaspoon finely chopped walnuts

1. Place pears in dessert dish. Top with whipped topping. Sprinkle with walnuts.

Per serving: 112 Cal, 3g Fat, 1g Sat F, 0mg Chol, 6mg Sod, 1g Pro, 16g Sug, 22g Carb, 3g Fib

Exchanges
Fat 1/2
Fruit 1-1/2

Net Carbs
19

Hint

Fresh pears can be used in above recipe. Place in oven, sprinkle with a small amount of water and bake at 350°F until tender. Cool before serving.

Mixed Fruit Dessert

MAKES 4 SERVINGS

A refreshing light dessert.

1 cup watermelon balls
1 cup cantaloupe balls
1 cup seedless green grapes
1 cup Bing cherries, pitted and halved
4 scoops of lemon sherbet (about 1/4 cup each)

1. Combine fruit in medium bowl. Spoon into small serving dishes; top with scoop of lemon sherbet.

Per serving: 130 Cal, 1g Fat, <1g Sat F, 0mg Chol, 25mg Sod, 2g Pro, 25g Sug, 31g Carb, 3g Fib

Exchanges   Net Carbs

Other Carbs 1/2   28
Fruit 1-1/2

Baked Cinnamon Pears

MAKES 1 SERVING

This recipe will satisfy your sweet tooth.

½ pear, remove core, but do not peel
1 teaspoon cinnamon sugar, made with Splenda
¼ cup nonfat vanilla ice cream

1. Preheat oven to 325°F. Place pear, skin-side down, in small baking pan. Sprinkle with cinnamon sugar. Bake for 35 to 40 minutes or until tender. Serve warm with a small scoop of ice cream.

Per serving: 95 Cal, 0g Fat, 0g Sat F, 0mg Chol, 32mg Sod, 2g Pro, 16g Sug, 23g Carb, 3g Fib

Exchanges   Net Carbs

Other Carbs 1/2   20
Fruit 1

Peachy Raspberry Dessert

White peaches (during season) are showing up in more and more supermarkets today.

2 **cups fresh raspberries**
¼ **cup Splenda (or to taste)**
4 **white peaches, peeled and sliced**
1 **pint nonfat vanilla ice cream**

1. Sweeten raspberries with Splenda to taste. Place in blender and blend just until smooth. Press mixture through a sieve to remove the seeds. Place peach slices in four dessert dishes. Top with a scoop of ice cream, then top with raspberry sauce.

Per serving: 168 Cal, <1g Fat, 0g Sat F, 0mg Chol, 64mg Sod, 5g Pro, 18g Sug, 38g Carb, 7g Fib

Exchanges   Net Carbs
Other Carbs 1-1/2   31
Fruit 1-1/2

Lemon Raspberry Dessert

MAKES 4 SERVINGS

A colorful dessert for that special dinner. So easy and so few calories

2 **cups raspberries (fresh or frozen)**
¼ **cup Splenda (or to taste)**
1 **pint lemon sorbet**
   small julienned pieces of lemon peel for garnish

1. Puree raspberries and sugar in a blender (do not let it turn to liquid.) Press mixture through a sieve, collecting puree in a bowl. Discard seeds. Place sorbet in individual bowls or wine glasses. Spoon sauce over top. Garnish with lemon peel.

Per serving: 130 Cal, <1g Fat, 0g Sat F, 0mg Chol, 9mg Sod, 1g Pro, 26g Sug, 32g Carb, 4g Fib

Exchanges   Net Carbs
Other Carbs 1-1/2   28
Fruit 1/2

Fruit & Yogurt Dessert

MAKES 1 SERVING

A satisfying dessert without all the fat and calories.

½ small cantaloupe
1 scoop nonfat frozen yogurt
1 tablespoon unsweetened coconut, toasted

1. Remove seeds from center of cataloupe. Fill with frozen yogurt; sprinkle with coconut. Place on attractive serving plate. Makes 1 serving.

Variation: Fill with ½ cup fresh raspberries; top with small scoop of lemon or pineapple sorbet.

Per serving: 188 Cal, 4g Fat, 3g Sat F, 0mg Chol, 77mg Sod, 5g Pro, 16g Sug, 37g Carb, 3g Fib

Exchanges   Net Carbs

Fat 1/2   34
Other Carbs 1
Fruit 1-1/2

Angel Cake Dessert

MAKES 8 SERVINGS

Keep an Angel Food cake in the freezer for this quick and easy dessert.

4 to 5 oranges (1 cup juice and 1 orange for slicing)
⅓ cup Splenda
1 tablespoon, plus 1 teaspoon cornstarch
1 large banana, sliced
2 kiwis, peeled and cut into chunks
1 small Angel Food cake

1. In medium saucepan, combine the 1 cup of orange juice, Splenda and cornstarch. Mix to thoroughly blend and dissolve cornstarch. Bring to a boil; reduce heat and cook until thickened, stirring frequently.

2. Remove from heat; stir in sliced bananas and kiwi. Peel remaining orange; cut into ¼-inch slices. Cut slices into quarters; add to sauce. Serve over cake slices.

Per serving: 163 Cal, <1g Fat, 0g Sat F, 0mg Chol, 319mg Sod, 3g Pro, 8g Sug, 38g Carb, 2g Fib

Exchanges   Net Carbs

Other Carbs 1-1/2   36
Fruit 1/2

Quick Angel Dessert

MAKES 1 SERVING

Wonderful on a hot summer day.

1   slice Angel Food cake
½   cup sliced fresh strawberries
2   tablespoon Lite frozen whipped
     topping, thawed

1. Place cake on attractive serving dish.
Top with strawberries and whipped topping.
If desired, garnish with a mint leaf.

Per serving: 120 Cal, 1g Fat, 1g Sat F,
0mg Chol, 213mg Sod, 2g Pro,
5g Sug, 25g Carb, 2g Fib

Exchanges   Net Carbs
Other Carbs 1   23
    Fruit 1/2

Strawberry Box Cake

MAKES 15 SERVINGS

If desired, top with a fresh strawberry.

1   Duncan Hines Moist Deluxe white
     cake mix
2   tablespoons oil
2   large egg whites
1   (3-oz) package sugar free strawberry
     gelatin
1   (8-oz) container Lite frozen whipped
     topping, thawed

1. Preheat oven to 350°F. In large mixing
bowl, combine dry mix, oil, 1⅓ cups water
and egg whites. Beat on low until blended.
Beat on medium 2 to 3 minutes or until
smooth. Pour into a sprayed 13x9-inch
baking dish. Bake for 30 to 35 minutes or
until cake tests done. Remove from oven;
pierce cake all over with long-tined fork.
  2. Dissolve gelatin in boiling water; pour
evenly over cake. Cover and chill. Spread
whipped topping over top. Cover; chill until
ready to serve.

Per serving: 214 Cal, 6g Fat, 3g Sat F,
0mg Chol, 360mg Sod, 5g Pro,
18g Sug, 32g Carb, 1g Fib

Exchanges   Net Carbs
    Fat 1   31
  Other Carbs 2
Very Lean Meat 1/2

Orange Cake

A simple yet festive dessert.

1   Duncan Hines Moist Deluxe white cake mix
2   tablespoons oil
1⅓ cups orange juice
2   large egg whites
1   (8-oz) container Lite frozen whipped topping, thawed
1   (16-oz) can Lite cherry pie filling.

1. Preheat oven to 350°F. In large mixing bowl, combine dry mix, oil, orange juice and egg whites. Beat on low until blended. Beat on medium 2 to 3 minutes or until smooth. Pour into a sprayed 13x9-inch baking dish. Bake for 25 to 30 minutes or until cake test done. Let cool.

2. Cut into 15 squares. Serve each square with 2 tablespoons pie filling topped with 2 tablespoons whipped topping.

Per serving: 219 Cal, 6g Fat, 3g Sat F, 0mg Chol, 234mg Sod, 2g Pro, 23g Sug, 37g Carb, 1g Fib

Exchanges   Net Carbs

Fat 1   36
Other Carbs 2

Orange Cheesecake Pie

This delicious dessert can be made ahead.

1   graham cracker pie crust, page 272
2   (8-oz) packages light cream cheese, softened
1   cup Splenda
½   cup fresh orange juice
1   (12-oz) container Lite frozen whipped topping, thawed

1. In large mixer bowl, beat cream cheese until smooth. Beat in Splenda. Gradually add orange juice to cream cheese mixture, beating until smooth. Add whipped topping; mix until well blended. Pour into pie crust. Chill at least two hours.

Per serving: 280 Cal, 17g Fat, 10g Sat F, 25mg Chol, 214mg Sod, 6g Pro, 8g Sug, 23g Carb, <1g Fib

Exchanges   Net Carbs

Fat 3-1/2   23
Meat 1
Other Carbs 1/2
Starch 1/2

Strawberry Pie

MAKES 8 SERVING

A wonderful dessert when strawberries are in season.

1 graham cracker pie crust, page 272
1 cup Splenda
3 tablespoons cornstarch
3 tablespoons strawberry gelatin (powder)
3 cups fresh whole strawberries

1. Place Splenda in small saucepan. Combine cornstarch with ¼ cup cold water, stirring until smooth. Add to saucepan along with ¾ cup water. Cook over medium low heat until thickened, stirring frequently. Add gelatin; stir to dissolve. Line pie shell with strawberries. Pour sauce over top. Chill until set.

Per serving: 161 Cal, 7g Fat, 1g Sat F, 0mg Chol, 109mg Sod, 2g Pro, 9g Sug, 25g Carb, 2g Fib

Exchanges   Net Carbs
Fat 1   23
Other Carbs 1/2
Starch 1
Fruit 1/2

Graham Cracker Crust

MAKES 1 PIE SHELL

Cheaper than store bought.

1¼ cups low-fat graham cracker crumbs
2 tablespoons Splenda
¼ cup reduced calorie margarine

1. Preheat oven to 350°F. Combine ingredients until well mixed. Press evenly into bottom and sides of 9-inch pie pan. Bake for 10 minutes. Let cool before filling.

Per $1/8^{th}$ shell: 105 Cal, 6g Fat, 1g Sat F, 0mg Chol, 99mg Sod, 1g Pro, 3g Sug, 11g Carb, 1g Fib

Exchanges   Net Carbs
Fat 1   10
Starch 1

Index

$\mathscr{A}$

S

Salads

Great Meals Begin With Six Ingredients Or Less

Six Ingredients or Less Diabetic - Over 400 delicious diabetic conscious, low-fat and low-carb recipes. Includes nutitional analysis and diabetic exchanges. 288 pages, Comb bound, $19.95.

Six Ingredients or Less Low-Carb - Over 600 easy recipes to help you creatively cook with 0 to 6 Net carbs per recipe. Includes nutritional analysis. 288 pages, Comb bound, $19.95.

Six Ingredients or Less - Revised, expanded edition of our best selling all-purpose cookbook. Over 600 delicious recipes from everyday cooking to company entertaining. 352 pages, $16.95.

Six Ingredients or Less Pasta and Casseroles - Main dish recipes for today's busy lifestyles. An original and low-fat version is given for each recipe. 224 pages, $14.95.

Six Ingredients or Less Slow Cooker - Easy stress-free recipes letting the slow cooker do the work for you. 224 pages, $14.95

SIX INGREDIENTS OR LESS
PO BOX 922
Gig Harbor, WA 98335
1-800-423-7184

Diabetic Cookbook	(____) # of copies	$19.95 each	$_____
Low -Carb Cooking	(____) # of copies	$19.95 each	$_____
Six Ingredients or Less	(____) # of copies	$16.95 each	$_____
Pasta & Casseroles	(____) # of copies	$14.95 each	$_____
Slow Cooker	(____) # of copies	$14.95 each	$_____

Plus Postage & Handling (First book $3.25, each add'l book, add $1.50) $_____
Washington residents add 8.5% sales tax or current tax rate $_____

Total $_____

Please Print or Type
(Please double-check addition, differences will be billed)

Name_____ Phone (____)_____

Address_____

City_____ State_____ Zip_____

MC or Visa_____ Exp _____

Signature_____

sixingredientsorless.com or carlean@sixingredientsorless.com